SAN FRANCISCO BAY AREA

Greenopia

the urban dweller's guide to green living

PUBLISHED BY The Green Media Group, LLC

The Green Media Group, LLC
P.O. Box 1706 Santa Monica CA 90406-1706 USA
(310) 917-1100 fax (310) 917-1109
www.greenopia.com

Greenopia™: the urban dweller's guide to green living, San Francisco Bay Area

Copyright © 2007 The Green Media Group, LLC

First Edition/First Printing

ISBN-10: 0-9785064-1-3
ISBN-13: 978-0-9785064-1-4

Greenopia guides are available at volume discounts and custom cover printing. Please contact The Green Media Group, LLC for further information at (310) 917-1100 fax (310) 917-1109, or e-mail us at orders@greenopia.com

Foreword

In 1994, my husband Tony and I built the first "green house" in our neighborhood. Because I was an asthmatic child, I wanted to create a contaminate-free home. We enlisted the help of environmental specialist Mary Cordaro to select the most eco-friendly building materials we could find at that time. It took almost three years to create a home that was as healthy and green as we could build and marked the beginning of my life-long journey to find the ultimate green everything.

As we had children, and our family expanded—from Alex, to Colin and Katey Ann—so did my quest. I started looking at the quality of our food, our water, the baby products we used, the cleaning supplies on our shelves. I wanted to be as conscious in these choices as I had been in the choices I made for the building materials in my home. It was not an easy task. There was no single place for me to go to find answers to my questions and no single source to guide me to local green services and businesses. So, after spending fifteen years in publishing, I decided to marry what I knew with what I loved. From this union of experience and passion, Greenopia™ was created.

The first edition of **Greenopia™: the urban dweller's guide to green living** was born in Los Angeles on Earth Day 2006 and began immediately to do what I had hoped it would—help people like myself make eco-friendly choices in all aspects of their everyday lives. Now I am thrilled to bring out a San Francisco Bay Area guide, second in a series that focuses on making the world a greener place, one city at a time.

My wish is that this guide will inspire you to look for new ways to make your world healthier and happier. By starting with our own lives, I believe we can inspire others to act, and in due course move closer to what we all want—a better world for ourselves and our children. Join me in supporting these eco-friendly businesses and services so we can help clean up our air and water, reverse global climate change, and lighten our footprint on this precious planet.

Gay Browne, Founder

Our Goal

It is our goal to help everyone live greener lives. We want to make our guide *your* guide. Its contents should reflect not only our view of these businesses and organizations, but yours as well. Please join our interactive community on the web (www.greenopia.com) and let us know what you think about our guide and about any of the businesses or organizations we've listed.

Our Belief

As consumers, we have power: power to drive demand, power to shape supply, and power to create a greener world. By changing our buying habits, we can change the world.

What This Guide Is

This is a consumer-friendly guide designed to help individuals locate "green" products and services in their cities. It is the result of our own research and it is designed to save you time and effort. We did the legwork so that you can now be more confident that your purchases are truly healthier, and more earth-friendly.

What This Guide Is Not

This guide is not a paid directory. Companies cannot pay to be included and no sponsorship is accepted. We are not specifically advocating any particular listee; rather we are simply informing you that they performed well in our green filtering process.

To Be Included in This Guide

To be listed in the guide is a big achievement. All listees are here because of their eco-friendliness. They have already been screened for their sustainability in the product or service arena and are now being compared with "the best of the best." Congratulations to all of the companies and people and services and groups that made it into this guide: We commend you!

Leaf Awards

Our goal is to provide you with answers to the questions that are of the highest priority to you. All categories are screened differently as each requires questions that are tailored to that particular type of service or business. In each section we outline the criteria we used in our evaluations. Our leaf awards are then calculated using a weighting system. The weighting for each category is customized to reflect the relative values of the responses to our questions.

For all businesses and services, there is a minimum requirement to get into the guide. It is clearly articulated in each section. Not all categories are leaf-awarded, but in those that are, listees can earn from one leaf ⌀ to a maximum of four leaves ⌀⌀⌀⌀. Where applicable, each category introduction has a summary of specific leaf award requirements.

About This Guide

A Pledge

Merchants and service providers are held to a pledge of honesty in their responses to our questions, and we work closely with the local community in an effort to ensure that no business is misrepresented.

Businesses with Green Certification

We urge you to extend the power of your pocketbook into other realms. Look for businesses certified by the agencies listed below. In doing so, you can be assured that you are supporting companies who operate in an environmentally sustainable way. These Bay Area certification programs encourage businesses to conserve resources, prevent pollution, and minimize waste. Those that pass the requirements for certification have made a commitment to a healthier and cleaner environment. (Look for the shared green certification seal below.) Let's recognize their achievement with our support.

Alameda County Green Business Program
Bay Area Green Business Program
Marin County Green Business Program
Marin Sustainable Partners Program
City of San Francisco Green Business Certification Program

Our Inspiration

We have been inspired and encouraged by the efforts of other organizations that have dedicated themselves to the health of the planet, paving the way for Greenopia. In particular, we would like to acknowledge Co-op America whose groundbreaking work to create an environmentally sustainable world through economic action provides a model for all of us. Other resources we hope you will find helpful include:

Edible East Bay	Om Organics
Green Zebra	Slow Food San Francisco
Idealist	Social Venture Network (SVN)
Local Harvest	Sustainable Business Alliance
Marin Organic	West Coast Green

We Invite Your Comments

Our best source of feedback about the products and services featured in the guide is you. It is our desire to make this guide and our website interactive so that you can play an active role in identifying and supporting the green merchants in your area, and encourage other businesses to become a part of the Greenopia community. You will find us at **www.greenopia.com**. As more businesses adopt green practices, we as consumers have increased opportunities to make ecologically smart choices. Together we will make a positive and powerful environmental impact. Join us in our efforts.

Nancy Arbuckle
Editor/Writer

We would like to recognize and thank our San Francisco Bay Area Advisory Council and the experts who contributed their wisdom to each section of the guide. We are indebted to this stellar group of individuals who gave us their time and shared their expertise to help us ensure the accuracy and quality of our listings and to give us input on the guide content and criteria overall. Their collaboration and guidance were invaluable. We are enormously grateful for their advice, experience, and enthusiasm.

Larry Bain, Founder and Executive Director, Nextcourse and Let's Be Frank

Jared Blumenfeld, Director, San Francisco Department of the Environment

Jesse Ziff Cool, Founder, CoolEatz Restaurants & Catering

Laurie David, Founder, Stop Global Warming Virtual March

Virginia Donohue and **Mark Klaiman**, Owners and Founders, Pet Camp®

Eric Corey Freed, Principal, organicARCHITECT

Gil Friend, President and CEO, Natural Logic

Susan Griffin-Black, Co-founder and Co-CEO, EO products

Lynda Grose, The Sustainable Cotton Project, Designer of the Esprit Ecollection

Elliot Helman, The Hotel Nonprofit Collaborative

Anna Lappé, Co-founder, Small Planet Institute

Adam Lowry, Co-founder, Method Products Inc.

Joel Makower, Founder and Executive Editor, GreenBiz.com

Patricia Monahan, Senior Analyst, Clean Vehicles Program, Union of Concerned Scientists

Stefan Muhle, General Manager, Orchard Hotel and Orchard Garden Hotel

Janet Nudelman, Policy Director, Breast Cancer Fund

Annie Somerville, Executive Chef, Greens Restaurant

Bryant Terry, Eco-chef and food justice activist

Special thanks also goes out to Greenopia's other friends and experts in the community who provided their input, namely **Mani Niall** from Just Desserts, **Zem Joaquin** from EcoFabulous, **Mary Cordaro** and **Scott Jones** from The Mary Cordaro Collection and H3 Environmental Corp., **Andre Carothers** from Rockwood Leadership, **Michelle L'Don** from Organic Vintners, and **Lincoln Pain** from the Sustainable Investment Forum. We are also indebted to everyone at the **San Francisco Department of the Environment** for their valuable input and guidance, and to the **Monterey Bay Aquarium Foundation** for the use of their Seafood Watch Guide, **Environmental Working Group** for permission to reprint their Pesticides in Produce data, and **CUESA** (Center for Urban Education about Sustainable Agriculture) for their Seasonality Charts.

To all of you—we couldn't have done it without you.

Acknowledgements

THE GREENOPIA TEAM

Greenopia is made up of dedicated professionals from diverse backgrounds who have devoted their lives to making our world greener, happier, and healthier.

We hope that the many hours of careful work that went into producing this guide is reflected in the pages that follow. The work of our publishing team was extensive: researching and developing criteria, identifying relevant markets and categories, going door-to-door to survey thousands of businesses, distilling all the collected data, determining which businesses should be included (based on our criteria), awarding leaves earned by listed businesses, interviewing contributors, and designing an accessible and useful format to put it all together. In addition, our web team worked hard to create a robust companion to the print guide that will build community, keep the guide current, capture user feedback, and offer our readers information for greening their lives even further.

The Green Media Group thanks everyone who made this guide what it is. This team set aside their lives and their sanity more often than can be measured.

Gay Browne (Founder)
Suzanne Biegel (Chief Catalyst)
Terrye Bretzke (Project Director)
Ferris Kawar (Research Director)
Moira Bartel (San Francisco Bay Area Manager)
Alison Edwards (San Francisco Research Coordinator)
Nancy Arbuckle (Book Editor/Writer)
Sally Coates (Designer)
Stephanie Hanford (Project Consultant, Advisory Council)
Craig Henderson (Technical Project Consultant)
Jacob Gordon (Writer)
Victoria Foraker (Project Assistant)
Elektra Grant (Project Assistant)
Basey Klopp (Project Assistant)
Susan Cohen (Indexer)

Our researchers, copy editors, and fact checkers: Laura Burstein, Pamela Cardin, Simone Cifuentes, Hannah Davey, Lori Gubera-Stengel, Colin Hudon, Sarah Million, Lindsay Nivens-Frosini, Michael Sandler, Heather Thompson, Nicole Vanoni, and Julia Weinberg.

A special thanks to the Excel Users Group and StockShop LLC who came to our rescue.

And from the Greenopia Team, a warm thanks to all of our family and loved ones for their support and understanding.

Being green just got a whole lot easier.

Welcome to Greenopia™

You've found *Greenopia™*, the definitive local source for green living. Whether you're looking for an organic muffin, to build or remodel an eco-friendly home, to cut your hair, or cut your energy bill, this guide is your key to finding the eco-friendliest in your area. We list restaurants, dry cleaners, pet stores, beauty salons, grocery stores, and so much more, with independent leaf awards that will help you find the greenest places in your neighborhood. We're *Greenopia™*, and our mission is to guide you to green.

All of the businesses, service providers, organizations, and resources in these pages offer green choices. None of them have paid to be here, and you won't find any ads, either. Our listings and evaluations are based on the work of our own research teams who, through interviews and surveys, have carefully considered each entry individually. The *Greenopia™* system of leaf awards ✐, which we have used in many categories, recognizes green businesses on a scale of one to four leaves, four being the "greenest." The number of leaves awarded a business is a measure of its sale or use of green products and services. At the beginning of each category, look for the criteria used to evaluate that group of listings.

Greenopia™ is more than a guide to greener living. It is a community of people who believe that the choices we make on a day-to-day basis—where we shop, eat, spend our dollars and time—makes a tangible difference in our health and in the health of our environment. We've done our best to provide the most thorough listings and the most useful information, but what's needed and valued are your opinions. There are a lot of folks out there who would like to know how you make your choices and what you think of these businesses and services. Share your thoughts with us. Add your comments and ratings to our website. Suggest businesses we might have missed. Let us hear about your personal experiences. And just as important, give us your reactions to our guide overall. To share your views about *Greenopia™* or pass on your own discoveries in the San Francisco Bay Area green community, visit www.greenopia.com.

Together we'll make the world greener.

Suzanne Biegel, Chief Catalyst
and the Greenopia Team

Contents

Foreword · iii
About This Guide · iv
Acknowledgments · vi
Welcome to Greenopia · ix

Eating Out 1
Restaurants · 2
Cafés, Tea Houses, and Juice Bars · 21
Bakeries · 28
Chocolatiers and Dessert Shops · 30
Seafood Guide · 32
Organic Standards for Food · 34

Eating In 37
Grocery Stores · 38
Farmers' Markets and Community-Supported Agriculture · 44
Grocery and Produce Delivery · 49
Specialty Markets · 50
Catering Services and Personal Chefs · 53
Wine, Beer, and Spirits · 56
Organic Standards for Wine, Beer, and Spirits · 58
Pesticides in Produce · 59
Eating in Season · 60

Being Beautiful 65
Beauty Product Suppliers · 66
Hair and Nail Salons · 70
Day Spas · 73
About Fragrance · 76

Getting Goods 79
Clothing/Shoes and Fabric/Yarn Stores · 80
Gifts, Accessories, and Baby Products · 85
Florists · 88
Office and Paper Products · 89
Low-Impact Fabrics and Fibers · 91
Fair Trade Certification · 92

Caring for Critters 95
Pet Food, Supplies, Grooming, and Other Services · 96
Green Pet Care · 100

Seeing the World 103
Travel Agents · 104
Hotels · 105

Sorting through Services **111**

Pharmacies	112
Personal Services	114
Dry Cleaners and Wet Cleaners	115
Cleaning Services	117
Pest Control	119
Banking and Finance	121
Real Estate	124
Telecommunications	125
Burial Services	126

Greening Your Space **129**

Furniture, Flooring, Carpeting, and Décor	130
Beds, Bedding, and Linens	134
Nurseries and Garden Supplies	135
Gardening and Landscaping	138
Architects/Tradespeople/Interior Designers/ Environmental Consultants	140
Alternative Energy Contractors (Design, Installation, Service, Repair)	148
Building Materials and Supplies	150
Recycling Centers/Recycling Services/Salvage Yards	152
Household Hazardous Waste Disposal	156
Reduce, Reuse, Recycle	158
What Goes in the Bin	159

Getting Around **161**

Eco-Friendly Vehicle Dealerships/ Service and Fueling Stations	162
Auto Clubs	166
Taxicabs and Limousines	166
Car Rentals/Car Share Services/ Alternative Transportation	167
Public Transportation	169
Carbon Offset Services	171
Going Carbon Neutral	173
Quick Guide to Alternative Transportation	175

Adding to Your Involvement **177**

Environmental Organizations	178
Educational Organizations	188
Books We Recommend	194

Regional Maps	196
Listings by Region	202
Alphabetical Index	222

Eating Out

Eating In

Being Beautiful

Getting Goods

Caring for Critters

Seeing the World

Sorting through Services

Greening Your Space

Getting Around

Adding to Your Involvement

Supporting the "Green Web"

Here in the Bay Area we have a wealth of extraordinary people producing incredible food. There are organic and eco-friendly growers, artisan cheese-makers, producers of traditional olive oils, organic vintners and wineries. When I go to the farmer's market, I am astounded by how hard people are working to produce these beautiful crops and create these delicacies. And it's so exciting to see how people respond to being directly in touch with the person who grew those beautiful apples or leafy greens, pressed that olive oil, or juiced that pomegranate. Unlike the supermarket, the farmer's market has a spontaneity and freshness that stimulates the senses and brings people to life.

As a restaurateur in the Bay Area, I have been working directly with small growers and producers for years. As time has passed and this region has become "food central," it's not only thrilling and fun to be here, it's also very meaningful. Being where we are and doing what we do means we're helping to support this "green web" of dedicated and talented people.

Providing fresh, healthy, organic food in a way that helps nurture and preserve the environment is what our business is all about. How we think about food, order and receive it, prepare and store it, is symbolic of a commitment to freshness, to sustainability. Maintaining our connection with the region and its many growers and small businesses is so important. We're conscious of working locally, within our own "foodshed," the area within 100 to 150 miles of where we're located.

When you enter a new restaurant, be receptive to basic observations. For instance, does the restaurateur shop locally? Are the ingredients sustainably produced? Are sustainable practices followed? Try to sense whether the staff is informed and invested in what's going on there. If people feel connected and committed to what they're doing, you'll detect a sense of vibrancy and vigor. This cohesion is the product of whole and healthy processes. It's not just about food, but about healthy lives, healthy ecosystems, and healthy societies.

ANNIE SOMERVILLE
Annie Somerville is an author, teacher, and the Executive Chef at Greens Restaurant in San Francisco's Fort Mason Center.

One of the most intimate moments we share with our planet is when we're holding a fork. The food we eat comes from the earth and turns into the stuff we're made of. Every day, more restaurants are recognizing that a healthy planet yields healthy food, which ends up making healthy people. That sounds tasty to us. But not every restaurant offering green eats makes a big deal out of it, so we looked below the surface to find healthy and natural fare from across the cuisine spectrum suitable for any type of budget

We chose to factor the sustainability features of the food over other areas in which a restaurant may demonstrate its commitment to the environment—such as green building design, the use of recyclable "to-go" containers, composting, or energy efficient kitchens. Future editions of the guide will reflect these important practices. However, since food is your main criteria when choosing a restaurant, we thought it should be ours as well.

Our leaf awards are based on the following:

- the percentage of produce purchased that is either certified organic and/or locally grown without pesticides and chemical fertilizers.

- the percentage of fresh poultry and eggs that is certified organic, free-range/cage-free OR locally raised, free-range/cage-free without the use of hormones and/or antibiotics.

- the percentage of dairy products and grains that are certified organic.

- the source of the seafood—whether it was wild-caught or farm-raised.

- the percentage of fresh meat that is certified organic and/or grass fed and produced without the use of hormones and antibiotics.

- the percentage of certified organic coffee, tea, juice, alcohol, soft drinks.

at least 25% of food and/or beverages served meets the above criteria.

at least 50% of food and/or beverages served meets the above criteria.

at least 75% of food and/or beverages served meets the above criteria.

90% or more of food and/or beverages served meets the above criteria.

Average price of an entrée:

$	$10 or less
$$	$11-$20
$$$	$21-$30
$$$$	$31 and up
C	Provides catering services

AMERICAN (INCLUDES SOUTHERN/CAJUN)

BALBOA CAFÉ 🌿🌿🌿 $$
3199 Fillmore St. SF (Cow Hollow) 94123 415-921-3944
Mon-Tue 11:30-10 Wed-Fri 11:30-11 Sat 9-11 Sun 9-10   www.plumpjack.com
Upscale American fare. Organic ingredients.

BUBBA'S DINER 🌿🌿🌿🌿 $$ C
566 San Anselmo Ave. San Anselmo 94960 415-459-6862
Wed-Fri 9-9 Sat-Sun 8-9 www.bubbas-diner.net
Classic American diner. Organic produce and coffee; grass-fed, hormone-free beef. Certified green business.

BULLSHEAD RESTAURANT 🌿🌿🌿 $$
840 Ulloa St. SF (Sunset) 94127 415-665-4350
4230 18th St. SF (Castro) 94114 415-431-4201
Mon-Tue 11-9:30 Wed-Sat 11-10 Sun 11-9 www.bullsheadrestaurant.com
Upscale diner. Organic meat and game, including buffalo.

COCK-A-DOODLE CAFÉ 🌿🌿🌿 $$ C
719 Washington St. Oakland (Lake Merritt/Downtown) 94607 510-465-5400
Mon-Fri 8-2:30 Sat-Sun 8-3 www.cockadoodlecafe.com
Locally grown produce. Breakfast, lunch, and brunch only.

COOL CAFÉ 🌿🌿🌿🌿 $ C
128 Lomita Dr. Stanford 94305 650-725-4758
Wed 11-5 Thu 11-8 Fri-Sun 11-5 www.cooleatz.com/cool-cafe
Indoor/outdoor restaurant next to sculpture garden on Stanford University campus.

FARMER BROWN 🌿🌿🌿 $$
25 Mason St. SF (Civic Center) 94102 415-409-3276
Daily 5-midnight Bar open until 2 a.m. www.farmerbrownsf.com
Classic Southern American fare. Organic ingredients.

JIMMY BEAN'S 🌿🌿🌿 $ C
1290 Sixth St. Berkeley 94710 510-528-3435
Mon-Fri 7-9 Sat-Sun 8-9 www.jimmybeans.com
Eclectic seasonal, organic comfort food.

LET'S BE FRANK DOGS 🌿🌿🌿 $ C
240 Hartford St. SF (Presidio/Presidio Heights) 94114 888-233-7265
Sat-Sun 11-4 (weather permitting) at the west end of Crissy Field
www.letsbefrankdogs.com
Hot dog cart that carries natural-fed beef dogs, organic buns, organic condiments, juices and sodas.

LOLA'S 🌿🌿 $ C
1585 Solano Ave. Berkeley 94707 510-558-8600
Wed-Sun 12-9 www.lolaspizza.com
Take-home pizza, entrees, roast chicken, sandwiches, salads, and desserts.

SUNNY SIDE CAFÉ 🌿🌿🌿 $
1499 Solano Ave. Albany 94706 510-527-5383
Mon-Fri 8-3 Sat-Sun 8:30-3
Modern American, largely organic fare. Breakfast served all day. Outdoor seating.

THREE DEGREES RESTAURANT 🌿 $$$ C
1651 Tiburon Blvd. Tiburon 94920 415-435-5996
140 South Santa Cruz Ave. Los Gatos 95030 408-884-1054
Hours vary by location www.threedegreesrestaurant.com
Fresh, seasonal comfort food.

TOWN HALL 🍃🍃🍃 **$$$**
342 Howard St. SF (SOMA) 94105 415-908-3900
Mon-Fri 11:30-10 Sat 5:30-10:30 Sun 5:30-9:30   www.townhallsf.com
Original American fare, heavy on organic ingredients.

T-REX BARBEQUE 🍃🍃 **$$ C**
1300 10th St. Berkeley 94710 510-527-0099
Mon-Thu 11:30-10 Fri 11:30-12:30 Sat 10:30-12:30 Sun 10:30-10
www.t-rex-bbq.com
Traditional bbq with a green twist. House smoked, grilled, and cured
all-organic, free-range meats. Local, organic produce.

VELO ROUGE 🍃🍃🍃 **$**
798 Arguello Blvd. SF (Richmond) 94118 415-752-7799
Mon-Tue 6:30 a.m.-3 p.m. Wed-Fri 6:30 a.m.-10 p.m. Sat-Sun 8-5
www.velorougecafe.com
Bicycle-themed restaurant serving organic and fair trade coffee and
comfort food. Local chef uses sustainable ingredients for a weekly event
called "Radio Africa."

AMERICAN (CONTEMPORARY)

2223 RESTAURANT 🍃🍃🍃🍃 **$$$ C**
2223 Market St. SF (Castro) 94114 415-431-0692
Mon-Thu 5-9:30 Fri-Sat 5-11 Sun 10:30-2:30, 5-9:30   www.2223restaurant.com
New American/Californian fare. Antibiotic-free meat; organic produce.
Seasonal ingredients.

BLUE PLATE, THE 🍃🍃🍃🍃 **$$$**
3218 Mission St. SF (Bernal Heights) 94110 415-282-6777
Mon-Thu 6-10 Fri-Sat 6-10:30 www.blueplatesf.com
Creative combinations of organic ingredients.

BOULETTES LARDER 🍃🍃🍃🍃 **$$ C**
One Ferry Building #48 SF (Embarcadero) 94111 415-399-1155
Mon-Fri 8-6 Sat 8-2:30 Sun 10-3 www.bouletteslarder.com
Restaurant, bakery, and deli. Prepared take-out foods, specialty spices.

CAPRICE, THE 🍃🍃🍃 **$$$$ C**
2000 Paradise Dr. Tiburon 94920 415-435-3400
Mon-Thu 5:30-10 Fri-Sun 5-10 www.thecaprice.com
Produce from local farms, wild-caught fish and hormone-free, grass-fed beef,
free-range chicken.

CENTRAL PARK BISTRO 🍃🍃 **$$$ C**
181 East Fourth Ave. San Mateo 94401 650-558-8401
Mon-Thu 11:30-3, 5-10 Fri-Sat 11:30-3, 5-10:30 Sun 5-10
www.centralparkbistro.com
Seasonal contemporary cuisine. Local ingredients.

DELANCEY STREET RESTAURANT 🍃🍃 **$$**
600 Embarcadero St. SF (SOMA) 94107 415-512-5179
Tue-Fri 11-11 Sat-Sun 10-11
Ethnic-inspired American bistro. Staffed by participants in the
Delancey Street Foundation job training program.

FIREFLY 🍃🍃🍃 **$$**
4288 24th St. SF (Noe Valley) 94114 415-821-7652
Mon-Thu 5:30-9:30 Fri-Sat 5:30-10 Sun 5:30-9 www.fireflyrestaurant.com
Locally purchased produce; grass-fed, hormone-free beef;
free-range poultry. Vegetarian dishes.

HOME 🍃🍃 $$$ C
2032 Union St. SF (Cow Hollow) 94123 415-931-5006
2100 Market St. SF (Castro) 94114 415-503-0333
Hours vary by location www.home-sf.com
Upscale comfort food. Organic ingredients.

LARK CREEK INN 🍃🍃 $$$ C
234 Magnolia Ave. Larkspur 94939 415-924-7766
Mon-Fri 11:30-2, 5:30-10 Sat 5-10 Sun 10-2, 5-9 www.larkcreek.com
Local purveyors; brunch, lunch and dinner, tasting menu, private parties.

LIBERTY CAFÉ, THE 🍃🍃🍃 $$
410 Cortland Ave. SF (Bernal Heights) 94110 415-695-8777
Tue-Fri 11:30-3, 5:30-9:30 Sat-Sun 10-2, 5:30-9:30
Neighborhood restaurant using local and organic produce and meat.

ONE MARKET 🍃 $$$$ C
1 Market St. SF (SOMA) 94105 415-777-5577
Mon-Fri 11:30-2, 5:30-9 Sat 5:30-9 www.onemarket.com
Exhibition kitchen; local purveyors. Tasting menu, private parties.

POSTRIO 🍃🍃 $$$$
545 Post St. SF (Nob Hill) 94102 415-776-7825
Daily 5:30-10 Lounge 11:30-11:30 www.postrio.com
Contemporary American Cuisine focusing on fish, meats, and produce
from small, local farms.

SLOW CLUB 🍃🍃 $$
2501 Mariposa St. SF (Mission) 94110 415-241-9390
Mon-Thu 8-2:30, 6:30-10 Fri 8-2:30, 6:30-11 Sat 10-2:30, 6-11 Sun 10-2:30
www.slowclub.com
Upscale dining in an industrial setting; some organic fare.

SMALL SHED FLATBREADS 🍃🍃 $$ C
17 Madrona St. Mill Valley 94941 415-383-4200
Sun-Thu 11-9 Fri-Sat 11-10 www.smallshed.com
Wood-fired flatbread pizzas, organic soups, salads, wine and beer; supports
local purveyors.

SUBCULTURE DINING 🍃🍃🍃🍃 $$$$
415-816-8787
Fri-Sun Seating times and locations vary www.dissidentchef.com
Underground, mobile restaurant that serves fine dining in private settings that
change from meal to meal. Multi-course meals with wine pairings.

TABLESPOON 🍃🍃 $$
2209 Polk St. SF (Russian Hill) 94109 415-268-0140
Mon-Thu 5:30-10:30 Fri-Sat 5:30-12 Sun 5-10 www.tablespoonsf.com
New American menu highlighting seasonal fare.

TOWN'S END RESTAURANT AND BAKERY 🍃🍃🍃 $$ C
2 Townsend St. SF (SOMA) 94107 415-512-0749
Tue-Thu 7:30-9 Fri 7:30-9:30 Sat 8-9:30 Sun 8-2:30
Casual New American; features local ingredients and hand-crafted
baked goods.

UNIVERSAL CAFÉ 🍃🍃🍃 $$$
2814 19th St. SF (Mission) 94110 415-821-4608
Tue-Fri 11:30-2:30 Tue-Thu 5:30-9:30 Fri 5:30-10:30
Sat 9-2:30, 5:30-10:30 Sun 9:00-2:30, 5:30-9:30 www.universalcafe.net
Wide-variety of seasonal dishes featuring fresh, local ingredients.

ASIAN

DELICA RF-1 🌿🌿🌿 **$**
One Ferry Building #45 SF (Embarcadero) 94111 415-834-0344
Mon-Fri 10-6 Sat 9-6 Sun 11-5 www.delicarf1.com
A Japanese delicatessen offering prepared side dishes, main courses,
fresh-fried foods, and substantial salads for take-away.

MEDICINE EATSTATION 🌿🌿🌿🌿 **$$$ C**
161 Sutter St. SF (Financial District) 94102 415-677-4405
Mon-Thu 11:30-2:30, 5:30-9 Fri 11:30-2:30, 5:30-10 Sat 5:30-10
www.medicinerestaurant.com
Vegan Japanese Zen Cuisine. All organic.

OUT THE DOOR 🌿🌿🌿🌿 **$**
One Ferry Building #3 SF (Embarcadero) 94111 415-321-3740
Mon-Fri 10-6 Sat 8:30-5 www.slanteddoor.com
The take-out version of The Slanted Door restaurant. Offers many of
the same dishes, but at lower prices.

RENEE'S PLACE 🌿🌿 **$**
1477 Solano Ave. Albany 94706 510-525-2330
Daily 11:30-3, 5-9:30
Szechuan and Hunan cuisine; mostly organic, free-range,
sustainable ingredients.

SIRAYVAH ORGANIC THAI CUISINE 🌿🌿🌿🌿 **$$ C**
366 El Camino Real San Carlos 94070 650-637-1500
Mon-Fri 11:30-2:30, 5-9:30 Sat-Sun 5-9:30
Traditional Thai combinations made with organic ingredients.

SLANTED DOOR, THE 🌿🌿🌿🌿 **$$$**
One Ferry Building #3 SF (Embarcadero) 94111 415-861-8032
Sun-Thu 11-10 Fri-Sat 11-10:30 www.slanteddoor.com
Modern Vietnamese restaurant that showcases fresh produce as well
as ecologically farmed meat, game, and poultry grown or raised at farms
around the San Francisco Bay Area.

THAI DELIGHT CUISINE 🌿 **$ C**
1700 Shattuck Ave. Berkeley 94709 510-549-0611
Daily 11:30-3, 4:30-9:45 www.thaidelightcuisine.com
Thai cuisine, featuring wild-caught fish, organic grains, and some
hormone-free meats.

ASIAN FUSION

AME RESTAURANT 🌿 **$$$ C**
St. Regis Hotel 689 Mission St. SF (SOMA) 94103 415-284-4040
Daily 5:30-10 www.amerestaurant.com
New American and Fusion cuisine; sashimi bar. Local ingredients.

CHAYA BRASSERIE 🌿🌿 **$$$**
132 The Embarcadero SF (Financial District) 94105 415-777-8688
Mon-Wed 11:30-10 Thu-Fri 11:30-10:30 Sat 5:30-10:30 Sun 5:30-10
www.thechaya.com
French-Japanese fusion. Restaurant has a formal dining room as well
as a more casual sushi bar.

EOS RESTAURANT 🌿🌿 **$$ C**
901 Cole St. SF (Cole Valley) 94117 415-566-3063
Sun-Thu 5:30-10 Fri-Sat 5:30-11 www.eossf.com
Asian fusion. Organic ingredients and wines.

O'CHAME ◊◊ $$
1830 Fourth St. Berkeley 94710 510-841-8783
Mon-Thu 11:30-3, 5:30-9 Fri-Sat 11:30-3, 5:30-9:30
Modern Japanese-fusion cuisine.

POMELO ◊ $$ C
1793 Church St. SF (Sunset) 94131 415-285-2257
92 Judah St. SF (Sunset) 94122 415-731-6175
Hours vary by location www.pomelosf.com
Eclectic global cuisine in small neighborhood bistro, featuring local ingredients.

BURGERS

BRICKHOUSE CAFE ◊◊◊ $ C
426 Brannan St. SF (SOMA) 94107 415-369-0222
Mon-Fri 7-10 Sat 10-10 www.brickhousesf.com
Specializes in all-natural Kobe beef burgers. Free-range chicken;
vegetarian dishes.

BURGER JOINT ◊ $
807 Valencia St. SF (Mission) 94110 415-824-3494
SFO International Terminal SF (SFO) 94128 650-583-5863
700 Haight St. SF (Lower Haight) 94117 415-864-3833
Hours vary by location www.burgerjointsf.com
Niman Ranch natural beef.

M&G BURGERS ◊ $ C
2017 Sir Francis Drake Blvd. Fairfax 94930 415-454-0655
989 Magnolia Ave. Larkspur 94939 415-461-2211
Mon-Sat 11-9 Sun 12-8
Organic beef and buffalo burgers, hot dogs, fish burgers, milk shakes,
soft-serve ice cream.

CALIFORNIAN

1550 HYDE CAFÉ & WINE BAR ◊◊◊ $$$
1550 Hyde St. SF (Russian Hill) 94109 415-775-1550
Tue-Thu 6-10 Fri-Sat 6-10:30 Sun 5:30-9:30 www.1550hyde.com
California-Mediterranean, simple, seasonal, organic cuisine. Award-winning
wine list.

ACME CHOPHOUSE ◊◊◊◊ $$$
24 Willie Mays Plaza SF (SOMA) 94107 415-644-0240
Tue-Fri 11-2:30, 5:30-10 Sat-Sun 5:30-10 (Expanded hours for Giants games)
www.acmechophouse.com
Fine American chophouse. Naturally raised meat and poultry; local fish;
sustainably grown produce. Recent green-friendly building renovation.

ADAGIA ◊◊◊ $$ C
2700 Bancroft Way Berkeley 94704 510-647-2300
Mon-Fri 11-5 Mon-Sun 5-10 Sat-Sun 10:30-3 www.adagiarestaurant.com
California-Mediterranean cuisine. Sustainable, local, organic ingredients;
outdoor patio.

B RESTAURANT AND BAR ◊◊◊◊ $
499 Ninth St. Oakland (Lake Merritt/Downtown) 94607 510-251-8770
720 Howard St. SF (SOMA) 94103 415-495-9800
Hours vary by location www.boxedfoodscompany.com
Simple, rustic cuisine. Organic produce and sustainably farmed or harvested
meats and fish sourced from within 100 miles. Small plates to go available as well.

BACAR ✿✿✿ $$$ C
448 Brannan St. SF (SOMA) 94107 415-904-4100
Mon-Thu 5:30-10 Fri 11-11 Sat 5:30-11 Sun 5:30-10
www.bacarsf.com
Organic ingredients sourced in the region; extensive wine list.

BOULEVARD RESTAURANT ✿✿ $$$
One Mission St. SF (Financial District) 94105 415-543-6084
Mon-Thu 11:30-10 Fri 11:30-10:30 Sat 5:30-10:30 Sun 5:30-10
www.boulevardrestaurant.com
California-French cuisine. Local organic produce, meats, and cheeses.

CHEZ PANISSE ✿✿✿✿ $$$$
1517 Shattuck Ave. Berkeley 94709 510-548-5525
Upstairs café: Mon-Thu 11:30-3, 5-10:30 Fri-Sat 11:30-3:30, 5-11:30 Downstairs:
Dinner by reservation only. www.chezpanisse.com
Upscale cuisine. Local organic ingredients. Prix fixe dinner menu downstairs;
a la carte menu upstairs.

CITIZEN CAKE ✿✿✿ $$$
399 Grove St. SF (Civic Center) 94102 415-861-2228
Tue-Fri 8-10 Sat 10-10 Sun 10-5 www.citizencake.com
Innovative cuisine with a focus on dessert items.

COCO 500 ✿✿✿✿ $$ C
500 Brannan St. SF (SOMA) 94107 415-543-2222
Mon-Thu 11:30-10 Fri 11:30-11 Sat 5:30-11 www.coco500.com
Upscale cuisine using seasonal, local and organic produce. Organic cocktails.

COI ✿✿✿✿ $$$$
373 Broadway SF (North Beach) 94133 415-393-9000
Tue-Sat 6-10 www.coirestaurant.com
Upscale California-French cuisine. Prix fixe and tasting menu; adjacent lounge
with a la carte menu.

COMFORTS ✿ $$ C
335 San Anselmo Ave. San Anselmo 94960 415-454-9840
Mon-Fri 6-7 Sat-Sun 7-7 www.comfortscafe.com
Eclectic cuisine. Organic, fair trade coffee; grass-fed beef;
wild salmon.

DE YOUNG CAFÉ ✿✿✿ $$
Golden Gate Park 50 Hagiwara Tea Garden Dr. SF (Sunset) 94118 415-750-2614
Tue-Sun 9:30-4 www.thinker.org/deyoung/visiting
All ingredients from Northern California organic farms and producers. Local
wines and coffee.

FLEA ST. CAFÉ ✿✿✿✿ $$$
3607 Alameda de las Pulgas Menlo Park 94025 650-854-1226
Tue-Sat 5:30-9:30 Sun 10-2, 5:30-8:30 www.cooleatz.com/flea-st-cafe
Fine dining. Organic wine and vodka cocktails. Reservations required.

FORK ✿✿ $$$ C
198 Sir Francis Drake Blvd. San Anselmo 94960 415-453-9898
Tue-Sat 5:30-9:30 Sun 4:45-9 www.marinfork.com
California-French cuisine. Local organic produce, free-range meat.

GARIBALDI'S ✿✿ $$$
5356 College Ave. Oakland (College Ave.) 94618 510-595-4000
Mon-Fri 11:30-2:30, 5:30-10 Sat 5:30-10:30 Sun 10-2, 5:30-9:30
www.garibaldis-eastbay.com
Free-range poultry, wild-caught fish, and locally grown produce.

GLOBE ✐✐✐ **$$ C**
290 Pacific Ave. SF (Financial District) 94111 415-391-4132
Mon-Fri 11:30-3, 6 p.m.-1 a.m. Sat 6 p.m.-1 a.m. Sun 6 p.m.-midnight
www.globerestaurant.com
California organic food with an Italian influence.

HARVEST & ROWE ✐✐✐✐ **$ C**
55 Second St. SF (SOMA) 94105 415-541-7771
Mon-Fri 8-3 www.harvestandrowe.com
Soups, salads, and sandwiches made from organic ingredients;
organic coffee and juices.

JACK FALSTAFF RESTAURANT ✐✐ **$$$ C**
598 Second St. SF (SOMA) 94107 415-836-9239
Mon-Thu 11:30-2, 5:30-10 Fri 11:30-2, 5:30-11 Sat 5:30-11
www.plumpjack.com/falstaff1.html
Upscale, Slow Food restaurant. All organic ingredients; energy
efficient establishment.

JZCOOL EATERY ✐✐✐✐ **$ C**
827 Santa Cruz Ave. Menlo Park 94025 650-325-3665
Mon 10-3 Tue-Sat 11-6 Sun 10-3 www.cooleatz.com
Casual breakfast, lunch, and dinner spot. Compostable utensils
and take-out packages.

LALIME'S ✐✐✐ **$$$**
1329 Gilman St. Berkeley 94706 510-527-9838
Mon-Thu 5:30-9:30 Fri-Sat 5:30-10 Sun 5-9 www.lalimes.com
Slow Food restaurant. Local, seasonal produce direct from farmers;
sustainable fish and meats.

LEGION OF HONOR CAFÉ ✐ **$$ C**
Lincoln Park 100 34th Ave. SF (Richmond) 94121 415-750-7639
Tue-Sun 9:30-4 Admission to museum required; no separate entry.
www.thinker.org/legion/visiting
Soups, salads, sandwiches, burgers, free-range poultry and wild fish entrees.
All showcase local, Northern California organic ingredients and flavors.

LETTUS CAFÉ ORGANIC ✐✐✐✐ **$ C**
3352 Steiner St. SF (Marina) 94123 415-931-2777
Mon–Fri 10:30-10 Sat-Sun 9-10 www.lettusorganic.com
Freshly made juices, salads, sandwiches, soups, entrees and desserts
using all organic ingredients. Serves breakfast, lunch, and dinner.

MIXT GREENS ✐✐✐✐ **$ C**
114 Sansome St. SF (Financial District) 94104 415-433-6498
475 Sansome St. SF (Financial District) 94104 (Opening May 2007)
Mon-Fri 10:30-3 www.mixtgreens.com
Innovative organic salads and sandwiches, juices and teas. Building
designed using environmentally-friendly materials.

MODERN TEA ✐✐✐✐ **$**
602 Hayes St. SF (Hayes Valley) 94102 415-626-5406
Tue-Fri 11:30-9 Sat 10:30-9 Sun 10:30-6 www.moderntea.com
Lunch, dinner, and weekend brunch in the heart of Hayes Valley.
Huge tea selection and related gifts.

MOUNTAIN HOME INN ✐✐ **$$$**
810 Panoramic Hwy. Mill Valley 94941 415-381-9000
Wed-Thu 11:30-8 Fri-Sat 11:30-9 Sun 11:30-8 www.mtnhomeinn.com
Creative cuisine highlighting local organic ingredients.

MYTH ⬩⬩ $$$
470 Pacific Ave. SF (Financial District) 94133 415-677-8986
Tue-Thu 5:30-9:30 Fri-Sat 5:30-10:30 www.mythsf.com
Eclectic California/French cuisine served in casual yet elegant surroundings.

PAPPO ⬩⬩ $$ C
2320 Central Ave. Alameda 94501 510-337-9100
Wed-Thu 5:30-9 Fri-Sat 5:30-10 Sun 10-1, 5:30-9 www.papporestaurant.com
Californian casual dining, featuring hormone-free meat, free range chicken, and locally grown produce.

PLUMPJACK CAFÉ ⬩⬩ $$$
3127 Fillmore St. SF (Cow Hollow) 94123 415-563-4755
Mon-Fri 11:30-2, 5:30-10 Sat-Sun 5:30-10 www.plumpjack.com
Upscale restaurant that features many small, organic, sustainable farms on the menu.

RANGE ⬩⬩⬩ $$
842 Valencia St. SF (Mission) 94110 415-282-8283
Sun-Thu 5:30-10 Fri-Sat 5:30-11 www.rangesf.com
Seasonal and hearty California cuisine.

RUBICON ⬩⬩ $$$
558 Sacramento St. SF (Financial District) 94111 415-434-4100
Mon-Sat 5:30-10:30 Wed 11:30-2 www.sfrubicon.com
California cuisine. Seasonal, organic ingredients.

SELLERS MARKETS ⬩⬩⬩⬩ $ C
388 Market St. SF (Financial District) 94111 415-956-3825
595 Market St. SF (Financial District) 94105 415-227-9850
Hours vary by location www.sellersmarkets.com
Eco-friendly food from local growers. Serving breakfast and lunch.

SIMMER ⬩ $$$ C
60 Corte Madera Ave. Corte Madera 94925 415-927-2332
Tue-Thu 6-9:30 Fri-Sat 6-10 Sun 10-2
Eclectic California-French bistro; organic greens, hormone-free meats.

SUTRO'S ⬩⬩⬩ $$$
Cliff House 1090 Point Lobos SF (Richmond) 94121 415-386-3330
Mon-Sat 11:30-9:30 Sun 11-10 www.cliffhouse.com
Fresh seafood and local ingredients served in a scenic ocean-view setting.

VENUS ⬩⬩⬩ $$
2327 Shattuck Ave. Berkeley 94704 510-540-5950
Mon 8-2:30 Tue-Fri 8-2:30, 5-9:30 Sat-Sun 8-2:15, 5-9:30
www.venusrestaurant.net
American bistro; organic, local, sustainable ingredients.

VIGNETTE ⬩⬩⬩ $$$ C
665 Bush St. SF (Nob Hill) 94108 415-956-2972
Daily 11:30-2, 5:30-10 www.vignetterestaurant.com
Seasonal fare from local farms and small growers. Meats are raised with no hormones or antibiotics.

VINO LOCALE ⬩⬩⬩⬩ $ C
431 Kipling St. Palo Alto 94301 650-328-0450
Tue-Sat 11-9 Sun 12-5 www.vinolocale.com
California cuisine served in a Victorian house. All-organic menu.

WEST BAY CAFÉ AND LOUNGE ✐✐✐ $$ C
Crowne Plaza Hotel - SFO 1177 Airport Blvd. Burlingame 94010 650-342-9200
Daily 5-10 www.sfocp.com
International coastal cuisine. A café for breakfast and lunch; fine dining and
lounge for dinner.

ETHIOPIAN

CAFÉ COLUCCI ✐✐✐✐ $$ C
6427 Telegraph Ave. Oakland (Lake Merritt/Downtown) 94609 510-601-7999
Daily 8 a.m.-10 p.m. www.cafecolucci.com
Organic Ethiopian cuisine in casual setting; vegetarian friendly; family operated.

FRENCH

ABSINTHE BRASSERIE AND BAR ✐✐✐ $$$
398 Hayes St. SF (Hayes Valley) 94102 415-551-1590
Tue-Sat 11:30-midnight Sun 11-10 www.absinthe.com
American-influenced brasserie. Late night café dining.

BISTRO 330 ✐ $$$ C
330 San Anselmo Ave. San Anselmo 94960 415-460-6330
Tue-Thu 5:30-9 Fri-Sat 5:30-10
Bistro serving free-range and hormone-free meat.

BUTLER AND THE CHEF BISTRO, THE ✐✐ $$ C
155A South Park SF (SOMA) 94107 415-896-2075
Mon-Sat 8-3 Sun 10-3 www.thebutlerandthechefbistro.com
Authentic French Bistro with sidewalk tables and charming atmosphere.
Biodegradable cutlery and eco-friendly atmosphere.

CHEZ ALEXANDER ✐ $$$
1136 Broadway Burlingame 94010 650-347-1053
Mon-Sat 5-10 Lunch by appt. www.chezalexander.com
Country French/European.

CHEZ MAMAN ✐✐✐ $$
2223 Union St. SF (Potrero Hill) 94123 415-771-7771
1453 18th St. SF (Potrero Hill) 94107 415-824-7166
Hours vary by location www.chezmamansf.com
Neighborhood restaurant. Crepes, salads, sandwiches, mussels.

CÔTÉ SUD ✐✐✐ $$
4238 18th St. SF (Castro) 94114 415-255-6565
Mon-Thu 5:30-9:30 Fri-Sat 5:30-10:30 www.cotesudsf.com
French bistro using organic ingredients.

CREPES CAFÉ ✐ $
1195 Merrill St. Menlo Park 94025 650-473-0506
Mon-Sat 8-9 Sun 8-4 www.crepescafe.com
Organic crepes and fillings.

FLEUR DE LYS ✐ $$$$
777 Sutter St. SF (Nob Hill) 94109 415-673-7779
Mon-Thu 6-9:30 Fri-Sat 5:30-10:30 www.fleurdelyssf.com
Contemporary cuisine served in an upscale setting.

FRINGALE ✐✐ $$
570 Fourth St. SF (SOMA) 94107 415-543-0573
Mon-Thu 11:30-2:30, 5:30-10 Fri 11:30-2:30, 5:30-11 Sat 5:30-11 Sun 5:30-10
www.fringalesf.com
Upscale, healthy cuisine.

GREGOIRE JACQUET 🌿🌿🌿 $ C
4001B Piedmont Ave. Piedmont 94611 510-547-3444
2109 Cedar St. Berkeley 94709 510-883-1893
Mon-Sun 11-9 www.gregoirerestaurant.com
French take-out food. Organic and locally purchased produce,
meat, and poultry.

JARDINIÈRE 🌿🌿🌿 $$$$
300 Grove St. SF (Civic Center) 94102 415-861-5555
Mon-Wed 5-10:30 Thu-Sun 5-11:30 www.jardiniere.com
Vibrant seasonal French-California cuisine using organic and
sustainable foods. Recycling and composting programs.
SF green certified business.

JOHN BENTLEY'S RESTAURANT 🌿🌿 $$$
2915 El Camino Real Redwood City 94061 650-365-7777
2991 Woodside Rd. Woodside 94062 650-851-4988
Hours vary by location www.johnbentleys.com
French-inspired American cuisine. Local organic and wild-grown ingredients.

JOJO 🌿🌿🌿 $$$
3859 Piedmont Ave. Piedmont 94611 510-985-3003
Tue-Thu 5:30-9:30 Fri-Sat 5:30-10:30 www.jojorestaurant.com
Country French dining. Locally grown and organic produce, free-range
chicken, wild-caught fish, hormone-free meat.

LUKA'S TAPROOM & LOUNGE 🌿🌿 $$
2221 Broadway Oakland (Lake Merritt/Downtown) 94612 510-451-4677
Mon-Tue 11:30-midnight Wed-Fri 11:30-2 a.m. Sat 5:30-2 a.m. Sun 11-midnight
www.lukasoakland.com
Restaurant, bar and lounge; California-French eclectic brasserie,
featuring locally grown produce, hormone-free meats and wild-caught fish.

MARCHÉ AUX FLEURS 🌿🌿 $$$ C
23 Ross Common Ross 94957 415-925-9200
Tue-Sat 5:30-close www.marcheauxfleursrestaurant.com
Fine French dining; organic, local produce and hormone-free meats.

MASA'S RESTAURANT 🌿🌿 $$$$
648 Bush St. SF (Financial District) 94108 415-989-7154
Tue-Thu 5:30-8:30 Fri-Sat 5:30-9 www.masasrestaurant.com
Fine French cuisine incorporating organic ingredients.
Inside the Executive Hotel.

MISTRAL ROTISSERIE PROVENCALE 🌿🌿🌿 $
One Ferry Building #41 SF (Embarcadero) 94111 415-399-9751
Mon-Fri 10-7 Sat 8-6 Sun 11-5 www.mistralrotisserie.com
Classic French rotisserie offering meats and poultry roasted with
Mediterranean flavors. Prepared foods available as well.

SOUTH PARK CAFÉ 🌿🌿 $$
108 South Park SF (SOMA) 94107 415-495-7275
Mon-Fri 11:30-2:30 Tue-Sat 5:30-10 www.southparkcafesf.com
French bistro and bar. Organic and local ingredients.

INDIAN/PAKISTANI

BREADS OF INDIA & GOURMET CURRIES 🌿🌿🌿 $$ C
2448 Sacramento St. Berkeley 94702 510-848-7684
Daily 11:30-2:30, 5:30-9:30
Regional Indian cuisine. Organic and locally grown produce, meat, grain;
wild-caught fish.

ROTI INDIAN BISTRO 🌿🌿🌿 $$
209 Park Rd. Burlingame 94010 650-340-7684
53 West Portal Ave. SF (West Portal) 94127 415-665-7684
Hours vary by location www.rotibistro.com
Modern Indian cuisine highlighting local and organic ingredients.

TABLE CAFÉ 🌿🌿🌿 $$ C
1167 Magnolia Ave. Larkspur 94939 415-461-6787
Tue-Fri 10:30-7 Sat 10:30-3:30
Indian cuisine. A specialty is dosai, or Indian crepes, filled with
a variety of local and organic ingredients. Also serves soups and salads.

ITALIAN

ACQUERELLO 🌿🌿🌿 $$$$
1722 Sacramento St. SF (Nob Hill) 94109 415-567-5432
Tue-Sat 5:30-10:30 www.acquerello.com
Haute Italian cuisine.

AMERICANO RESTAURANT AND BAR 🌿 $$$$ C
Hotel Vitale 8 Mission St. SF (SOMA) 94105 415-278-3777
Mon-Thu 6:30-10 Fri 6:30-11 Sat 7:30-11 Sun 7:30-10
www.americanorestaurant.com
Rustic Italian and Californian cuisine. Produce, meat, and cheese
purchased directly from farmers.

ANGELINO RESTAURANT 🌿🌿 $$$ C
621 Bridgeway Sausalito 94965 415-331-5225
Mon-Tue 5-9:30 Wed-Sun 11:30-9:30
www.angelinorestaurant.com
Old-world Italian restaurant. Local organic produce; wild-caught and
sustainably farmed fish; hormone-free meat.

APERTO 🌿🌿 $$ C
1434 18th St. SF (Potrero Hill) 94107 415-252-1625
Mon-Fri 11:30-2:30, 5:30-10 Sat 11-2:30, 5:30-10 Sun 10-2:30, 5-9
www.apertosf.com
Neighborhood restaurant. Local, seasonal, and organic ingredients; seasonal
herb garden and olive bushes.

BACCO RISTORANTE ITALIANO 🌿🌿🌿 $$
737 Diamond St. SF (Noe Valley) 94114 415-282-4969
Mon-Thu 5:30-9:30 Fri-Sat 5:30-10 Sun 5-9 www.baccosf.com
Regional Italian cuisine. Organic pastas and breads; local produce;
free-range meat.

BENISSIMO RISTORANTE & BAR 🌿 $$$ C
18 Tamalpais Dr. Corte Madera 94925 415-927-2316
Daily 4-10 www.benissimos.com
Organic salad greens, wild salmon.

CAFÉ 817 🌿🌿🌿🌿 $$ C
817 Washington St. Oakland (Lake Merritt/Downtown) 94607 510-271-7965
Mon-Fri 7:30-3 Sat 8:30-3 www.cafe817.com
Local and organic produce, meat.

C'ERA UNA VOLTA 🌿🌿 $$ C
1332 Park St. Alameda 94501 510-769-4828
Tue-Sat 9-3, 5:30-10 Sun 9-3 www.ceraunavolta.us
Organic produce; hormone-free meat, fish.

CUGINI 🌿🌿 $$
1556 Solano Ave. Albany 94707 510-558-9000
Tue-Fri 11-2:30, 5-10 Sat 5-10 Sun 4-9
Southern Italian cuisine. Variety of wood-fired pizzas and pasta.

DELFINA 🌿🌿 $$
3621 18th St. SF (Mission) 94110 415-552-4055
Mon-Thu 5:30-10 Fri-Sat 5:30-11 Sun 5-10 www.delfinasf.com
Neighborhood trattoria. Organic ingredients, all-natural meat.

DIVINO RISTORANTE ITALIANO 🌿🌿🌿 $$
968 Ralston Ave. Belmont 94002 650-620-9102
Tue-Fri 11:30-2, 5:30-9:30 Sat 5:30-9:30 Sun 5-9 www.divinobelmont.com
Traditional Italian cuisine. Organic pasta and bread; free-range meat; local organic produce.

DOPO 🌿🌿🌿🌿 $$
4293 Piedmont Ave. Piedmont 94611 510-652-3676
Mon-Thu 11:30-2:30, 5:30-10 Fri 11:30-2:30, 5:30-11 Sat 5:30-11
Seasonal Italian dishes. Organic and locally grown produce; hormone-free meat.

ECCOLO 🌿🌿🌿🌿 $$$
1820 Fourth St. Berkeley 94710 510-644-0444
Mon-Thu 11:30-9:30 Fri 11:30-10 Sat 11-10 Sun 11-9 www.eccolo.com
Modern Italian cuisine. All organic, local, sustainable ingredients.

EMMY'S SPAGHETTI SHACK 🌿 $$
18 Virginia St. SF (Bernal Heights) 94110 415-206-2086
Sun-Thu 5:30-11 Fri-Sat 5:30-12
Italian food. Some organic dishes.

FRANTOIO RISTORANTE & OLIVE OIL CO. 🌿 $$$ C
152 Shoreline Hwy. Mill Valley 94941 415-289-5777
Daily 5:30-10 www.frantoio.com
Modern Tuscan cuisine. Organic produce, hormone-free meat, house-made extra virgin olive oil.

OLIVETO'S 🌿🌿🌿🌿 $$$
5655 College Ave. Oakland (College Ave.) 94618 510-547-5356
Mon-Wed 11:30-2, 5:30-9:30 Thu-Fri 11:30-2, 5:30-10 Sat 5:30-10 Sun 5-9
www.oliveto.com
Italian fine dining, featuring organic and locally grown produce, hormone-free meats and poultry.

PIATTI LOCALI 🌿 $$$ C
625 Redwood Hwy. Mill Valley 94941 415-380-2525
Mon-Thu 11:30-9 Fri-Sat 11:30-10 Sun 11:30-9 www.piatti.com
Italian restaurant emphasizing hormone-free beef and poultry, and organic and/or local produce when possible.

PIZZAIOLO 🌿🌿🌿🌿 $$
5008 Telegraph Ave. Oakland (Temescal) 94609 510-652-4888
Mon-Sat 5:30-10 www.pizzaiolo.us
Southern Italian trattoria cuisine, featuring organic and locally grown produce, meats, poultry, fish, and coffee.

RIVOLI 🌿🌿 $$$
1539 Solano Ave. Berkeley 94707 510-526-2542
Mon-Thu 5:30-9:30 Fri 5:30-10 Sat 5-10 Sun 5-9 www.rivolirestaurant.com
French-Italian inspired menu; local, seasonal, sustainable ingredients.

VINOROSSO 🌿🌿 **$$**
629 Cortland Ave. SF (Bernal Heights) 94110 415-647-1268
Tue-Sun 4-11 www.vinorossosf.com
Enoteca Italiana. Wine shop, wine bar, Italian eatery. Largely organic.

ZUPPA 🌿🌿🌿 **$$$ C**
564 Fourth St. SF (SOMA) 94107 415-777-5900
Mon-Fri 11:30-3, 5:30-11 Sat 5:30-11 Sun 5:30-10:30 www.zuppa-sf.com
Gourmet Italian cuisine in unique setting.

LATIN AMERICAN (INCLUDES CARIBBEAN/CUBAN)

CAFÉ DE LA PAZ 🌿🌿🌿 **$$ C**
1600 Shattuck Ave. Berkeley 94709 510-843-0662
Mon-Thu 11:30-9:30 Fri 11:30-10 Sat 11-10 Sun 11-9:30 www.cafedelapaz.net
Nuevo Latino and Spanish tapas. Organic and locally grown produce, meats,
poultry, and fish.

CHA CHA CHA 🌿 **$$**
1801 Haight St. SF (Haight) 94117 415-386-7670
2327 Mission St. SF (Haight) 94110 415-824-1502
Hours vary by location www.cha3.com
Caribbean-style tapas.

CHARANGA 🌿🌿 **$$ C**
2351 Mission St. SF (Mission) 94110 415-282-1813
Tue-Wed 5:30-10 Thu-Sat 5:30-11 www.charangasf.com
Pan-Latin-Caribbean food. Organic and seasonal ingredients. Small plates.

FONDA 🌿🌿🌿 **$$**
1501A Solano Ave. Albany 94707 510-559-9006
Mon-Fri 5:30-12:30 Sat-Sun 4:30-12:30 www.fondasolano.com
Latin-American cuisine. Some organic produce; hormone-free meat.
Seasonal ingredients.

FRONT PORCH, THE 🌿🌿🌿 **$$**
65A 29th St. SF (Mission) 94110 415-695-7800
Daily 5:30-10:30 www.thefrontporchsf.com
Organic Caribbean soul food.

LIMON 🌿🌿 **$$**
524 Valencia St. SF (Mission) 94110 415-252-0918
Mon-Thu 5:30-10:30 Fri 5:30-11 Sat 12-11 Sun 12-10 www.limon-sf.com
Nuevo Latino/Peruvian Cuisine. Emphasis on fresh seafood.

PEÑA PACHAMAMA 🌿🌿🌿 **$$**
1630 Powell St. SF (North Beach) 94133 415-646-0018
Wed-Thu 5:30-10:30 Fri-Sat 5:30-11:30 Sun 10:30-3:30, 5:30-11:30
www.penapachamama.com
Authentic Bolivian cuisine. Live music and dancing nightly.

RAMBLAS TAPAS RESTAURANT AND BAR 🌿🌿 **$$ C**
557 Valencia St. SF (Mission) 94110 415-565-0207
Mon-Thu 5-10 Fri 5-midnight Sat 3-midnight Sun 11-10 www.ramblastapas.com
Authentic Spanish tapas featuring local California growers and farmers.
SF green certified business.

SOL FOOD PUERTO RICAN CUISINE 🌿 **$ C**
732 Fourth St. San Rafael 94901 415-451-4765
901 Lincoln Ave. San Rafael 94901 415-256-8903
Hours vary by location www.solfoodrestaurant.com
Puerto Rican fare and sandwiches with some organic produce and
vegan options in the mix. Steak sandwiches made with hormone-and
antibiotic-free beef.

MEDITERRANEAN (INCLUDES GREEK)

À CÔTÉ 🍃🍃 $$

5478 College Ave. Oakland (College Ave.) 94618 510-655-6469
Sun-Tue 5:30-10 Wed-Thu 5:30-11 Fri-Sat 5:30-midnight
www.acoterestaurant.com
Mediterranean, small-plate cuisine. Organic, locally purchased produce.

AZIZA 🍃🍃🍃 $$$

5800 Geary Blvd. SF (Richmond) 94121 415-752-2222
Mon, Wed-Sun 5:30-10 www.aziza-sf.com
Upscale contemporary Moroccan with Californian influences.
Features organic and locally produced ingredients.

BAR TARTINE 🍃🍃🍃🍃 $$$

561 Valencia St. SF (Mission) 94110 415-487-1600
Tue-Wed 6-10 Thu-Sat 11-2, 6-11 Sun 11-2, 6-10
www.tartinebakery.com/bar_tartine.htm
Gourmet restaurant and bar. Emphasis on organic ingredients.

BIA'S RESTAURANT AND WINE BAR 🍃🍃🍃🍃 $$

1640 Haight St. SF (Haight) 94117 415-861-8868
Tue-Sun 11-11 www.biasrestaurantandwinebar.com
Mediterranean-influenced California cuisine with wine bar. Casual atmosphere.

CAFÉ ROUGE 🍃🍃🍃🍃 $$$ C

1782 Fourth St. Berkeley 94710 510-525-1440
Mon 11:30-3 Tue-Thu 11:30-9:30 Fri-Sat 11:30-10 Sun 10-9:30
www.caferouge.net
Casual, rustic Mediterranean/American cuisine. Organic produce,
free-range meat, house-aged steaks.

CAMPTON PLACE 🍃🍃 $$$$ C

340 Stockton St. SF (Union Square) 94108 415-955-5555
Mon-Thu 7 a.m.-9:30 p.m. Fri 7 a.m.-10 p.m. Sat-Sun 8 a.m.-9:30 p.m.
www.camptonplace.com
High-end cuisine with a Mediterranean influence.

DI BARTOLO 🍃🍃🍃 $$$

3308 Grand Ave. Oakland (Lake Merritt/Downtown) 94610 510-451-0576
Tue-Thu 5:30-10 Fri-Sat 5:30-11 Sun 5:30-10 www.restaurantdibartolo.com
California-Mediterranean fusion. Locally purchased produce, wild-caught fish,
sustainable meats.

FAZ 🍃🍃 $$$ C

155 Steuart St. SF (SOMA) 94105 415-495-6500
Mon-Fri 11:30-10 Sat 5-10 www.fazrestaurants.com
Mediterranean cuisine. Full bar.

GREENS RESTAURANT 🍃🍃🍃🍃 $$$ C

Fort Mason Center Building A SF (Marina) 94123 415-771-6222
Mon 5:30-9 Tue-Sat 12-2:30, 5:30-9 Sun 10:30-2 www.greensrestaurant.com
Creative vegetarian cuisine. Mediterranean, Mexican, and
Southwestern influences.

KOKKARI 🍃🍃 $$$

200 Jackson St. SF (Financial District) 94111 415-981-0983
Mon-Thu 11:30-10 Fri 11:30-11 Sat 5-11 www.kokkari.com
Upscale Greek with Mediterranean and California influences.

MANDALOUN 🍃🍃🍃🍃 $$

2021 Broadway St. Redwood City 94063 650-367-7974
Mon-Thu 11:30-10 Fri-Sat 11:30-11 Sun 4-9 www.mandaloun.biz
Tapas, antipasti. Wood-fired pizza, grill, and rotisserie. Seafood.
Local organic meats and produce. Patio garden.

PARÉA WINE BAR AND CAFÉ 🍃🍃🍃 $
795 Valencia St. SF (Mission) 94110 415-255-2102
Wed-Mon 5-midnight www.pareawinebar.com
Organic home-style Mediterranean dishes with an extensive wine selection.

TOMATINA 🍃🍃 $$
1338 Park St. Alameda 94501 510-521-1000
Daily 11:30-10 www.tomatina.com
California-Mediterranean dishes, featuring 100% organic wheat pizzas,
pasta, and piadini.

TRAPEZE RESTAURANT 🍃🍃 $$$ C
266 Lorton Ave. Burlingame 94010 650-344-4242
Daily 11-10:30 www.trapezerestaurant.com
Free range beef, poultry, seafood, homemade pasta and bread.
Vegetarian dishes.

YUMMA'S MEDITERRANEAN GRILL 🍃🍃🍃 $ C
721 Irving St. SF (Sunset) 94122 415-682-0762
Daily 11-10
Organic produce; grass-fed, all-natural meat. Casual dining grill.

ZATAR 🍃🍃🍃🍃 $$ C
1981 Shattuck Ave. Berkeley 94704 510-841-1981
Wed-Sat 5:30-9:30 Fri 11:30 a.m.-2:30 p.m. www.zatarrestaurant.com
Eclectic Mediterranean cuisine. All-organic ingredients; herbs and
vegetables from on-site garden.

MEXICAN

DON PICO'S ORIGINAL MEXICAN BISTRO 🍃🍃 $$
461 El Camino Real San Bruno 94066 650-589-1163
Tue-Sat 11-9
Traditional Mexican food. Made with organic ingredients.

DOÑA TOMAS 🍃🍃🍃 $$
5004 Telegraph Ave. Oakland (Temescal) 94609 510-450-0522
Tue-Thu 5:30-9:30 Fri-Sat 5:30-10 www.donatomas.com
Mexican food highlighting local ingredients. Organic produce, sustainably
raised beef, pork, and chicken. Fresh-squeezed lime margaritas.

GREEN CHILE KITCHEN 🍃🍃🍃🍃 $ C
601 Baker St. SF (Western Addition) 94117 415-614-9411
Mon-Fri 11:30-9 Sat-Sun 11-9 www.greenchilekitchen.com
New Mexican-inspired fare.

HAPPY BURRITO 🍃🍃 $ C
1616 Webster St. Oakland (Lake Merritt/Downtown) 94612 510-763-9174
Mon-Fri 9-5:45 Sat 11-4
Mexican food. Locally grown produce.

LA ESTRELLITA CAFE 🍃🍃 $$ C
446 East 12th St. Oakland (East Oakland) 94606 510-465-7188
Mon-Thu 8 a.m.-10 p.m. Fri-Sat 8 a.m.-11 p.m. www.laestrellitacafe.com
Mexican fare featuring locally grown produce, hormone-free meats,
and wild-caught fish.

MIJITA 🍃🍃 $
One Ferry Building #44 SF (Embarcadero) 94111 415-399-0814
Mon-Fri 10-8 Sat 9-8 Sun 10-4 www.mijitasf.com
Cocina Mexicana using local, seasonal ingredients and sustainable
seafood and meats.

ROOSEVELT TAMALE PARLOR 🌿🌿 $
2817 24th St. SF (Mission) 94110 415-824-2600
Tue-Thu 11:30-9 Fri 11:30-10 Sat 9-10 Sun 9-9
Mexican food, with an emphasis on fresh and seasonal ingredients.

TACUBAYA 🌿🌿 $$
1788 Fourth St. Berkeley 94710 510-525-5160
Mon, Wed-Fri 10-9 Tue 10-4 Sun 9-9
Mexican taqueria; homemade tortillas, organic, sustainable meats.

TAMARINDO ANTOJERIA MEXICANA 🌿🌿 $$$
468 Eighth St. Oakland (Lake Merritt/Downtown) 94607 510-444-1944
Mon-Fri 11-3, 5-9:30 Sat 10-3, 5-10 www.tamarindoantojeria.com
Fine Mexican dining, featuring organic and locally grown produce,
hormone-free meats, and free range poultry.

MIDDLE EASTERN

JERUSALEM ORGANIC KITCHEN & BURGERS 🌿🌿🌿🌿 $ C
1897 Solano Ave. Berkeley 94707 510-525-7888
Daily 11-9
Organic Middle-Eastern and American food. Salads, kebabs, and burgers.

RAZAN'S ORGANIC KITCHEN 🌿🌿🌿🌿 $ C
2119 Kittridge St. Berkeley 94704 510-486-0449
Daily 10-10
Middle-Eastern wraps and plates.

PIZZA

CHEESEBOARD PIZZA COLLECTIVE, THE 🌿🌿 $
1512 Shattuck Ave. Berkeley 94709 510-549-3055
Tue-Fri 11:30-2, 4:30-7 Sat 12-3, 4:30-7 www.cheeseboardcollective.com
Features organic, vegetarian toppings. Take-out but no delivery.

DELFINA PIZZERIA 🌿🌿🌿🌿 $$
3611 18th St. SF (Mission) 94110 415-437-6800
Mon 5:30-10 Tue-Thu 11:30-10 Fri 11:30-11 Sat 12-11 Sun 12-10
www.pizzeriadelfina.com
Neighborhood pizzeria. Organic ingredients, all natural meat.

GIOIA 🌿🌿 $
1586 Hopkins St. Berkeley 94707 510-528-4692
Mon-Sat 11-8
New York-style pizzeria. Organic flour crust. Take-out but no delivery.

PAULINE'S PIZZA 🌿🌿 $$ C
260 Valencia St. SF (Mission) 94103 415-552-2050
Tue-Sat 5-10 www.paulinespizza.com
Unusual and mostly organic pizza. Take-out but no delivery.

PIZZA PAZZA 🌿🌿 $$
3905 Piedmont Ave. Piedmont 94611 510-653-0157
Mon-Thu 11:30-9 Fri-Sat 11:30-10 Sun 5-9
Organic flour pizzas. Many organic toppings. Delivery after 5 p.m.

PIZZETTA 211 🌿🌿🌿🌿 $$
211 23rd Ave. SF (Richmond) 94121 415-379-9880
Wed-Fri 12-2:30, 5-9 Sat-Sun 12-9 Mon 5-9 www.pizzetta211.com
Thin-crust pizza and other Italian specialties featuring organic ingredients.
Take-out but no delivery.

SEAFOOD

FERRY PLAZA SEAFOOD 🍃🍃🍃 **$$**
One Ferry Building #18 SF (Embarcadero) 94111 415-274-2561
Tue-Wed 10:30-7 Thu-Fri 10:30-8 Sat 7-6 Sun 10-5 www.ferryplazaseafood.com
Local fresh fish and seafood.

HOG ISLAND OYSTER COMPANY 🍃🍃🍃🍃 **$$**
One Ferry Building #11A SF (Embarcadero) 94111 415-391-7117
20215 Hwy. 1 Marshall 94940 415-663-9218
Hours vary by location www.hogislandoysters.com
Practices sustainable aquaculture.

HORIZON'S 🍃 **$$$ C**
558 Bridgeway First Floor Sausalito 94965 415-331-3232
Mon-Fri 11:30-9 Sat 10:30-10 Sun 10:30-9 www.horizonssausalito.com
Seafood on the water in Sausalito.

ONDINE 🍃 **$$$**
558 Bridgeway Second Floor Sausalito 94965 415-331-1133
Special events and private parties only. www.ondinesausalito.com
Private dining venue on the waterfront. Features seasonal ingredients,
wide selection of seafood, and an extensive wine list.

PACIFIC CATCH 🍃 **$$ C**
2027 Chestnut St. SF (Marina) 94123 415-440-1950
133 Corte Madera Town Center Corte Madera 94925 415-927-3474
Hours vary by location www.pacificcatch.com
Fresh seafood dishes and house-made sauces.

PARADISE BAY RESTAURANT & BAR 🍃 **$$$**
1200 Bridgeway Sausalito 94965 415-331-3226
Mon-Fri 11:30-10:30 Sat-Sun 10:30-10:30 www.paradisebaysausalito.com
Asian-inspired seafood restaurant. Some organic items.

PISCES CALIFORNIA CUISINE 🍃 **$$**
3414 Judah St. SF (Sunset) 94122 415-564-2233
Tue-Sun 4-10
Fusion of different styles featuring wild-caught fish.

SAM'S ANCHOR CAFÉ 🍃🍃🍃 **$$ C**
27 Main St. Tiburon 94920 415-435-4527
Mon-Fri 11-10 Sat-Sun 9:30-10 www.samscafe.com
American cuisine; wild-caught fish, sustainable meats, local, organic produce.
Vegetarian options. Bayside seating.

SEA SALT 🍃🍃🍃 **$$$**
2512 San Pablo Ave. Berkeley 94702 510-883-1720
Daily 11:30-10 www.seasaltrestaurant.com
Sustainable seafood-based menu; heated outdoor patio.

WEIRD FISH 🍃🍃🍃 **$$**
2193 Mission St. SF (Mission) 94110 415-863-4744
Mon-Thu 9-10 Fri-Sat 9-midnight Sun 9-10 www.weirdfishsf.com
Small vegetarian and seafood restaurant focused on sustainable seafood.
Selection of organic wine and beer.

VEGETARIAN/RAW

ALIVE! 🌿🌿🌿 **$$**
1972 Lombard St. SF (Marina) 94123 415-923-1052
Wed-Sun 5-10 www.aliveveggie.com
Raw/living vegan cuisine featuring organic ingredients.

CAFÉ GRATITUDE 🌿🌿🌿🌿 **$$ C**
1730 Shattuck Ave. Berkeley 94709 415-824-4652 ext. 3
2400 Harrison St. SF (Mission) 94110 415-824-4652 ext. 1
1336 Ninth Ave. SF (Sunset) 94122 415-824-4652 ext. 2
2200 Fourth St. San Rafael 94901 415-824-4652 ext. 4
Hours vary by location www.cafegratitude.com
Organic, raw, vegan food. Juice bar, cold-press coffee.

DAILY HEALTH 🌿🌿🌿🌿 **$**
1235 Ninth Ave. SF (Sunset) 94122 415-681-7675
Mon-Fri 10-8 Sat-Sun 11-5
Organic, raw, vegan food in restaurant attached to alternative health store.

GREENS RESTAURANT 🌿🌿🌿🌿 **$$$ C**
Fort Mason Center Building A SF (Marina) 94123 415-771-6222
Mon 5:30-9 Tue-Sat 12-2:30, 5:30-9 Sun 10:30-2 www.greensrestaurant.com
Creative vegetarian cuisine. Mediterranean, Mexican, and
Southwestern influences.

JUDAHLICIOUS 🌿🌿🌿🌿 **$**
3906 Judah St. SF (Sunset) 94122 415-665-8423
Daily 9-7 www.judahlicious.com
Vegan organic food, smoothies, drinks, and juice bar. SF green certified business.

JUICEY LUCY'S 🌿🌿🌿🌿 **$$ C**
Farmer's Market at 24th St. and Sanchez SF (Noe Valley)
703 Columbus Ave. SF (North Beach) 94133 415-786-1285
Farmer's Market at St. Joseph Way and Geary SF (Richmond)
Hours vary by location
Organic, vegan, raw, kosher food. Juice bar.

MANZANITA RESTAURANT 🌿🌿🌿🌿 **$$ C**
4001 Linden St. Oakland (Lake Merritt/Downtown) 94608 510-985-8386
Daily 11:30-2:30, 5:30-9 www.manzanitarestaurant.com
Organic, vegan, macrobiotic cuisine.

MILLENNIUM 🌿🌿🌿🌿 **$$$ C**
580 Geary St. SF (Union Square) 94102 415-345-3900
Mon-Thu 5:30-9:30 Fri-Sat 5:30-10:30 Sun 5:30-9:30 www.millenniumrestaurant.com
Vegetarian fine dining with local, organic, and sustainably farmed food that is
GMO free. Recycling and composting programs.

NEW WORLD VEGETARIAN CUISINE 🌿 **$$ C**
464 Eighth St. Oakland (Lake Merritt/Downtown) 94607 510-444-2891
Mon-Thu 11-9 Fri-Sat 11-9:30 Sun 11-9
Vegetarian and vegan cuisine.

PRISM CAFÉ 🌿🌿🌿🌿 **$ C**
1918 Park Blvd. Oakland (Lake Merritt/Downtown) 94606 510-251-1453
Mon-Thu 8-8 Fri-Sat 8 a.m.-11 p.m. Sun 8-8 www.prismcafe.com
Organic vegetarian cuisine, featuring cornmeal and wheat-free pizza crusts.
Microbrew beer, music.

QUE SERAW SERAW 🌿🌿🌿🌿 **$ C**
1160 Capuchino Ave. Burlingame 94010 650-348-7298
Mon-Fri 10-6 Sat 10-4 www.queserawseraw.com
Take-out only. Soup, salad, wraps, pizza, desserts. All food organic, vegan, raw.
Wheat and gluten free. No dairy.

CAFÉS, TEA HOUSES, AND JUICE BARS

Coffee and tea are the most commonly consumed beverages in the world after water. Cafés themselves have played a major role in human civilization ever since people got the hankering for something hot to drink and something good to eat.

Coffee and tea also have huge ecological and social impacts. Growing coffee and tea organically preserves healthy ecosystems, and fair trade certification (see page 92) helps to ensure that growers get a living wage for their harvest. Organic ingredients and food prepared with an eye toward what's local and sustainable can make that meal or snack one to remember.

In short, there's a long story behind that little latté and, we hope, a happy planet behind that healthy helping. And should you desire something cold, look for juice bars that offer concoctions made from organic fruits and veggies. (Oh, and don't forget to bring your own mug or cup if that coffee, tea, or juice is to go!)

We have determined leaf awards based primarily on the percentage of coffees, teas, and juices offered that are certified organic. However, because many of these establishments also offer a wide range of milk products and prepared food items, we have sought to factor in whether or not there are certified organic options in these areas as well.

at least 25% of the coffee, tea, and juice served meets the above criteria.

at least 50% of the coffee, tea, and juice served meets the above criteria.

at least 75% of the coffee, tea, and juice served meets the above criteria, plus over 25% of all dairy is certified organic, and 25% of prepared food items are made with certified organic ingredients.

90% or more of the coffee, tea, and juice served meets the above criteria, plus at least 50% of all dairy is certified organic, and 50% of prepared food items are made with certified organic ingredients.

ACRE CAFÉ
1013 Turney Ave. SF (Presidio/Presidio Heights) 94129 415-561-2273
Mon-Fri 7:30-3 www.acregourmet.com
Soups, sandwiches, salads, quesadillas, pizza. Organic ingredients.
Also offers catering.

ARC CAFÉ
1890 Bryant St. SF (Mission) 94114 415-437-2233
Mon-Fri 7:30-6 Sat-Sun 8-4 www.arccafesf.com
Organic coffee and tea; sandwiches, salads, handmade pastries.
Hosts special events.

ARIZMENDI BAKERY COOPERATIVE
4301 San Pablo Ave. Emeryville 94608 510-547-0550
3265 Lakeshore Ave. Oakland (Lake Merritt/Downtown) 94610 510-268-8849
1331 Ninth Ave. SF (Sunset) 94122 415-566-3117
Hours vary by location www.arizmendibakery.org
Breads, pastries, and pizza made with organic ingredients. Organic,
fair trade coffee and tea. Worker-owned.

AXIS CAFÉ ⌀⌀⌀⌀
1201 Eighth St. SF (SOMA) 94107 415-437-2947
Mon-Fri 7-7 Sun 1-4 www.axis-cafe.com
Organic café. Fireplace, outdoor patio.

BAKE SHOP, THE ⌀⌀
1926 Shattuck Ave. Berkeley 94704 510-841-0773
Mon-Fri 8-6 Sat 9-5 Sun 9-3 www.thebakeshopberkeley.com
Artisan pizza, sandwiches, salads, cakes, and pastries.

BITTERSWEET ⌀⌀⌀
5427 College Ave. Oakland (College Ave.) 94618 510-654-7159
2123 Fillmore St. SF (Pacific Heights) 94115 415-346-8715
Hours vary by location www.bittersweetcafe.com
Specialty chocolate shop. Fair trade, organic tea and coffee.

BLUE BOTTLE COFFEE CO. ⌀⌀⌀⌀
315 Linden St. SF (Hayes Valley) 94102 415-252-7535
Mon-Fri 7-5:30 Sat-Sun 8-5 www.bluebottlecoffee.net
Organic coffee and pastries. Also has carts at several Bay Area
farmers' markets. Offers espresso catering for events.

BOXED FOODS COMPANY ⌀⌀⌀⌀
245 Kearny St. SF (Financial District) 94108 415-981-9376
Mon-Fri 8-3 www.boxedfoodscompany.com
Boxed lunches, organic salads, tea, coffee.

CAFÉ BENALLY ⌀
1131 Taraval St. SF (Sunset) 94116 415-682-3686
Mon-Fri 7-7 Sat-Sun 8-7
Organic coffee and tea.

CAFÉ CAPUCHINO ⌀⌀⌀⌀
1158 Capuchino Ave. Burlingame 94010 650-342-2669
Mon-Fri 7:30-4 Sat 9-3
Organic, fair trade coffee, tea, juice, and snacks.

CAFÉ CRESCENDO ⌀⌀⌀⌀
233 14th St. SF (Mission) 94103 415-503-1093
Mon-Fri 7-3 Sat 9-3 www.cafecrescendo.com
Organic food and coffee.

CAFÉ DEL SOUL ⌀⌀⌀⌀
247 Shoreline Hwy. Mill Valley 94941 415-388-1852
Mon-Sat 11-7 www.cafedelsoul.net
Health-oriented café serving California cuisine. Organic food;
yoga classes, events.

CAFÉ FANNY ⌀⌀⌀⌀
1603 San Pablo Ave. Berkeley 94702 510-524-5451
Mon-Fri 7-3 Sat 8-4 Sun 8-3 www.cafefanny.com
Meat and produce from local, sustainable farms. Sister café to Chez Panisse.
Organic coffee, tea, and hot chocolate.

CAFÉ GRATITUDE ⌀⌀⌀⌀
1730 Shattuck Ave. Berkeley 94709 415-824-4652 ext. 3
2400 Harrison St. SF (Mission) 94110 415-824-4652 ext. 1
1336 Ninth Ave. SF (Sunset) 94122 415-824-4652 ext. 2
2200 Fourth St. San Rafael 94901 415-824-4652 ext. 4
Hours vary by location www.cafegratitude.com
Organic, raw, vegan food. Juice bar, cold-press coffee.

CAFÉ GRILLADES ✑✑✑✑

BayHill Shopping Center 851 Cherry Ave. San Bruno 94066 650-589-3778
501 Hayes St. SF (Civic Center) 94102 415-553-8500
Hours vary by location   www.cafegrillades.com
Organic Mediterranean fare. Organic coffee and juice.

CAFÉ LO CUBANO ✑✑✑✑

3401 California St. SF (Laurel Heights) 94118 415-831-4383
Mon-Fri 6 a.m.-11 p.m. Sat-Sun 7a.m.-midnight www.cafelocubano.com
Organic, Cuban-style coffee and pressed sandwiches.

CAFÉ QUE TAL ✑✑✑

1005 Guerrero St. SF (Mission) 94110 415-282-8855
Mon-Fri 7-7 Sat-Sun 8-7
Neighborhood café. Some organic, fair trade coffee and tea.

CAFFÉ DEL DOGE ✑✑

419 University Ave. Palo Alto 94301 650-323-3600
Mon-Wed 7 a.m.-10 p.m. Thu-Sat 7 a.m.-11 p.m. Sun 8 a.m.-10 p.m.
www.caffedeldoge.com
Indoor/outdoor coffee house. American location of Italian-based
coffee roastery.

CHAT'S OF SAN FRANCISCO ✑✑✑

301 Arkansas St. SF (Potrero Hill) 94107 415-206-0300
215 Second St. SF (SOMA) 94105 415-357-1514
Hours vary by location
Coffee roasting company. Imported organic coffee and tea;
Mitchell's ice cream.

COFFEE TO THE PEOPLE ✑✑✑✑

1206 Masonic Ave. SF (Haight) 94117 415-626-2435
Mon-Fri 6-8 Sat-Sun 7-8 www.coffeetothepeople.com
Organic, fair trade coffee and tea.

COLE COFFEE ✑✑

6255 College Ave. Oakland (Rockridge) 94618 510-653-5453
Daily 7-7 www.colecoffee.com
Organic coffee, juice, and tea.

COMFORTS ✑

335 San Anselmo Ave. San Anselmo 94960 415-454-9840
Mon-Fri 8:30-2:30 Sat-Sun 8:30-3 www.comfortscafe.com
Eclectic California cuisine. Organic, fair trade coffee; grass-fed beef;
wild salmon.

CRISSY FIELD CENTER CAFÉ ✑✑✑✑

603 Old Mason St. SF (Presidio/Presidio Heights) 94123 415-561-7756
Daily 9-5 www.crissyfield.org/cafeshop
Organic sandwiches, soups, baked goods, and juices.

DISH CAFÉ ✑✑✑✑

39 Mesa St. SF Film Centre SF (Presidio/Presidio Heights) 94129 415-561-2336
Mon-Fri 8-4
Breakfast and lunch. Soup, sandwiches, salads, pasta, and pizza.

FAR LEAVES TEA ✑

2979 College Ave. Berkeley 94705 510-665-9409
5677 Horton St. Emeryville 94608 510-601-5928
Hours vary by location   www.farleaves.com
Teahouse offering loose tea and equipage.

FROG HOLLOW FARMS ✐✐✐✐
One Ferry Building #46 SF (Embarcadero) 94111 415-445-0990
Mon-Sat 7-6 Sun 9-5 www.froghollow.com
Locally grown organic fruit; organic baked goods; tea and coffee.

GROVE, THE ✐✐✐
2250 Chestnut St. SF (Marina) 94123 415-474-4843
2016 Fillmore St. SF (Pacific Heights) 94115 415-474-1419
Mon-Fri 11-7 Sat-Sun 8-11
Café offering organic prepared foods, coffee, teas, and juices.
Also serves beer and wine.

GUERILLA CAFÉ ✐✐✐
1620 Shattuck Ave. Berkeley 94709 510-845-CAFE
Tue-Sun 8-8 www.guerillacafe.com
Blue Bottle coffee, organic food. Fair trade products.

HARVEST & ROWE ✐✐✐✐
55 Second St. SF (SOMA) 94105 415-541-7771
Mon-Fri 8-3 www.harvestandrowe.com
Soups, salads, and sandwiches made from organic ingredients;
organic coffee and juices.

HUDSON BAY CAFFE ✐✐
5401 College Ave. Oakland (Rockridge) 94618 510-658-0214
Mon-Fri 6-9 Sat-Sun 7-9
Organic, fair trade coffee and tea.

JAVA BEACH ✐✐✐
1396 La Playa St. SF (Sunset) 94122 415-665-5282
Mon-Fri 5:30-11 Sat-Sun 6-11 www.javabeachcafe.com
Organic, fair trade coffee.

JUDAHLICIOUS ✐✐✐✐
3906 Judah St. SF (Sunset) 94122 415-665-8423
Daily 9-7 www.judahlicious.com
Vegan organic food, smoothies, drinks, and juice bar.
SF green certified business.

JUICE BAR COLLECTIVE ✐✐✐✐
2114 Vine St. Berkeley 94709 510-548-8473
Mon-Sat 10-4:30
Organic prepared foods and fresh-squeezed juices.

JUICEY LUCY'S ✐✐✐✐
Farmer's Market at 24th St. and Sanchez SF (Noe Valley)
703 Columbus Ave. SF (North Beach) 94133 415-786-1285
Farmer's Market at St. Joseph Way and Geary SF (Richmond))
Hours vary by location
Organic, vegan, raw, kosher food. Organic juice bar and kiosks.

JULIE'S COFFEE AND TEA GARDEN ✐✐✐✐
1223 Park St. Alameda 94501 510-865-2385
Mon-Fri 7-9 Sat-Sun 8-7 www.juliestea.com
Organic coffee, tea, herbs, and herbal products. Small selection of
prepared foods.

KAILA'S CORNER CUP ✐✐✐
3655 Lawton St. SF (Sunset) 94122 415-753-1941
Mon-Fri 6-5 Sat 7-5 Sun 7-4
Organic French coffee and soy milk; organic baked goods.

L'AMYX TEA BAR 🌿🌿
3437 Lakeshore Ave. Oakland (Lake Merritt/Dowtown) 94610 510-835-8332
4179 Piedmont Ave. Piedmont 94611 510-594-8322
Daily 10 a.m.-midnight www.lamyx.com
Wide range of organic and fair trade teas and some coffees.

LETTUS CAFÉ ORGANIC 🌿🌿🌿🌿
3352 Steiner St. SF (Marina) 94123 415-931-2777
Mon-Fri 10:30-10 Sat-Sun 9-10 www.lettusorganic.com
Freshly made juices, salads, sandwiches, soups, entrees and desserts using all
organic ingredients. Serves breakfast, lunch, and dinner.

MARIN COFFEE ROASTERS 🌿🌿
4 Bolinas Rd. Fairfax 94930 415-451-1825
635 San Anselmo Ave. San Anselmo 94960 415-258-9549
Hours vary by location
Some organic, fair trade coffee. Roasts their own beans. Some organic baked
goods and breakfast items. Full kitchen at San Anselmo location.

MISSION CREEK CAFÉ, THE 🌿🌿
968 Valencia St. SF (Mission) 94110 415-641-0888
Daily 7-9
Neighborhood café, organic tea and some organic fair trade coffee.

MOKKA 🌿🌿🌿🌿
3075 Telegraph Ave. Berkeley 94705 510-848-8909
Mon-Fri 7-6 Sat-Sun 8-5
Organic coffees and teas.

MUFFIN MANIA 🌿🌿
2 Bayview St. San Rafael 94901-4913 415-485-1027
Mon-Fri 6-3 Sat 7-2
More than 30 types of muffins. Full lunch menu featuring local and
organic produce.

NELLY'S JAVA 🌿🌿🌿🌿
1952 Mountain Blvd. Oakland (Montclair) 94611 510-338-0388
Mon-Fri 6-6 Sat 7-6 Sun 7:30-3:30
100% organic and fair trade coffees and teas. Some food items available.

NERVOUS DOG COFFEE 🌿🌿
3438 Mission St. SF (Mission) 94110 415-282-4364
Tue-Fri 7:30-6 Sat 8-6 Sun 8-5
Neighborhood café serving organic coffee.

NEW COLLEGE CAFÉ 🌿🌿🌿
777 Valencia St. SF (Mission) 94110 415-437-3401
Mon-Thu 9-9 Fri-Sun 9-4
Small café used primarily by students at the school. Some organic sweets,
coffee, and tea.

NOMAD CAFÉ 🌿🌿🌿🌿
6500 Shattuck Ave. Oakland (Temescal) 94609 510-595-5344
Mon-Sat 7-10 Sun 8-10 www.nomadcafe.net
100% organic Mediterranean café and restaurant serving breakfast, lunch, and
dinner; organic and fair trade coffees and teas.

NORTHPOINT COFFEE COMPANY 🌿🌿🌿
1250 Bridgeway Sausalito 94965 415-331-8777
Daily 6:30-6:30 www.northpointcoffee.com
Coffee, smoothies, panini, salads, gelato.

ORGANIC COFFEE COMPANY ✑✑✑✑
88 Fourth St. SF (SOMA) 94103 415-512-7436
Mon-Thu 6-8:30 Friday 6-7 Sat 7-7 Sun 7-3 www.organiccoffeecompany.com
Sandwiches, salads, and soup prepared by Culinary Academy students.
Organic ingredients when possible; all-organic coffee.

PEACE CAFÉ ✑✑✑✑
1665 Haight St. SF (Haight) 94117 415-864-1978
Daily 9-9 www.redvic.com
Organic, vegetarian food, coffee and tea.

PEOPLE'S CAFÉ ✑✑✑✑
1419 Haight St. SF (Haight) 94117 415-553-8842
Daily 7-10
Organic coffee, tea, and food.

PHILZ COFFEE ✑
3901 18th St. SF (Castro) 94114 415-552-8378
3101 24th St. SF (Mission) 94110 415-282-9155
Daily 7-7 www.philzcoffee.com
Handmade coffee blends by local artisan coffee maker.

POWER SOURCE ✑✑✑✑
81 Fremont St. SF (SOMA) 94105 415-896-1312
Mon-Fri 7-3:30 www.powersourcecafe.com
Organic fresh-squeezed fruit and vegetable juices, smoothies, and
lunch items. Organic coffee and tea.

PRI PRI CAFÉ ✑✑✑
1309 Solano Ave. Albany 94706 510-528-7002
Mon-Fri 8-5 Sat-Sun 9-5 www.pripricafe.com
Kid-friendly café. Mediterranean fare, Spanish tapas, fresh juices.
Available for private events.

PROGRESSIVE GROUNDS ✑✑
400 Cortland Ave. SF (Bernal Heights) 94110 415-282-6233
2301 Bryant St SF (Mission) 94110 415-647-0103
Daily 6:30 a.m.-8 p.m.
Classic coffee shop also serving sandwiches and snacks.

RAW ENERGY ORGANIC JUICE CAFÉ ✑✑✑✑
2050 Addison St. Berkeley 94704 510-665-9464
Mon-Fri 7:30-7:30 Sat 11-4 www.rawenergy.net
All-organic juices, smoothies, raw food.

RIGOLO CAFÉ ✑✑✑
3465 California Street SF (Presidio/Presidio Heights) 94118 415-876-7777
Mon-Sat 8-9 Sun 8-8 www.rigolocafe.com
Upscale breakfast, lunch, and dinner café. Casual and
family-friendly.

RITUAL COFFEE ROASTERS ✑✑
1026 Valencia St. SF (Mission) 94110 415-641-1024
Mon-Fri 6-11 Sat 7-11 Sun 7-9 www.ritualroasters.com
Café serving variety of organic coffee, roasted in the café.

ROCKIN' JAVA ✑✑✑✑
1821 Haight St. SF (Haight) 94117 415-831-8842
Daily 7:30-7:30 www.rockinjava.com
Organic, fair trade coffee and tea. Selection of organic sandwiches and snacks.

SAMOVAR TEA LOUNGE ✑✑✑✑
730 Howard St. SF (SOMA) 94103 415-227-9400
498 Sanchez St. SF (Castro) 94114 415-626-4700
Hours vary by location www.samovartea.com
Organic teas from around the world; eclectic menu. Frequent special events.

SIDEWALK JUICE ✑✑✑✑
3287 21st St. SF (Mission) 94110 415-341-8070
Mon-Fri 9-6 Sat 10-7 Sun 10-6 (seasonal hours)
Organic smoothies, juices, and vegan food.

SPASSO COFFEEHOUSE ✑✑✑
6021 College Ave. Oakland (College Ave.) 94618 510-428-1818
Mon-Fri 6:45-7:30 Sat-Sun 7:30-7:30 www.spassocoffeehouse.com
Organic and fair trade coffees and teas, dairy, and juices. Small selection of
prepared food items.

SPIKE'S COFFEES & TEAS ✑
4117 19th St. SF (Castro) 94114 415-626-5573
Mon-Sat 6:30-7 Sun 7:30-7 www.spikescoffee.com
Artisanal and gourmet coffees, teas, and chocolates.

SUNDANCE COFFEE ✑✑
2295 Third St. SF (Potrero Hill) 94107 415-503-1446
Mon-Fri 7-6 Sat 8-1 Sun 8-12 www.sundancecoffeesf.com
Café serving organic coffee and tea.

SUNSET CAFÉ ✑✑✑✑
1722 Taraval St. SF (Sunset) 94116 415-283-7528
Mon-Fri 7-7 Sat 8-7 Sun 8-5 www.thesunsetcafe.com
Café food, organic tea and coffee.

TAY TAH CAFÉ ✑✑✑
1182 Solano Ave. Albany 94706 510-527-8104
Mon-Fri 8-6 Sat 9-6
Coffee and teas; tapioca bubble tea, Mitchell's ice cream,
Asian and American snacks.

VILLAGE GROUNDS ✑✑✑
1797-A Shattuck Ave. Berkeley 94709 510-486-2877
Mon-Thu 7-10 Sat 8-8 Sun 8-10 www.villagegrounds.com
Organic, fair trade drinks; biodegradable cups.

WARMING HUT, THE ✑✑✑✑
Fort Mason Building 983 SF (Presidio/Presidio Heights) 94123 415-561-3042
Closed due to fire. Will reopen Summer 2007. Call 415-561-7756 for more information.
www.crissyfield.org/cafeshop/warminghut.html
Organic soups, sandwiches, salads, baked goods, and coffee drinks.
Green design. SF green certified business.

WELL GROUNDED TEA & COFFEE ✑✑✑✑
6925 Stockton Ave. El Cerrito 94530 510-528-4709
Mon-Fri 6-5 Sat 7-4 Sun 7-3 www.well-grounded.com
Organic coffee and tea house. Compostable containers.

ZAZEN COFFEE TEA & ORGANICS ✑✑✑✑
2314 Clement St. SF (Richmond) 94121 415-221-8283
Mon-Fri 7-6 Sat-Sun 8-6
All organic teas and coffees.

ZEMOCHA ✑✑✑✑
1959 Shattuck Ave. Berkeley 94704 510-644-4464
Mon-Sat 11-7 www.zemocha.com
Organic, fair trade hot chocolate, coffees, and teas.

ZOCALO COFFEEHOUSE 🌿🌿

645 Bancroft   San Leandro 94577 510-569-0102
Mon-Fri 6-6 Sat-Sun 8-6 www.zocalocoffeehouse.com
Coffeehouse and roastery; organic, fair trade coffee, pastries and bagels.
Alameda County certified green business.

BAKERIES

Enter a bakery that serves up organic treats and you've entered a
world where good taste and good health join in perfect combination.
And they do so in a sustainable way.

A loaf of whole grain bread, a pie plump with organic apples, some
wholesome breakfast muffins—look for food that is both delicious and
environmentally friendly. It's out there waiting for you.

The bakeries included here were given leaf awards based on the total
percentage of baked goods offered that are made with certified
organic ingredients (particularly grains, dairy products, and produce).

🌿 at least 25% of the baked goods meet the above criteria.

🌿🌿 at least 50% of the baked goods meet the above criteria.

🌿🌿🌿 at least 75% of the baked goods meet the above criteria.

🌿🌿🌿🌿 90% or more of the baked goods meet the above criteria.

ACME 🌿🌿🌿🌿

1601 San Pablo Ave. Berkeley 94702 510-524-1021
One Ferry Building #15 SF (Embarcadero) 94105 415-288-2978
Hours vary by location www.acmebread.com
Artisan bread made from organic flour.

ARIZMENDI BAKERY COOPERATIVE 🌿🌿🌿🌿

4301 San Pablo Ave. Emeryville 94608 510-547-0550
3265 Lakeshore Ave. Oakland (Lake Merritt/Downtown) 94610 510-268-8849
1331 Ninth Ave. SF (Sunset) 94122 415-566-3117
Hours vary by location www.arizmendibakery.org
Worker-cooperative bakery serving organic pastries, breads, cookies, pizzas,
and fair trade organic coffee. Uses only compostable utensils.

BOULANGERIE BAY BREAD 🌿🌿🌿

800 Redwood Hwy. Suite 125 Mill Valley 94941 415-381-1260
1000 Cole St. SF (Cole Valley) 94117 415-242-2442
1909 Union St. SF (Cow Hollow) 94123 415-440-4450
2310 Polk St. SF (Marina) 94109 415-345-1107
543 Columbus Ave. SF (North Beach) 94133 415-399-0714
2043 Fillmore St. SF (Pacific Heights) 94115 415-928-1300
2325 Pine St. SF (Pacific Heights) 94115 415-440-0356
Hours vary by location www.baybread.com
Artisan breads and specialty pastries made with organic flour;
organic coffees and teas.

CHURRO STATION ✐✐✐
2 Fifer Ave. Suite 110 Corte Madera 94925 415-927-7141
26 Medway Rd. Suite 3 San Rafael 94901 415-459-8000
Mon-Fri 6-6 Sat 7-6 Sun 7-2 www.churrostation.com
Organic churros; six varieties available.

FAT ANGEL BAKERY ✐✐✐✐
71 Broadway Blvd. Fairfax 94930 415-455-0590
Daily 6-4 www.fatangelbakery.com
Mostly organic bakery. Wheat-free, vegan options. Serves Thanksgiving coffee.
Wedding cakes prepared on special order.

FEEL GOOD BAKERY ✐✐✐
1650 Park St. Alameda 94501 510-864-2733
Mon-Fri 6-8 Sat 8-8 Sun 9-7 www.feelgoodbakery.com
Organic breads and pastries; fair trade coffee.

GREAT HARVEST BREAD ✐✐
5800 College Ave. Oakland (College Ave.) 94618 510-655-4442
Mon-Fri 7-7 Sat 7-6 Sun 10-5 www.greatharvestoakland.com
Organic breads and pastries.

NABOLOM BAKERY ✐✐✐
2708 Russell St. Berkeley 94705 510-845-2253
Mon 7-2 Tue-Fri 7-6 Sat 7:30-6 Sun 7:30-3 www.nabolom.com
Worker-collective bakery and café; pastries, organic breads, pizza and soups.

PETITE PATISSERIE ✐✐✐✐
1415 18th St. SF (Potrero Hill) 94107 415-821-9378
Tues 7-3 Wed-Sat 7-7 Sun 8-3 www.petitepatisserie.com
All-organic bakery offering pastries, cookies, croissants, bread, and sweets.

RUSTIC BAKERY ✐✐
1139 Magnolia Ave. Larkspur 94939 415-925-1556
Mon-Fri 7-4 Sat 8-4 Sun 8-2 www.rusticbakery.com
Organic breads and treats, with a particular focus on a range of flatbreads
that are made with organic yeasts. Organic coffee.

TARTINE BAKERY ✐✐✐
600 Guerrero St. SF (Mission) 94110 415-487-2600
Mon 8-7 Tue-Wed 7:30-7 Thu-Fri 7:30- 8 Sat 8-8 Sun 9-8
www.tartinebakery.com
Baked goods made with organic flour, sugar, and local eggs. Prepared foods
using organic, seasonal produce and meat.

TOWN'S END RESTAURANT AND BAKERY ✐✐
2 Townsend St. SF (SOMA) 94107 415-512-0749
Tue-Thu 7:30-9 Fri 7:30-9:30 Sat 8-9:30 Sun 8-2:30
A mostly organic bakery.

VITAL VITTLES ✐✐✐✐
2810 San Pablo Ave. Berkeley 94702 510-644-2022
Tue-Fri 8-3 www.vitalvittles.com
Organic mill and bakery. Alameda County certified green business.

YOUR BLACK MUSLIM BAKERY ✐✐✐
5832 San Pablo Ave. Oakland (Lake Merritt/Downtown) 94608 510-658-7080
365 17th St. Oakland (Lake Merritt/Downtown) 94610 510-355-5750
4915 Telegraph Ave. Piedmont 94609 510-652-1738
Hours vary by location www.ybmb.com
100% organic grain breads and pastries. The Telegraph store serves
certified organic coffees, juices, and prepared foods.

CHOCOLATIERS AND DESSERT SHOPS

A masterfully made dessert rich in organic ingredients, a piece of chocolate made from cacao grown without harm to the planet, ice cream made from milk free of hormones and other additives, these are not only delicious and pleasurable treats for you, they also treat the planet well. Maybe your diet is at odds with your dessert, but there's no need to go off your green values when it's time for pie.

The dessert purveyors included here were given leaf awards based on the percentage of certified organic food on their menu. To determine this, we looked into the percentage of dairy products, chocolate, flour, fruit, and other ingredients that are certified organic and/or sustainably produced.

✿	at least 25% of the ingredients in the desserts/chocolate goods is certified organic.
✿✿	at least 50% of the ingredients in the desserts/chocolate goods is certified organic.
✿✿✿	at least 75% of the ingredients in the desserts/chocolate goods is certified organic.
✿✿✿✿	90% or more of the ingredients in the desserts/chocolate goods is certified organic.

BI-RITE CREAMERY AND BAKESHOP ✿✿✿✿
3692 18th St. SF (Mission) 94110 415-626-5600
Mon-Tue, Thu 11-9 Fri-Sat 11-10 Sun 11-9 (seasonal hours) www.biritecreamery.com
Ice cream shop using organic dairy products from Straus Organic Creamery and other local ingredients. Organic cones.

BITTERSWEET ✿✿
5427 College Ave. Oakland (College Ave.) 94618 510-654-7159
2123 Fillmore St. SF (Pacific Heights) 94115 415-346-8715
Hours vary by location www.bittersweetcafe.com
Specialty chocolate shop. Fair trade, organic tea and Blue Bottle organic coffee.

CITIZEN CAKE ✿✿✿
399 Grove St. SF (Civic Center) 94102 415-861-2228
Tue-Fri 8-10 Sat 10-10 Sun 10-5 www.citizencake.com
Patisserie, restaurant, and bar specializing in desserts and cakes.

FAIRFAX SCOOP ✿✿✿✿
63 Broadway Blvd. Fairfax 94930 415-453-3130
Daily 12-10
Organic ice cream. Compostable utensils and containers.

ICI ✿✿✿✿
2948 College Ave. Berkeley 94705 510-665-6054
Mon 2-9 Tue-Thu 12-9 Fri-Sat 12-9:30 Sun 12-9 www.ici-icecream.com
Ice cream shop. Organic ingredients.

KARA'S CUPCAKES ✿✿✿
3249 Scott St. SF (Marina) 94123 415-563-2253
Tue-Sat 10-6 Sun 11-5 www.karascupcakes.com
Cupcakes made from organic, local ingredients. Wedding tower of cupcakes; custom designs and delivery available.

MAGGIE MUDD 🍃
903 Cortland Ave. SF (Bernal Heights) 94110 415-641-5291
Mon-Thu 3-10 Fri 3-11 Sat 11-11 Sun 11-9 www.maggiemudd.com
Vegan ice cream.

MIETTE 🍃🍃🍃
One Ferry Building #10 SF (Embarcadero) 94111 415-837-0300
Mon-Fri 10-6 Sat 9-6 Sun 11-5 www.miettecakes.com
Cakes, Parisian macaroons, cupcakes, tarts, pot de crème and cookies,
all made with organic ingredients.

PETITE PATISSERIE 🍃🍃🍃🍃
1415 18th St. SF (Potrero Hill) 94107 415-821-9378
Tue 7-3 Wed-Sat 7-7 Sun 8-3 www.petitepatisserie.com
All organic bakery offering pastries, cookies, croissants, bread, and sweets.

SAN FRANCISCO CHOCOLATE FACTORY, THE 🍃
286 12th St. SF (SOMA) 94103 888-732-4626
Mon-Sat 12-6 www.sfchocolate.com
Limited selection of organic, fair trade chocolate.

SKETCH ICE CREAM 🍃🍃🍃
1809A Fourth St. Berkeley 94710 510-665-5650
Mon-Thu 12-6 Fri-Sat 12-8 Sun 12-6 (seasonal hours) www.sketchicecream.com
Gelato-style ice cream; Straus organic milk; seasonal organic fruit; Blue Bottle
coffee and tea.

TARTINE BAKERY 🍃🍃🍃
600 Guerrero St. SF (Mission) 94110 415-487-2600
Mon 8-7 Tue-Wed 7:30-7 Thu-Fri 7:30-8 Sat 8-8 Sun 9-8 www.tartinebakery.com
Baked goods made with organic flour, sugar, and local eggs.

THREE TWINS ICE CREAM 🍃🍃🍃
641 Del Ganado Rd. San Rafael 94903 415-492-TWIN
Mon-Thu 12-8 Fri-Sat 12-9:30 Sun 12-8 www.threetwinsicecream.com
All-organic ice cream; ingredients from local, organic dairies and farms.

Tell us what you think about the businesses and services we've
listed: How was the food? How was the service? What did you
think of the ambiance? What was your experience overall? Visit
www.greenopia.com to rate a business, to post your review, to
see what other people think, or to tell us about your favorite place.

HOW TO USE THIS GUIDE

The seafood in this guide may occur in more than one column based on how it is caught, where it is from, etc. Please read all columns and be sure to check labels or ask questions when shopping or eating out: Where is the seafood from? Is it farmed or wild-caught? How was it caught?

MAKE CHOICES FOR HEALTHY OCEANS

Your consumer choices make a difference:

Best Choices are abundant, well managed and caught or farmed in environmentally friendly ways.

Good Alternatives are an option,but there are concerns with how they're caught or farmed—or with the health of their habitat due to other human impacts.

Avoid for now as these items are caught or farmed in ways that harm other marine life or the environment.

BEST CHOICES

Abalone (farmed)
Barramundi (US farmed)
Catfish (US farmed)
Clams, Mussels, Oysters (farmed)
Cod: Pacific (Alaska longline)*
Crab: Dungeness, Snow (Canada)
Halibut: Pacific
Lobster: Spiny (US)
Pollock (wild-caught from AK)*
Rockfish: Black (CA, OR)
Sablefish/Black Cod (AK, BC)
Salmon (wild-caught from AK)*
Sardines
Scallops: Bay (farmed)
Shrimp: Pink (OR)
Spot Prawn (BC)
Striped Bass (farmed)
Sturgeon, Caviar (farmed)
Tilapia (US farmed)
Trout: Rainbow (farmed)
Tuna: Albacore (BC, US troll/pole-caught)
Tuna: Skipjack (troll/pole-caught)
White Seabass

AK=Alaska BC=British Columbia CA=California OR=Oregon
WA=Washington US=United States
† Limit consumption due to concerns about mercury or other contaminants. Visit www.oceansalive.org/eat.cfm.
* Certified as sustainable to the Marine Stewardship Council. Visit www.msc.org. Contaminant information provided by Environmental Defense.

GOOD ALTERNATIVES

Basa/Tra (farmed)
Clams, Oysters† (wild-caught)
Cod: Pacific (trawled-caught)
Crab: King (AK), Snow (US), imitation
Dogfish (BC)†
Flounders, Soles (Pacific)
Lingcod
Lobster: American/Maine
Mahi mahi/Dolphinfish (US)
Rockfish (hook & line caught from AK, BC)†
Sablefish/Black Cod (CA, OR, WA)
Salmon (CA, OR, WA wild-caught)
Sanddabs: Pacific
Scallops: Bay, Sea (Canada and Northeast)
Shrimp (US farmed or wild-caught)
Spot Prawn (US)
Squid
Sturgeon (wild-caught from OR, WA)
Swordfish (US longline)†
Tuna: Bigeye, Yellowfin (troll/pole)†
Tuna: canned light
Tuna: canned white/Albacore†

AVOID

Chilean Seabass/Toothfish†
Cod: Atlantic
Crab: King (imported)
Dogfish (US)†
Grenadier/Pacific Roughy
Lobster: Spiny (Caribbean imported)
Mahi mahi/Dolphinfish (imported)
Monkfish
Orange Roughy†
Rockfish (trawl-caught)†
Salmon (farmed, including Atlantic)†
Scallops: Sea (Mid-Atlantic)
Shark†
Shrimp (imported farmed or wild-caught)
Sturgeon†, Caviar (imported wild-caught)
Swordfish (imported)†
Tuna: Albacore, Bigeye, Yellow fin (longline)†
Tuna: Bluefin†

ORGANIC STANDARDS FOR FOOD

In the words of the U.S. Department of Agriculture, "Organic food is produced by farmers who emphasize the use of renewable resources and the conservation of soil and water to enhance environmental quality for future generations." Thus "organic" refers to a specific set of standards used throughout the entire process of food production. Food that is certified organic comes from farms that have been inspected and approved under the USDA's guidelines (by a third-party agent). Organic certification prohibits the use of most conventional pesticides, synthetic fertilizers, sewage sludge, bioengineering, and irradiation (also called "ionizing radiation" or "cold pasteurization"). Organic meat, eggs, poultry, and dairy come from animals not treated with antibiotics or growth hormones. Certified organic food is, by definition, free from genetically modified organisms (GMOs). Also, any handling or processing of organic food must be done by certified companies.

UNDERSTANDING ORGANIC LABELING

In the U.S., federal organic legislation defines three levels of organics. Products made entirely with certified organic ingredients and methods can be labeled "100% organic." Products with 95% organic ingredients can use the word "organic" on packaging, advertising, etc. Both may also display the USDA organic seal. A third category, containing a minimum of 70% organic ingredients, can be labeled "made with organic ingredients." In addition, products can also display the logo of the individual certification body that approved them. Products made with less than 70% organic ingredients cannot advertise this information to consumers and can only mention this fact in the product's ingredient statement. Similar percentages and labels apply in the European Union.

SMALL AND TRANSITIONAL FARMERS

Although organic certification is typically an excellent way to ensure the quality and eco-friendliness of the food you buy, not all farmers and food producers are officially certified. The organic certification process is rigorous and often expensive. Small farms in particular may not be certified, or may be "transitional," meaning they are on their way to certification. If you go to local farmers' markets, the best way to understand what you're buying and how it is grown is to ask the farmer or vendor questions. Local farmers may be happy to show you around their farms so you can see for yourself as well.

Getcha Grub On!

Sorry to break it to you folks, but most of us have been the unwitting participants in a grand dietary experiment—and we, the guinea pigs, aren't faring so well. In just under two generations, the American diet has become overrun with highly processed, high-fat, high-sugar, high-salt foods, which are culprits in a litany of health problems. Our "get big or get out" farm policy has also meant small farmers have been pushed off the land faster than you can say, "Super Size Me!" Our industrial agriculture is also one of the globe's largest contributors of greenhouse gas emissions and one of the worst polluters of air, soil, and water.

Thankfully, this conundrum is something we can each work to improve. We can choose what we call grub—local, sustainably raised, whole foods. The best part is that grub is not just good for the earth and for farmers; it's good for your body, too. Plus, grub tastes damn good.

Choosing grub may just mean that within our lifetime we'll be able to look back with incredulity at this strange and failed American dietary experiment. Food will no longer be a source of illness and unhappiness; what little "conventional" produce remains will be labeled "grown with chemicals," and funding for sustainable farming will surpass that for the newest chemical cocktail or genetically modified twist.

While we're striving for this day, we can improve our own health and limit our exposure to toxins by making smart food choices. Seek out food co-ops where you have a say in what goes onto the shelves, find a farm near you and join your neighbors in supporting it through community supported agriculture, or visit your local farmers' market and taste freshly picked produce bursting with flavor and put a face to the farmer who feeds you.

Guinea pigs of the world unite! We have nothing to lose but waste, pollution, illness, environmental devastation...and our love handles.

ANNA LAPPÉ AND BRYANT TERRY

Anna Lappé of the Small Planet Institute and Bryant Terry, Eco-chef and food justice activist, are coauthors of *Grub: Ideas for an Urban Organic Kitchen.* (www.eatgrub.org)

Eating In

Most of us spend a significant percentage of our food budget every week at our local grocery store. We recommend spending that all-important grocery money on products that are healthier for you and the planet.

For a grocery store to be included in the guide and so recognized with a one-leaf award, its overall stock (food and non-food items) must meet at least 25% of the criteria outlined below.

We've evaluated our grocery stores with nine product areas in mind: produce, meat and poultry, fish, dairy products, non-dairy beverages, prepared foods, canned and dry goods, personal care items, cleaning products and household goods.

- For food items, we based our leaf awards on the overall percentage of brands and products offered that are certified organic and free of genetically modified organisms (GMOs); or are locally grown and produced without the use of chemical fertilizers, herbicides, or pesticides. (The chart on page 60, *Eating in Season*, will help you identify fruits and vegetables in season in the Bay Area so you can buy locally grown and, ideally, organic produce, year-round.)

- For meat, poultry, and dairy products, we looked at the percentage raised organically, without the use of antibiotics or hormones.

- With fish, we checked into whether it was wild caught, or sustainably farm raised and processed without chemical treatment. (We have included a *Seafood Guide* on page 32 to help you make healthy and sustainable seafood choices.)

- Non-food items (personal care products and tools, household cleaning supplies, and paper products) were rated based on the total percentage offered that is environmentally sound, non-toxic, sustainably produced, and, where appropriate, made with recycled content.

> ✿ at least 25% of products meet the above criteria.
> ✿✿ at least 50% of products meet the above criteria.
> ✿✿✿ at least 75% of products meet the above criteria.
> ✿✿✿✿ 90% or more of products meet the above criteria.

Genetic Engineering (GE) and Genetically Modified Organisms (GMOs): *Genetic Engineering is a radical new way to grow food. Unlike traditional breeding, genetic engineering manipulates the genes and DNA of plants and animals to create new life forms, or Genetically Modified Organisms, that would never occur in nature. This creates new and unpredictable health and environmental risks. To create GE crops, genes from bacteria, viruses, plants, and animals are inserted into plants like soybeans, corn, canola, and cotton. Try to avoid all products containing GMOs. However, since GE products are not generally labeled, the best way to avoid eating them is to purchase organically grown food.*

26TH AND GUERRERO MARKET ✍✍✍✍
1400 Guerrero St. SF (Mission) 94110 415-282-6274
Mon-Fri 8-9 Sat-Sun 9-9 www.26thandguerreromarket.com
Small neighborhood grocer; organic produce, health food.

ALAMEDA NATURAL GROCERY ✍✍✍✍
1650 Park St. Alameda 94501 510-865-1500
Mon-Sat 8-8 Sun 8-7 www.alamedamarketplace.com
Organic and locally grown foods; eco-friendly home and personal products.

ANDRONICO'S MARKET ✍
1550 Shattuck Ave. Berkeley 94709 510-841-7942
1850 Solano Ave. Berkeley 94707 510-524-1673
2655 Telegraph Ave. Berkeley 94704 510-845-1062
1414 University Ave. Berkeley 94702 510-548-7061
690 Los Altos Rancho Ctr. Los Altos 94024 650-948-6648
500 Stanford Shopping Ctr. Palo Alto 94304 650-327-5505
100 Center Blvd. San Anselmo 94960 415-455-8186
1200 Irving St. SF (Sunset) 94122 415-661-3220
Hours vary by location www.andronicos.com
Grocery store; extensive selection of organic foods.

BERKELEY BOWL ✍✍✍✍
2020 Oregon St. Berkeley 94703 510-843-6929
Mon-Sat 9-8 Sun 10-6 www.berkeleybowl.com
Organic, local, and exotic produce; sustainable meat, poultry, fish; extensive
bulk food section.

BERKELEY NATURAL GROCERY ✍✍✍
1336 Gilman St. Berkeley 94706 510-526-2456
Daily 9-8 www.naturalgrocery.com
Organic produce; natural personal care and cleaning products.

BI-RITE MARKET ✍✍✍✍
3639 18th St. SF (Mission) 94110 415-241-9760
Mon-Fri 9-9 Sat-Sun 9-8 www.biritemarket.com
Neighborhood grocer; organic produce; natural meats; prepared organic
specialty food.

BUFFALO WHOLE FOOD & GRAIN COMPANY ✍✍✍
598 Castro St. SF (Castro) 94114 415-626-7038
Mon-Sat 9-8 Sun 10-8 www.buffalowholefoods.com
Premium vitamins, natural bodycare, fresh dairy, bakery and deli foods, and
organically-grown produce.

CHURCH STREET GROCETERIA ✍✍
300 Church St. SF (Castro) 94114 415-626-1653
Daily 8-11
Carries a wide selection of organic produce and canned goods.

COUNTRY SUN NATURAL FOODS ✍✍✍✍
440 South California Ave. Palo Alto 94306 650-324-9190
Mon-Fri 9-8 Sat 9-7 Sun 10-7 www.countrysun.com
Local and organic produce and groceries; wine; body care; supplements;
bulk foods.

DRAEGER'S SUPERMARKETS, INC. ✍✍
342 First St. Los Altos 94022 650-948-4425
1010 University Dr. Menlo Park 94025 650-324-7700
222 East Fourth Ave. San Mateo 94401 650-685-3700
Hours vary by location www.draegers.com
International foods and wines; gift baskets; deli; gluten-free and specialty
bakery; cooking school.

EARTHBEAM NATURAL FOODS ✑✑✑✑
1399 Broadway Burlingame 94010 650-347-2058
Mon-Sat 9-7 Sun 10-6 www.earthbeamfoods.com
Full-service grocery. Organic produce; bulk foods; seasonal soups.

EEZY FREEZY ✑✑
25 West Portal Ave. SF (West Portal) 94127 415-566-6000
Daily 7 a.m.-11 p.m.
General grocer; some organic produce.

EL CERRITO NATURAL GROCERY ✑✑✑
10367 San Pablo Ave. El Cerrito 94530 510-526-1155
Daily 9-8 www.naturalgrocery.com
Organic produce; natural personal care and cleaning products.

ESSENTIAL FOODS ✑✑✑✑
403 Irving St. SF (Sunset) 94122 415-242-1936
Daily 9 a.m.-10 p.m.
Neighborhood health food store; mostly organic products.

FALLETTI FOODS ✑✑
308 Broderick St. SF (Alamo Square) 94117 415-626-4400
Daily 7 a.m.-9 p.m. www.fallettifoods.com
Offers locally grown produce, a meat and seafood department, as well as an
extensive grocery selection.

FOOD MILL, THE ✑✑✑
3033 MacArthur Blvd. Oakland (East Oakland) 94602 510-482-3848
255 West MacArthur Blvd. Piedmont 94611 510-595-3633
Hours vary by location www.foodmillonline.com
Health food, frozen foods, and pharmacy; some eco-friendly
household products.

FRESH ORGANICS ✑✑✑✑
1023 Stanyan St. SF (Noe Valley) 94117 415-564-2800
Daily 9-8
Organic, natural foods; juice bar; health section.

FRUIT BARN ✑
1616 Ocean Ave. SF (Ingleside) 94112 415-469-8010
Mon-Sat 8-7 Sun 9-5
Small grocer; some local produce.

GOLDEN PRODUCE ✑✑✑
172 Church St. SF (Castro) 94114 415-431-1536
Daily 9-8
Small general grocer; conventional and organic produce.

GOOD EARTH NATURAL & ORGANIC FOODS ✑✑✑✑
1966 Sir Francis Drake Blvd. Fairfax 94930 415-454-0123
Daily 9-8 www.goodearthnaturalfoods.net
Organic produce and poultry; grass-fed beef; wine and beer; bulk foods;
health and body care. Vegetarian and vegan to-go bar.

GOOD LIFE GROCERY ✑✑
448 Cortland Ave. SF (Bernal Heights) 94110 415-648-3221
Daily 8-9
Neighborhood grocery store with organic produce and well-stocked
meat department.

HAIGHT FILLMORE WHOLE FOODS ✑✑
501 Haight St. SF (Haight) 94117 415-552-6077
Daily 8 a.m.-10 p.m.
Neighborhood grocery store with some organic products.

HARVEST URBAN MARKET 🍃🍃🍃
2285 Market St. SF (Castro) 94114 415-626-0805
191 Eighth St. SF (SOMA) 94103 415-621-1000
Hours vary by location www.harvesturban.com
Organic health food store and cafe; organic coffee.

HEALTH HAVEN PRODUCE AND NATURAL FOOD 🍃🍃
621 Divisadero St. SF (Western Addition) 94117 415-351-1267
Daily 9-9
Sells mostly organic produce and products.

LAKESHORE NATURAL FOODS 🍃🍃🍃🍃
3321 Lakeshore Ave. Oakland (Lake Merritt/Downtown) 94610 510-452-1079
Mon-Fri 9:30-7 Sat 9:30-6 Sun 10-5
Natural health products; dry and frozen foods; personal care products;
fair trade coffees and teas.

LUNARDI'S 🍃🍃🍃
Carlmont Village Shopping Ctr. 1085 Alameda de las Pulgas Belmont 94002
650-591-5768
1825 El Camino Real Burlingame 94010 650-697-5306
100 Skycrest Shopping Ctr. San Bruno 94066 650-952-2851
Hours vary by location www.lunardis.com
Local, natural meats; line-caught seafood; artisanal cheeses; heirloom produce,
deli, bakery.

MARKET HALL PRODUCE 🍃🍃🍃
5655 College Ave. Oakland (College Ave.) 94618 510-601-8208
Mon-Fri 9-8 Sat 9-7 Sun 9-6 www.markethallproduce.com
Locally grown produce; free-range eggs; organic dairy; dry goods;
non-dairy beverages.

MOLLIE STONE'S 🍃
1477 Chapin Ave. Burlingame 94010 650-558-9992
270 Bon Air Shopping Ctr. Greenbrae 94904 415-461-1164
164 South California Ave. Palo Alto 94306 650-323-8361
22 Bayhill Shopping Ctr. San Bruno 94066 650-873-8075
49 West Forty-Second Ave. San Mateo 94403 650-372-2828
2435 California St. SF (Pacific Heights) 94115 415-567-4902
Tower Market 635 Portola Dr. SF (Twin Peaks) 94127 415-664-1600
100 Harbor Dr. Sausalito 94965 415-331-6900
Hours vary by location www.molliestones.com
A full-line grocery store offering some organic produce, natural meats,
and fresh seafood.

NABILAS 🍃
559 Hayes St. SF (Alamo Square) 94102 415-864-6514
Mon-Sat 9-9 Sun 9-8
Family-run neighborhood health food market.

NATURE STOP 🍃🍃
1336 Grant Ave. SF (North Beach) 94133 415-398-0257
Mon-Fri 9-9 Sat-Sun 10-9
Small natural food store. Organic products, artisan bread, juice/smoothie bar.

NORIEGA PRODUCE MARKET 🍃🍃🍃🍃
3821 Noriega St. SF (Sunset) 94122 415-564-0370
Daily 8-8
Organic, natural health food.

OASIS NATURAL FOODS 🍃
2021 Novato Blvd. Novato 94947 415-897-4706
Mon-Fri 9-7 Sat 9:30-6 Sun 10-6 www.oasisnaturalhealth.com
Small local market with dry goods, frozen section, beauty products.

OTHER AVENUES ✐✐✐✐
3930 Judah St. SF (Sunset) 94122 415-661-7475
Daily 10-8 www.otheravenues.org
Worker-owned co-op. Organic grocery; housewares; supplements;
beer and wine.

PARADISE FOODS ✐✐
5627 Paradise Dr. Corte Madera 94925 415-945-8855
Mon-Sat 8-8 www.foodsofparadise.com
Full-service grocery store with some local and organic offerings.

PIAZZA'S FINE FOODS ✐✐
Charleston Shopping Ctr. 3922 Middlefield Rd. Palo Alto 94303 650-494-1629
Laurelwood Shopping Ctr. 1218 West Hillsdale Blvd. San Mateo 94403
650-341-9496
Hours vary by location www.piazzasfinefoods.com
Full-service grocery store with some organic and natural products.

PIEDMONT GROCERY ✐✐
4038 Piedmont Ave. Piedmont 94611 510-653-8181
Mon-Sat 9-8 Sun 9-7
Organic and natural products; meats; poultry; seafood; hot and
cold take-out food.

PRODUCE CENTER, THE ✐✐
1500 Shattuck Ave. Berkeley 94709 510-848-8100
Mon-Sat 8-7 Sun 10-5:30
Organic and conventional produce.

RAINBOW GROCERY ✐✐✐✐
1745 Folsom St. SF (Mission) 94103 415-863-0620
Daily 9-9 www.rainbowgrocery.org
Worker-owned co-op. Organic, natural vegetarian food; eco-friendly products.
SF green certified business.

REAL FOOD COMPANY, THE ✐✐✐✐
3060 Fillmore St. SF (Cow Hollow) 94123 415-567-6900
2140 Polk St. SF (Russian Hill) 94109 415-673-7420
Hours vary by location www.realfoodco.com
Organic, natural foods; health and beauty section.

SAVEMORE MARKET ✐✐
4219 Park Blvd. Oakland (East Oakland) 94602 510-530-6296
Daily 7:30 a.m.-11 p.m.
Neighborhood market with some organic and natural produce; eco-friendly
household products; fair trade coffees and teas.

TARAVAL MARKET ✐✐
1215 Taraval St. SF (Sunset) 94116 415-664-7388
Daily 8:30-8
All-natural grocer; some organic products.

THOM'S NATURAL FOODS ✐✐✐✐
5843 Geary Blvd. SF (Richmond) 94121 415-387-6367
Daily 8:30-8
All organic products, from groceries to health and beauty products.

TRADER JOE'S 🍃🍃

2217 South Shore Ctr. Alameda 94501 510-769-5450
417 Westlake Ctr. Daly City 94015 650-755-3825
225 El Cerrito Plaza El Cerrito 94530 510-524-7609
5700 Christie Ave. Emeryville 94608 510-658-8091
765 Broadway Millbrae 94030 650-259-9142
1820 South Grant St. San Mateo 94402 650-570-6140
401 Bay St. SF (North Beach) 94133 415-351-1013
7514 Redwood Blvd. Novato 94945 415-898-9359
555 Ninth St. SF (SOMA) 94103 415-863-1292
3 Masonic Ave. SF (Western Addition) 94118 415-346-9964
301 McLellan Dr. South SF 94080 650-583-6401
337 Third St. San Rafael 94901 415-454-9530
Hours vary by location www.traderjoes.com
Some organic and natural foods. Non-toxic cleaning products. Unbleached
and recycled paper products.

VALENCIA WHOLE FOODS 🍃🍃🍃

999 Valencia St. SF (Mission) 94110 415-285-0231
Daily 8-9
Neighborhood grocery store with organic foods; deli; botanicals; fresh bread;
vitamins; bulk spices.

VILLAGE MARKET 🍃🍃

5885 Broadway Terrace Piedmont 94618 510-547-3200
Mon-Sat 7 a.m.-9 p.m. Sun 8-8 www.villagemkt.com
Non-hormone meats and poultry; fresh fish; organic produce; eco-friendly
household and personal care products. Weekend BBQ.

VILLAGE MARKET, THE 🍃🍃🍃🍃

One Ferry Building #29 SF (Embarcadero) 94111 415-989-9200
4555 California St. SF (Richmond) 94118 415-221-0445
Hours vary by location www.villagemarketsf.com
Wine and specialty items. California Street location also has organic produce,
fresh-cut flowers; espresso drinks; small seating area.

WHOLE FOODS MARKET 🍃🍃🍃🍃

3000 Telegraph Ave. Berkeley 94705 510-649-1333
4800 El Camino Real Los Altos 94022 650-559-0300
414 Miller Ave. Mill Valley 94941 415-381-1200
774 Emerson St. Palo Alto 94301 650-326-8676
1250 Jefferson Ave. Redwood City 94062 650-367-1400
399 Fourth St. SF (SOMA) 94107 415-618-0066
1765 California St. SF (Pacific Heights) 94109 415-674-0500
1010 Park Pl. San Mateo 94403 650-358-6900
340 Third St. San Rafael 94901 415-451-6333
Hours vary by location www.wholefoodsmarket.com
A full-service grocery store offering many organic and fair trade products.
Bulk selection; natural meats and fresh seafood; natural body care products;
alternative pharmacy; organic beer and wine.

WHOLE LIFE NATURAL FOODS 🍃🍃🍃

344 Woodside Plaza Redwood City 94061 650-364-4946
744 Laurel Ave. San Carlos 94070 650-593-7927
Hours vary by location
Packaged, dry, canned, and frozen natural foods; baby products.

WILLIAM'S NATURAL FOODS 🍃🍃🍃

12249 San Pablo Ave. Richmond 94805 510-232-1911
Mon-Fri 9-7 Sat 9-6 Sun 11-6
Organic food; vitamins and supplements; non-toxic household goods.

WOODLANDS MARKET 🍃

735 College Ave. Kentfield 94904 415-457-8160
Daily 7-9 www.woodlandsmarket.com
Full-service, family-owned grocery store.

There's nothing like a good farmers' market and there are many in the area. Farmers' markets are about the food and about the community. You'll find fresh produce, tasty treats, locally made goods, and many products you can't get at the grocery store. Plus, food items at the farmers' markets change naturally with the seasons.

You may notice that some of the produce at a farmers' market is not organic. Often small farmers cannot afford to go through the organic certification process. Some are making great strides by carrying produce that is grown without synthetic chemical fertilizers, herbicides, or pesticides.

We urge you to support the farmers who have made this effort. Some vendors will clearly mark their area with signs that say "organic" or "pesticide free." If you're not sure, ask. Because the mix of vendors changes quite frequently at farmers' markets, we have not awarded leaves.

When you buy a share in a local farm operation, you are part of what is called Community-Supported Agriculture (CSA). This means you have joined a regional community of growers and consumers and are sharing in both the risks and the benefits of food production.

Typically, members or "share holders" of the farm pay in advance to cover the costs of the farm. In return, they receive shares of the farm's produce throughout the growing season. By direct sales to community members, growers receive better prices for their crops and gain some financial security.

The farmers' markets in this category were not leaf-awarded due to the great variation among vendors. As for CSAs, we have listed some of the best, but there are many others from which to choose.

Visit our website (www.greenopia.com) and tell us about your local farmers' market—what you buy there and why. And let us know if you are a CSA shareholder and what you like best about being a part of that movement.

Certified Farmers' Market (CFM): *These are locations that have been approved by the county agricultural commissioner for farmers to sell agricultural products directly to consumers.*

FARMERS' MARKETS

ALAMEDA CFM
Taylor Ave. and Webster St. Alameda 94501 800-949-FARM
Tue 9:30-1 Year-round Thu 4-8 May-Sep www.pcfma.com

BAYVIEW/HUNTER'S POINT FARMERS' MARKET
Third St. and Oakdale Ave. 4705 Third Street SF (Bayview/Hunter's Point) 94124
415-355-3723
Call for days and hours www.sfenvironment.org/farmmkt06.pdf

BELMONT CFM
El Camino Real and O'Neill St. Belmont 94002 800-949-FARM
Sun 9-1 May-Nov www.pcfma.com

BERKELEY SATURDAY CFM
Center St. and Martin Luther King Way Berkeley 94704 510-548-3333
Sat 10-3 Year-round www.cafarmersmarkets.com

BERKELEY SHATTUCK ORGANIC CFM
Shattuck Ave. and Rose St. Berkeley 94709 510-548-3333
Thu 3-7 Year-round www.cafarmersmarkets.com

BERKELEY TUESDAY CFM
Derby St. and Martin Luther King Jr. Way Berkeley 94704 510-548-3333
Tue 2-6 Year-round www.cafarmersmarkets.com

BURLINGAME FRESH MARKET CFM
Burlingame Ave. and Park Rd. Burlingame 94010 650-344-1735
Sun 9-1 May-Dec www.cafarmersmarkets.com

CORTE MADERA CFM
Tamalpais Dr. and Hwy. 101 Corte Madera 94925 415-382-7846
Wed 12-5 Year-round www.cafarmersmarkets.com

DALY CITY CFM
3 Serramonte Ctr. Daly City 94015 800-806-FARM
Thu, Sat 9-1 Year-round www.cafarmersmkts.com

EAST OAKLAND CFM
73rd Ave. and International Blvd. Oakland (East Oakland) 94621 510-638-1742
Fri 10-2 May-Nov www.cafarmersmarkets.com

EAST OAKLAND SENIOR CENTER CFM
9255 Edes Ave. Oakland (East Oakland) 94603 510-562-8989
Wed 10:30-2:30 Apr-Nov www.cafarmersmarkets.com

EL CERRITO PLAZA FARMERS' MARKET
San Pablo Ave. and Fairmount Ave. El Cerrito 94530 510-528-7992
Tue, Sat 9-1 Year-round www.elcerritoplaza.com

FAIRFAX CFM
Bolinas Rd. and Broadway Blvd. Fairfax 94930 415-472-6100
Wed 4-8 Jun-Oct www.marincountyfarmersmarkets.org

FARM FRESH CHOICE
2530 San Pablo Ave. Berkeley 94702 510-848-1704
Hours vary by location www.ecologycenter.org/ffc
Community produce stands located at four after-school and summer school
locations (see website for locations and hours).

FREMONT CENTERVILLE CFM
Bonde Way and Fremont Blvd. Fremont 94536 800-549-5227
Sat 9-1 Year-round www.fremontfarmersmarket.com

FREMONT IRVINGTON CFM
Bay St. and Fremont Blvd. Fremont 94538 415-472-6100
Sun 9-1 Year-round www.marincountyfarmersmarkets.org

FREMONT KAISER CFM
39400 Paseo Padre Parkway Fremont 94538 800-949-FARM
Thu 10-2 Year-round www.pcfma.com

FREMONT NUMMI CFM
Grimmer Blvd. and Fremont Blvd. Fremont 94538 800-549-5227
Fri 2-6 May-Oct www.cafarmersmarkets.com

HAYWARD CFM
Main St. and B St. Hayward 94541 415-472-6100
Sat 9-1 Year-round www.marincountyfarmersmarkets.org

HAYWARD KAISER CFM
Hesperian Blvd. and West Tennyson Rd. Hayward 94545 800-949-FARM
Wed 10-2 Year-round www.pcfma.com

LARKSPUR CFM
Larkspur Landing Circle Larkspur 94939 415-382-7846
Sat 10-2 May-Oct www.cafarmersmarkets.com

MENLO PARK CFM
Crane St. and Chestnut St. Menlo Park 94025 831-688-8316
Sun 9-1 Year-round www.cafarmersmarkets.com

MILLBRAE CFM
Broadway and Victoria Ave. Millbrae 94030 650-697-7324
Sat 8-1 Year-round www.cafarmersmarkets.com

MO' BETTER FOOD
Seventh St. and Mandela Parkway Oakland (West Oakland) 94607 510-776-4178
Sat 10-3 Year-round www.mobetterfood.com

NOVATO DOWNTOWN CFM
Sherman Ave. and Grant Ave. Novato 94945 800-897-FARM
Tue 4-8 Apr-Sep www.marincountyfarmersmarkets.org

OAKLAND FRUITVALE CFM
34th Ave. and 12th St. Oakland (West Oakland) 94601 510-535-6926
Sun 10-3 Year-round; Thu 2-7 Jun-Nov www.unitycouncil.org

OAKLAND GRAND LAKE CFM
Grand Ave. and Lake Park Way Oakland (Lake Merritt/Downtown) 94610
415-472-6100
Sat 9-2 Year-round www.marincountyfarmersmarkets.org

OAKLAND JACK LONDON CFM
Broadway and Embarcadero Oakland (Lake Merritt/Downtown) 94607
800-949-FARM
Sun 10-2 Year-round and Wed 10-2 May-Oct www.pcfma.com

OAKLAND KAISER CFM
Howe St. (btw MacArthur Blvd. and 40th St.) Oakland (Lake Merritt/Downtown)
94611 800-949-FARM
Fri 10-2 Year-round www.pcfma.com

OAKLAND MONTCLAIR SUNDAY CFM
LaSalle Ave. and Moraga Ave. Oakland (Montclair) 94611 510-745-7100
Sun 9-1 Year-round www.urbanvillangeonline.com

OAKLAND TEMESCAL CFM
5300 Claremont Ave. Oakland (Temescal) 94618 510-745-7100
Sun 9-1 Year-round www.urbanvillageonline.com

OLD OAKLAND CFM
Ninth St. and Broadway Oakland (Lake Merritt/Downtown) 94607 510-745-7100
Fri 8-2 Year-round www.urbanvillageonline.com

REDWOOD CITY CFM
850 Winslow St. Redwood City 94063 650-592-4103
Sat 8-12 Apr-Nov www.rwckfm.com

REDWOOD CITY KAISER CFM
Veterans Blvd. and Maple St. Redwood City 94063 800-949-FARM
Wed 10-2 Year-round www.pcfma.com

RICHMOND CFM
Civic Center Plaza Dr. and MacDonald Ave. Richmond 94804 510-758-2336
Fri 11-5 Year-round www.cafarmersmarkets.com

SAN CARLOS CFM
Laurel St. and Olive St. San Carlos 94070 800-949-FARM
Thu 4-8 May-Sep www.pcfma.com

SAN FRANCISCO ALEMANY CFM
100 Alemany Blvd. SF (Bernal Heights) 94110 415-647-9423
Sat 6-5 Year-round www.cafarmersmkts.com

SAN FRANCISCO CROCKER GALLERIA
50 Post St. SF (Union Square) 94104 800-806-FARM
Thu 11-3 Year-round www.cafarmersmkts.com

SAN FRANCISCO FERRY PLAZA FARMERS MARKET
One Ferry Building SF (Embarcadero) 94111 415-291-3276
Tue 10-2 Sat 8-2 Year-round
www.cuesa.org/markets

SAN FRANCISCO FILLMORE CFM
O'Farrell St. and Fillmore St. SF (Japantown) 94115 800-949-FARM
Sat 9-1 May-Nov www.pcfma.com

SAN FRANCISCO HEART OF THE CITY FARMERS' MARKETS
Market St. and Hyde St. SF (Civic Center) 94103 415-558-9455
Sun 7-5 Wed 7-5:30 Year-round www.cafarmersmarkets.com

SAN FRANCISCO KAISER CFM
2425 Geary Blvd. SF (Western Addition) 94115 800-949-FARM
Wed 10-2 Year-round www.pcfma.com

SAN FRANCISCO MARINA CFM
Fillmore St. and Chestnut St. SF (Marina) 94123 800-806-FARM
Call for days and hours www.cafarmersmkts.com

SAN FRANCISCO NOE VALLEY CFM
3861 24th St. SF (Noe Valley) 94114 415-248-1332
Sat 8-1 Year-round www.noevalleyfarmersmarket.com

SAN LEANDRO BAYFAIR MALL CFM
Fairmont Dr. and East 14th St. San Leandro 94578 800-806-FARM
Sat 9-1 Year-round www.cafarmersmkts.com

SAN MATEO CFM
West Hillsdate Blvd. and Campus Dr. San Mateo 94403 800-949-FARM
Wed, Sun 9-1 Year-round www.pcfma.com

SAN RAFAEL CIVIC CENTER-MARIN COUNTY CFM
Hwy. 101 and North San Pedro Rd. San Rafael 94903 415-472-6100
Thu, Sun 8-1 Year-round www.marincountyfarmersmarkets.org

SAN RAFAEL DOWNTOWN CFM
Fourth St. and B St. San Rafael 94901 415-492-8007
Thu 6 p.m.-9 p.m. Apr-Sep www.sanrafaelmarket.org

SANTA CLARA KAISER CFM

710 Lawrence Expressway Santa Clara 95051 800-949-FARM
Thu 10-2 Year-round www.pcfma.com

SAUSALITO CFM

Bridgeway and Tracy Sausalito 94065 415-382-7846
Fri 4-8 May-Oct www.cafarmersmarkets.com

SOUTH SAN FRANCISCO CFM

West Orange Ave. and Tennis Dr. South SF 94080 800-949-FARM
Sat 9-1 May-Oct www.pcfma.com

UNION CITY KAISER CFM

3553 Whipple Rd. Union City 94587 800-949-FARM
Tue 10-2 Year-round www.pcfma.com

UNION CITY-OLD ALVARADO CFM

Smith St. and Watkins St. Union City 94587 800-949-FARM
Sat 9-1 Year-round www.pcfma.com

COMMUNITY-SUPPORTED AGRICULTURE

EATING WITH THE SEASONS CSA

3739 Balboa St. PMB 157 SF (Richmond) 94121 831-245-8125
Mon-Fri 9-5 Year-round www.eatwiththeseasons.com
Organic produce, grass-fed beef, eggs, chicken; fair trade coffee and tea.
Home delivery or drop off points throughout the Bay Area.

FULL BELLY FARM CSA

P.O. Box 220 Guinda 95637 800-791-2110
Year-round www.fullbellyfarm.com
Organic produce farm. Home delivery in select East Bay regions; delivery to
drop-off points in greater Bay Area.

HIDDEN VILLA CSA

26870 Moody Road Los Altos 94022 650-949-8647
Tue, Thu Hours Vary May-Nov www.hiddenvilla.org/csa.php
Organic CSA with an environmental education program and summer camp for
children. Serves Peninsula.

RIVERDOG FARM CSA

P.O. Box 42 Guinda 95637 530-796-3802
By appt. Year-round www.riverdogfarm.com
Certified organic produce; drop-off points at various locations. Serves East Bay.

SAN GERONIMO VALLEY CSA

P.O. Box 134 San Geronimo 94963 415-488-0124
Wed 1-7 June-Oct
Cooperative CSA representing Marin organic farmers. Serves Marin.

TERRA FIRMA FARMS CSA

P.O. Box 836 Winters 95694 530-756-2800
By appt. Year-round www.terrafirmafarm.com
Organic produce; neighborhood drop-off points. Serves East Bay and SF.

TWO SMALL FARMS CSA

P.O. Box 2065 Watsonville 95077 831-761-8380
By appt. Apr-Nov www.twosmallfarms.com
Collaborative CSA between Mariquita and High Ground Organics Farms. Serves
Peninsula and SF.

These grocery and produce delivery services will deliver fresh, healthy food and sustainably made non-food items to your door. They offer a service that will save you hours every week. Many also offer on-line ordering capabilities that are fast and convenient.

We have reviewed these delivery services in nine product areas: produce, meat and poultry, fish, dairy products, non-dairy beverages, prepared foods, canned and dry goods, personal care supplies, cleaning products and household goods.

- For food items, we looked at the overall percentage of brands and products offered that are certified organic and free of genetically modified organisms (GMOs); or are locally grown and produced without the use of chemical fertilizers, herbicides, or pesticides.

- For meat, poultry, and dairy products, we looked at the percentage raised organically, without the use of antibiotics or hormones.

- With fish, we checked into whether it was wild caught, or sustainably farm raised and processed without chemical treatment.

- For non-food items (personal care products, household cleaning supplies, and paper products), we looked at the total percentage offered that is environmentally sound, non-toxic, sustainably produced and, where appropriate, made with recycled content.

---

at least 25% of products meet the above criteria.

at least 50% of products meet the above criteria.

at least 75% of products meet the above criteria.

90% or more of products meet the above criteria.

AHA-YES!
1931 Old Middlefield Way Suite 202 Mountain View 94043 650-641-0003
Mon-Sat by appt. www.aha-yes.com
Organic, natural household products; local delivery or warehouse pick-up. Percentage of sales donated to charity. Serves Peninsula.

EATING WITH THE SEASONS CSA
3739 Balboa St. PMB 157 SF (Richmond) 94121 831-245-8125
Year-round www.eatwiththeseasons.com
Organic produce, grass-fed beef, eggs, chicken; fair trade coffee and tea. Home delivery or drop off points throughout Bay Area.

FARM FRESH TO YOU
23808 State Hwy. 16 Capay 95607 800-796-6009
By appt. www.farmfreshtoyou.com
Organic produce; home delivery throughout Bay Area which includes recipes.

FULL BELLY FARM CSA
P.O. Box 220 Guinda 95637 800-791-2110
Year-round www.fullbellyfarm.com
Organic produce farm. Home delivery in select East Bay regions; delivery to drop-off points in greater Bay Area.

GOURMET GARDEN TO GO ✐✐

419 Miller Ave. Mill Valley 94941 415-381-4267
Mon-Sat 11-8 www.gourmetgardentogo.com
Take-out gourmet dinners and desserts; no additives or preservatives. Pick-up
or delivery. Serves Marin and SF.

GUERRILLA ORGANICS ✐✐✐✐

736 Alcatraz Ave. Suite 7 Oakland (North Oakland) 94609 415-240-7212
By appt. www.guerrillaorganics.com
Home-delivered organic produce boxes; raw and sattvic (yogic) options. Serves
East Bay, Peninsula, SF.

ORGANIC EXPRESS ✐✐✐✐

P.O. Box 460411 SF 94146 415-ORGANIC
Mon-Fri 9-5 www.organicexpress.com
Local, organic produce and dry goods delivery; pre-selected and
custom packages.

WESTSIDE ORGANICS ✐✐✐✐

3202 Investment Blvd. Hayward 94545 866-ALL-ORGANIC
Mon 12-5 Tue-Fri 10-5 www.westsideorganics.com
Home-delivered organic produce and eco-friendly household supplies.

SPECIALTY MARKETS

Businesses in this category vary widely due to the many specialized
food areas they focus on. We looked for stores that are not just
specialists in their niche but also make sure what they offer is mostly
organic and healthy, as well as delicious.

Where there is one primary product area at a given market, we
focused exclusively on that in awarding our leaves. If a market offers
goods in several product categories, we have evaluated all major ones.

Specialty markets can be rated in all food areas, depending on what
they offer: produce, meat and poultry, fish, dairy products, non-dairy
beverages, canned and dry goods, and/or prepared foods.

We based our leaf awards on the percentage of brands and
products offered that are certified organic and free of genetically
modified organisms (GMOs); or are locally grown and produced
without the use of chemical fertilizers, herbicides, or pesticides.

For specialty stores where meat, poultry, and/or dairy products were
offered, we looked at the percentage raised organically, without the
use of antibiotics or hormones.

Where fish was available, we checked into whether it was wild
caught, or sustainably farm raised and processed without
chemical treatment.

✐	at least 25% of products meet the above criteria.
✐✐	at least 50% of products meet the above criteria.
✐✐✐	at least 75% of products meet the above criteria.
✐✐✐✐	90% or more of products meet the above criteria.

AK MEATS 🌿🌿🌿🌿
2346 Clement St. SF (Richmond) 94121 415-933-6328
Mon-Fri 8-7 Sat-Sun 10-7
Specializing in natural and organic meats, poultry, and fish.

BARON'S MEAT AND POULTRY 🌿🌿🌿🌿
1650 Park St. Alameda 94501 510-864-1915
Mon-Sat 10-8 Sun 10-7 www.baronsmeats.com
Organic and hormone-free meat, poultry, and game.

CHEESE PLUS 🌿
2001 Polk St. SF (Russian Hill) 94109 415-921-2001
Mon 11-7 Tue-Sat 10-7:30 Sun 11-7 www.cheeseplus.com
Specialty cheese shop carrying small variety of other organic products
including chocolate, and specialty condiments.

CHEESEBOARD COLLECTIVE, THE 🌿🌿🌿
1504 Shattuck Ave. Berkeley 94709 510-549-3183
Mon 7-1 Tue-Fri 7-6 Sat 8:30-5 www.cheeseboardcollective.coop
Worker-owned artisan cheese shop; baked pizzas daily.

COWGIRL CREAMERY 🌿🌿🌿🌿
One Ferry Building #17 SF (Embarcadero) 94111 415-362-9354
Tomales Bay Foods 80 Fourth St. Point Reyes Station 94956 415-663-9335
Hours vary by location www.cowgirlcreamery.com
All handmade and artisan cheeses, as well as prepared foods and accessories.

CRYSTAL SPRINGS FISH & POULTRY 🌿🌿🌿
116 De Anza Blvd. San Mateo 94402 650-573-0335
Mon-Fri 9-6:30 Sat 9-5:30
Meat, fish, poultry; prepared foods.

DE MARTINI ORCHARD 🌿
66 N. San Antonio Rd. Los Altos 94022 650-948-0881
Daily 8-7 www.demartiniorchard.com
Fresh and dried locally grown produce, nuts, and dairy; artisan breads
and spreads.

DREWES BROS. MEATS 🌿🌿🌿🌿
1706 Church St. SF (Noe Valley) 94131 415-821-0515
Mon-Fri 9:30-7 Sat 9-6 Sun 10-5 www.drewesbros.com
All-natural, free-range meats and fresh fish.

ECOEXPRESS 🌿🌿🌿🌿
85 Galli Dr. Novato 94949 800-733-3495
Mon-Fri 9:30-6 www.ecoexpress.com
Wide selection of fair trade, sweatshop free, and/or organic gifts, wine,
chocolate, coffee and tea, kitchen, bath, body, and baby products.

FAR WEST FUNGI 🌿🌿🌿
One Ferry Building #34 SF (Embarcadero) 94111 415-989-9090
Mon-Fri 10-6 Sat 8-6 Sun 11-5 www.farwestfungi.com
Full line of quality organic mushroom products.

GOLDEN GATE MEAT COMPANY 🌿🌿🌿
One Ferry Building #13 SF (Embarcadero) 94111 415-983-7800
Mon-Fri 6:30-7 Sat 7-6 Sun 8-5 www.goldengatemeatco.co
100% natural and organic. A wide variety of meats, poultry and seafood.
Butcher counter and hot prepared foods.

HAPUKU FISH SHOP 🌿🌿🌿
5655 College Ave. Oakland (College Ave.) 94618 510-654-3474
Mon-Fri 10-8 Sat 10-7 Sun 10-6 www.hapukufish.com
Wild-caught, organic, and farm-raised fish; shellfish.

MCEVOY RANCH 🌿🌿🌿🌿

One Ferry Building #16 SF (Embarcadero) 94111 415-291-7224
Mon 11-6 Tue-Fri 10-7 Sat 8-6 Sun 10-5 www.mcevoyranch.com
Certified organic olives, olive oil, and specialty products direct from their
Marin County ranch.

MISSION MARKET FISH AND POULTRY 🌿

2590 Mission St. SF (Mission) 94110 415-282-3331
Mon-Sat 9-6
Free-range poultry; wild-caught fish.

NUMI ORGANIC 🌿🌿🌿🌿

2230 Livingston St. Oakland (Lake Merritt/Downtown) 94606 510-534-6864
Mon-Fri 9-5 www.numitea.com
Numi organic tea.

PRATHER RANCH MEAT COMPANY 🌿🌿🌿🌿

One Ferry Building #32 SF (Embarcadero) 94111 415-391-0420
Mon-Fri 10-7 Sat 8-6 Sun 11-5 www.prmeatco.com
Offers variety of sustainably-raised meats from small, local ranchers.
No GMOs, antibiotics, or hormones.

SAN FRANCISCO FISH COMPANY 🌿🌿🌿

One Ferry Building #31 SF (Embarcadero) 94111 415-399-1111
Mon-Fri 10-7 Sat 8-6 Sun 11-5 www.sanfranfishco.com
Full-service fish market offering all types of seafood, mostly wild caught.
Sells lunch daily, from soups and salads to prepared foods.

SIGONA'S FARMERS MARKET 🌿

2345 Middlefield Rd. Redwood City 94063 650-368-6993
Stanford Shopping Ctr. 180 El Camino Real Palo Alto 94304 650-329-1340
Hours vary by location www.sigonas.com
Produce and specialty foods; some organic produce; dried fruits and nuts;
jam, olive oil, and sauces.

STONEHOUSE CALIFORNIA OLIVE OIL COMPANY 🌿🌿🌿🌿

1717 Fourth St. Berkeley 94710 510-524-1400
One Ferry Building #28 SF (Embarcadero) 94111 415-765-0405
San Francisco Centre 845 Market St. 2nd Floor SF (Union Square) 94103 415-538-9424
Hours vary by location www.stonehouseoliveoil.com
Organic California olive oils, balsamic vinegars, fleur de sel, and other
specialty offerings.

TSAR NICOULAI CAVIAR CAFÉ 🌿🌿🌿

One Ferry Building #12 SF (Embarcadero) 94111 415-288-8630
Mon-Fri 11-7 Sat 9-6 Sun 11-5 www.tsarnicoulai.com
Sustainable, domestic caviar and champagne.

VER BRUGGE FOODS 🌿🌿

6321 College Ave. Oakland (College Ave.) 94618 510-658-6854
Mon-Fri 9-6:30 Sat 9-6 Sun 10-5
Mostly hormone-free meats; free-range poultry; wild-caught fish. Some
organic, prepared foods.

VILLAGE MARKET, THE 🌿🌿🌿🌿

One Ferry Building #29 SF (Embarcadero) 94111 415-989-9200
4555 California St. SF (Richmond) 94118 415-221-0445
Hours vary by location www.villagemarketsf.com
Wine and specialty items. California Street location also has organic produce,
fresh-cut flowers; espresso drinks; small seating area.

CATERING SERVICES AND PERSONAL CHEFS

Catering your events with certified organic food or food that is locally grown in a sustainable manner is a great way to be healthy and kind to the planet, and to turn people on to sustainable products.

This section contains caterers and personal chefs whose primary focus is just that. Readers should also check the restaurant section for other catering options.

In this category, we looked at the percentage of food offered that is either certified organic or locally grown and produced without the use of chemical fertilizers, herbicides, or pesticides and, in the case of meat and poultry, without antibiotics and hormones.

If fish is offered, it must be wild caught or sustainably farm raised and processed without chemical treatment.

To be listed, at least 25% of products offered must meet the above criteria.

ALIVE AND RADIANT FOODS
Berkeley 510-527-8916 www.blessingsaliveandradiantfoods.com
Caterer; specializes in raw, vegan foods.

AMIEE ALAN CUSTOM CATERING
Emeryville 510-655-2355
www.amieealan.com
Catering and event planning; uses organic ingredients.

ARE YOU BEING SERVED
Novato 415-898-0163
www.areyoubeingservedcatering.com
Organic produce; hormone-free meats; wild-caught and sustainably farmed fish. Biodegradable utensils available.

AUBERGINE CATERING
2142 Stuart St. Berkeley 94705 510-704-8847
www.auberginecatering.com
Catering and event planning. Weekly home delivery, rotating menu.

BACK TO EARTH
P.O. Box 10104 Berkeley 94709 510-652-2000
www.backtoearth.com
Ecologically-sound catering and event design; fresh, seasonal cuisine using local organic ingredients.

COMPONERE FINE CATERING
6613 Hollis St. Emeryville 94608 925-429-2400
www.componerefinecatering.com
Organic produce; free range, hormone-free meat; sustainable seafood. Waste from test kitchen and events is composted.

COOK! SF
21 Stillman St. Suite 4 SF 94107 415-513-5328
www.cook-sf.com
Ready-to-cook, home-delivered meals; organic and free-range ingredients when possible.

Eating In

COOL EATZ CATERING
827 Santa Cruz Ave. Menlo Park 94025 650-325-2068
By appt. www.cooleatz.com/catering/index.html
Catering and special events management; corporate catering. Uses local, organic ingredients.

DEBBIE DOES DINNER
SF 415-468-3323
www.debbiedoesdinner.com
Full-service caterer; seasonal ingredients. Specializes in cookies, brownies, and bars; mail order available.

EARTHEN FEAST
SF 415-317-2005
www.earthenfeast.com
Vegan chef; personal cooking, catering, private lessons.

GARDEN GOURMET
Oakland 510-985-1065
www.gardengourmetchef.com
In-home vegetarian chef service. Local, organic and seasonal ingredients; packaged in reusable glass containers.

GREEN TABLE, THE
831-345-2676
www.thegreentable.net
Organic, seasonal catering service. Sustainable event planning; organic flowers; party and food design.

HEALING HEARTH, THE
SF 415-407-4689
www.thehealinghearth.com
In-home personal chef during illness recovery. Serves East Bay, Marin, and San Francisco.

JANE PEAL CUISINIÈRE
SF 415-826-2133
www.pealcuisine.com
Home-delivered vegetarian meals. Serves San Francisco.

LIVING ROOM EVENTS
SF 415-522-1417
www.livingroomevents.com
Organic, sustainable caterer. Ingredients purchased directly from local growers; biodegradable plates, utensils; composts all waste.

MARCUS RIOS PERSONAL CHEF & CATERER
SF 415-350-3113
www.chefmarcusrios.com
Events and personal cooking. Organic, seasonal, local ingredients. Serves San Francisco.

NOURISHING THE WHOLE
Oakland 510-333-5007
www.nourishingthewhole.blogspot.com
Nutritional coach and personal chef. Cooking classes.

ORGANIC CHEF CATERING
SF 415-563-1292
www.organicchefcatering.com
Organic cuisine made with farm fresh ingredients.

RISING SUN CATERING

1294 Bello Ave. St. Helena 94574 650-589-0157
www.risingsuncatering.com
Local and sustainable ingredients; specializes in green weddings.
Serves entire Bay Area.

SEASON: CONSCIOUS CATERING (BRYANT TERRY)

SF www.eatgrub.org
Menu planning and catering for small dinner parties, business meetings,
and on-site retreats. Uses fresh local, seasonal, organic food.

THERAPEUTIC CHEF

SF 415-680-4041
www.therapeuticchef.com
Vegan personal chef; works exclusively with ill clients. Nutritional education,
cooking classes. Serves Marin, Peninsula, and San Francisco.

WORK OF ART CATERING

1226 Folsom St. SF (SOMA) 94103 415-552-1000
www.woacatering.com
Full-service catering and event planning. All organic menus on request.
SF green certified business.

Many restaurants also offer catering services—probably some of your
favorites. Look for the "C" designation next to a restaurant's name in the
Eating Out - Restaurants section of the guide.

Top Ten Reasons to Buy Organic

1. Protect the health of future generations.
2. Protect water quality.
3. Nurture soil quality and prevent erosion.
4. Save energy.
5. Keep poisons off your plate.
6. Protect farm worker health.
7. Help small farmers.
8. Promote biodiversity.
9. Expose the hidden environmental and social costs of conventional foods.
10. Enjoy better flavor and greater nourishment.

WINE, BEER, AND SPIRITS

Eating In

In spite of the trend toward organics in the last decade, growers and producers, as well as consumers, largely ignored organic alcoholic beverages. Many thought organic production methods were incompatible with quality beer and wine. Indeed, those who sampled the first attempts may not have been too pleased.

However, all of this is changing. An increasing number of growers and producers are rediscovering what many brewers, vintners, and distillers have known for centuries: the joys and challenges of growing and processing beer, wine, and spirits without the use of artificial ingredients, chemical pesticides and fertilizers, or synthetic additives.

We have not awarded leaves in this category because it is an emerging area with evolving standards. But the shops listed here have made an extra effort to carry an assortment of organic wines, beers, and spirits.

They also carry products from "old world" purveyors whose brands may not be labeled "organic," but who have been making all-natural alcoholic beverages in the same way for centuries. You may also find a selection of biodynamic wines in these stores.

Most of the owners and managers of the stores listed here are enthusiastic about the organic and sustainably produced products they carry and possess a wealth of information they would be happy to share.

Biodynamic: *Begun about seventy years ago, biodynamic farming uses basic organic practices but adds special plant, animal, and mineral preparations to the land and uses the rhythm of the sun, moon, planets, and stars to create a healthy, self-supporting farming eco-system.*

ARLEQUIN WINE MERCHANT
384 Hayes St. SF (Civic Center) 94102 415-863-1104
Mon-Sat 11-8 Sun 12-6 www.arlequinwine.com
Organic and artisan wines.

BISON BREWERY
2598 Telegraph Ave. Berkeley 94704 510-697-1537
By appt. www.bisonbrew.com
Microbrewery offering multiple varieties of all-organic beer.

ELIXIR
3200 16th St. SF (Mission) 94103 415-552-1633
Mon-Fri 4 p.m.-2 a.m. Sat noon-2 a.m. Sun 11 a.m.-2 a.m. www.elixirsf.com
Neighborhood bar serving organic wine, beer, and vodka.
SF green certified business.

FERRY PLAZA WINE MERCHANT
One Ferry Building #23 SF (Embarcadero) 94111 866-991-9400
Mon 11-8 Tue-Wed 10-8 Thu-Fri 10-9 Sat 9-9 Sun 10-7 www.fpwm.com
Artisan and organic wines. Wine shop and wine bar.

JUG SHOP, THE

1590 Pacific Ave. SF (Pacific Heights) 94109 415-885-2922
Mon-Sat 9-9 Sun 10-7 www.jugshop.com
Comprehensive selection of fine wine, beer and spirits. Small percentage is
organic or biodynamic.

K&L WINE MERCHANTS

3005 El Camino Real Redwood City 94061 650-364-8544
638 Fourth Street SF (SOMA) 94107 415-896-1734
Hours vary by location www.klwines.com
Artisanal wines, some organic.

PARÉA WINE BAR AND CAFÉ

795 Valencia St. SF (Mission) 94110 415-255-2102
Wed-Mon 5-midnight www.pareawinebar.com
Organic home-style Mediterranean dishes with an extensive wine selection.

SWIRL ON CASTRO

572 Castro St. SF (Castro) 94114 415-864-2226
Mon-Fri 12-8 Sat 12-9 Sun 12-7 www.swirloncastro.com
Wine shop and wine bar. Carries a variety of organic and biodynamic wines.

VINOROSSO

629 Cortland Ave. SF (Bernal Heights) 94110 415-647-1268
Tue-Sun 4-11 www.vinorossosf.com
Wine shop, wine bar, and Italian eatery. Large selection of certified and non-
certified organic wines.

VINTAGE BERKELEY

2113 Vine St. Berkeley 94709 510-665-8600
Mon-Sat 11-8 Sun 12-6 www.vintageberkeley.com
Wine shop with small organic wine selection.

WILLIAM CROSS

2253 Polk St. SF (Russian Hill) 94109 415-346-1314
Sun-Mon 11-7 Tue, Thu 11-8 Wed 11-9 Fri-Sat 11-10
Wine merchant and wine bar that carries organic wines and beer.

YIELD WINE BAR

2490 Third St. SF (Dog Patch) 94107 415-401-8984
Tue-Fri 5 p.m.-12 midnight Sat 6 p.m.-12 midnight Sun 4-8 www.yieldsf.com
Wine bar featuring 100% organic, biodynamic, and sustainable wines.
Limited organic food menu available.

**The following merchants also carry a selection of organic wine, beer, and/or
spirits. See our listings under the *Grocery Stores* and *Specialty Markets* in the
Eating In sections and *Pharmacies* in the *Sorting through Services* section.**

Berkeley Bowl
Bi-Rite Market
Country Sun Natural Foods
EcoExpress
Elephant Pharmacy
Good Earth Natural Organic Foods
Good Life Grocery

Mollie Stone's
Nature Stop
Other Avenues
Rainbow Grocery
Real Food Company, The
Village Market, The (Ferry Plaza)
Whole Foods Market

We've done our best to compile a list of the merchants and service
providers who offer local, sustainable, and organic food and
beverages. We'd like you to tell us about your experiences: How
were the variety and quality of the food and goods? What about
your service experience? Was the price in keeping with what you
got? Go to www.greenopia.com and post your review.

ORGANIC WINE

Made with Organic Grapes—Grapes have been grown in accordance with the strict organic rules set by the USDA National Organic Program. In addition, the wine is produced and bottled in a certified organic facility. Low levels of added sulfites are allowed, up to 100 parts per million (ppm), as opposed to conventional wines which may contain up to 350 ppm.

Organic Wine—Grapes have been grown in accordance with the strict organic rules set by the USDA National Organic Program. In addition, the wine is produced and bottled in a certified organic facility. Contrary to traditional winemaking, this category has no added sulfites. Organic wine may carry the USDA ORGANIC green logo.

Most wines making an organic claim are in the "Made with Organic Grapes" category because the United States is the only country that has limited the growth of the organic wine industry by adding the sulfites technicality to the labeling guidelines. Therefore, only domestic wines can be found labeled as "Organic Wine." Learn to read labels carefully and you'll find some great organic wines: If it doesn't say organic on the label then it's not!

Our thanks to Organic Vintners for the above information.

ORGANIC BEER

Organic beer is made from certified organic malted barley, hops, and yeast. These ingredients are grown without the use of synthetic pesticides, herbicides, and fertilizers.

ORGANIC SPIRITS

Organic spirits are made from organic ingredients such as grains or potatoes. In the U.S. there are only a few producers and distributors of organic spirits but these products are available. You can find vodka, rum, grappa, gin, whiskey, and a variety of liqueurs that are organic. Some spirits are made with some organic ingredients, but may not qualify for full organic certification.

Look for the USDA certified organic seal for U.S. made products, or an internationally recognized organic seal for those made overseas.

Eating In

Lowest in Pesticides	Highest in Pesticides
Asparagus	Apples
Avocados	Bell Peppers
Bananas	Celery
Broccoli	Cherries
Cauliflower	Grapes (imported)
Corn (sweet)	Nectarines
Kiwi	Peaches
Mangos	Pears
Onions	Potatoes
Papaya	Red Raspberries
Pineapples	Spinach
Peas (sweet)	Strawberries

WHY SHOULD YOU CARE ABOUT PESTICIDES?

There is growing consensus in the scientific community that small doses of pesticides and other chemicals can adversely affect people, especially during vulnerable periods of fetal development and childhood when exposures can have long lasting effects. Because the toxic effects of pesticides are worrisome, not well understood, or in some cases completely unstudied, shoppers are wise to minimize exposure to pesticides whenever possible.

WILL WASHING AND PEELING HELP?

Nearly all of the data used to create these lists already considers how people typically wash and prepare produce (for example, apples are washed before testing, bananas are peeled). While washing and rinsing fresh produce may reduce levels of some pesticides, it does not eliminate them. Peeling also reduces exposures, but valuable nutrients often go down the drain with the peel. The best option is to eat a varied diet, wash all produce, and choose organic when possible to reduce exposure to potentially harmful chemicals.

HOW THIS GUIDE WAS DEVELOPED

The produce ranking was developed by analysts at the not-for-profit Environmental Working Group (EWG) based on the results of nearly 43,000 tests for pesticides on produce collected by the U.S. Department of Agriculture and the U.S. Food and Drug Administration between 2000 and 2004. A detailed description of the criteria used in developing the rankings is available as well as a full list of fresh fruits and vegetables that have been tested (see above tables).

ENVIRONMENTAL WORKING GROUP

Reprinted with the permission of the Environmental Working Group (EWG). EWG is a not-for-profit environmental research organization dedicated to improving public health and protecting the environment by reducing pollution in air, water and food. For more information, visit www.ewg.org.

VEGETABLES

Dark green indicates that a product is available and is being harvested.

	Jan	Feb	Mar	Apr	May	Jun	Jul	Aug	Sep	Oct	Nov	Dec
Artichokes			■	■	■	■		■	■	■	■	■
Arugula	■	■	■	■	■	■	■	■	■	■	■	
Asian Greens	■	■	■	■	■	■	■	■	■	■	■	■
Asparagus		■	■	■	■	■		■	■		■	
Avocados	■	■	■	■	■	■	■	■	■	■	■	■
Basil		■	■		■	■	■	■	■	■		■
Beans	■	■	■	■	■	■	■	■	■	■	■	■
Beets	■	■	■	■	■	■	■	■	■	■	■	■
Bok Choy	■	■	■	■	■	■			■	■	■	■
Broccoli	■	■	■	■	■	■	■	■	■	■	■	■
Brussels Sprouts	■	■	■						■	■	■	■
Burdock							■	■	■	■	■	■
Cabbage	■	■	■	■	■	■	■	■	■	■	■	■
Cactus Pads					■	■	■	■	■	■		■
Cardoons	■	■	■	■	■	■	■	■	■	■	■	■
Carrots	■	■	■	■	■	■	■	■	■	■	■	■
Cauliflower	■	■	■	■	■	■			■	■	■	■
Celery				■	■	■	■	■	■	■	■	■
Chard	■	■	■	■	■	■	■	■	■	■	■	■
Collards	■	■	■		■	■	■	■	■	■	■	■
Corn					■	■	■	■	■	■	■	
Cress	■	■	■		■							
Cucumbers					■	■	■	■	■	■	■	
Dandelion/Chicory	■	■	■	■	■	■						
Eggplant					■	■	■	■	■	■		
Endive	■	■	■	■	■	■	■	■	■	■	■	■
Fava Beans				■	■	■						
Fennel	■	■	■	■	■	■	■	■	■	■	■	■
Garlic	■	■	■	■	■	■	■	■	■	■	■	■
Gourds				■	■	■	■	■	■	■	■	
Green Garlic	■		■	■	■			■	■	■	■	■
Greens, Various	■	■	■	■	■	■	■	■	■	■	■	■
Herbs	■	■	■	■	■	■	■	■	■	■	■	■

Light green indicates that it is available but is not within its natural harvest season (possible through storage or hot house production).

	Jan	Feb	Mar	Apr	May	Jun	Jul	Aug	Sep	Oct	Nov	Dec
Horseradish	■	■	■	■	■	■	■	■	■	■	■	■
Kale	■	■	■	■	■	■	■	■	■	■	■	■
Kohlrabi				■	■	■	■	■		■	■	■
Leeks	■	■	■	■	■	■	■	■	■	■	■	■
Lettuces	■	■	■	■	■	■	■	■	■	■	■	■
Mushrooms	■	■	■	■	■	■	■	■	■	■	■	■
Nettles	■	■	■	■	■	■	■					■
Mustard					■	■	■	■	■	■	■	
Okra						■	■	■	■	■		
Olives	▨	▨	▨	▨	▨	▨	▨	■			▨	▨
Onions	■	■	■	■	■	■	■	■	■	■	■	■
Parsnips	■	■	■						■	■	■	■
Peas				■	■	■	■	■	■			
Peppers, Bell						▨	■	■	■	■		
Peppers, Chili						▨	■	■	■	■		
Potatoes	■	■	■	■	■	■		■	■	■	■	■
Purslane					■	■	■	■	■			
Radicchio				■	■	■	■	■	■	■	■	
Radish	■	■	■	■	■	■	■	■	■	■	■	■
Rapini	■	■	■	■	■	■		■	■	■	■	■
Rhubarb				■	■	■	■	■				■
Rutabaga	■	■	■	■					■	■	■	■
Salsify	■	■	■	■	■	■	■		■	■	■	■
Scallions	■	■	■	■	■	■	■	■	■	■	■	■
Shallots				■		■	■	■	■	■		■
Spinach	■	■	■	■	■	■	■	■	■	■	■	■
Squash, Summer					■	■	■	■	■			
Squash, Winter	▨							■	■	■	■	■
Sunchokes	■											
Sweet Potatoes												
Tomatillos						■	■	■	■	■		■
Tomatoes				▨	▨	■	■	■	■	■		
Turnips	■	■	■	■					■	■	■	■

FRUIT AND NUTS

Eating In

	Jan	Feb	Mar	Apr	May	Jun	Jul	Aug	Sep	Oct	Nov	Dec
Almonds	■	■						■	■	■	■	
Apples	■	■						■	■	■	■	■
Apricots					■	■	■					
Apriums					■	■	■					
Asian Pears	■	■					■	■	■	■	■	■
Blackberries					■	■	■	■	■	■		
Blueberries					■	■	■	■				
Boysenberries						■	■					
Cactus Pears						■	■					
Cherimoyas	■	■	■	■	■						■	■
Cherries				■	■	■						
Chestnuts									■	■	■	■
Dates	■							■	■	■	■	■
Dried Fruit	■	■	■	■	■	■	■	■	■	■	■	■
Figs						■	■	■	■	■	■	
Grapefruit	■	■	■									
Grapes							■	■	■	■	■	
Guavas	■	■	■							■	■	■
Jujubes									■	■	■	■
Kiwi	■	■	■								■	■
Kumquats	■	■	■								■	■
Lemons	■	■	■	■	■	■	■	■	■	■	■	■
Limes	■	■	■	■						■	■	■

Light green indicates that it is available but is not within its natural harvest season (possible through storage or hot house production).

	Jan	Feb	Mar	Apr	May	Jun	Jul	Aug	Sep	Oct	Nov	Dec
Loquats					X	X						
Mandarins	X	X	X									
Melons							X	X	X	X	X	
Mulberries						X	X	X				
Nectarines						X	X	X	X			
Oranges	X	X	X	X	X							
Peaches						X	X	X	X			
Pears	X	X						X	X	X	X	X
Persimmons	X									X	X	X
Pistachios	L	L	L	L	L	L	L	L	X	X	L	
Plums						X	X	X	X			
Pluots						X	X	X	X	X		
Pomegranates									X	X	X	X
Pomelos	X	X	X	X								X
Quince									X	X	X	X
Raspberries						X	X	X	X	X	X	
Rhubarb				X	X	X	X	X	X			
Strawberries				X	X	X	X	X	X	X	X	
Tangerines	X	X	X								X	X
Tayberries						X	X					
Tomatillos							X	X	X	X	X	X
Tomatoes			L	L	L	X	X	X	X	X		
Walnuts	X	X	X	X	X	X	X		X	X	X	X

CUESA

Reprinted with the permission of the Center for Urban Education about Sustainable Agriculture. CUESA is dedicated to promoting a sustainable food system through the operation of the Ferry Plaza Farmers Market and its educational programs. To learn more about regional agriculture, seasonal eating, and the Ferry Plaza Farmer Market, visit www.cuesa.org.

The Roots of Vitality

Natural beauty care is about taking care of our bodies and our planet. As simple as the idea sounds, it flies in the face of a multi-billion-dollar industry based upon making artificial products in a chemical laboratory. Healthy, wholesome, sustainable products come from companies built around healthy, wholesome, and sustainable principles. So look for and purchase products you believe in. In so doing, you will uncover companies whose values are in alignment with your own.

The most important thing to look for in personal care products is, first of all, no artificial colors or fragrances. Period. Truly natural products are based on essential oils, which means no synthetic ingredients. The fragrance should come from the plant world, not the industrial lab or chemical factory. Obtaining essential oils from plants brings us in touch with vital constituents, linking us back to the biological world from which we come. There is a definite relationship of connection and vitality.

The second most important principle when searching for the right products is to understand whom you are buying from. Since there are no official organic standards for personal care products, consumers need to be especially observant of what they buy. Companies practicing a holistic and natural approach are more conscious of the long-term effects of what they do; they are crafting products that are more artisan-like, more local, and more healthful. They take into consideration how the plants were grown, how the oils were distilled, whether the ingredients are organic, if they are wild-crafted. These are businesses that strive to be integrated and whole, that are more interested in the far-reaching implications of what they do, and consider all the principles of natural body care on a daily basis.

The choices we make in our own personal care should help enrich and enliven us. It's easy to forget about the joy we can find in taking care of ourselves. Something as simple as the scent of lavender, a smell that might not even consciously register in our awareness, can somehow reconnect us to how and why we're here. And by staying in touch with that natural root of vitality, by simply paying attention to the things that make up everyday life, our awareness can shift and we can better keep track of what we truly value. Revelations can come from just paying attention. Enjoy it. It's your daily life.

SUSAN GRIFFIN-BLACK
Susan Griffin-Black and her husband are the founders of EO, a line of body and face care products specializing in traditional healing and essential oils. (www.eoproducts.com)

The cosmetics industry is, in many ways, self-regulating. That means makers of cosmetics do not need approval from the Food and Drug Administration (FDA) for every chemical they use in their products. It's up to us to make sure we're getting products that are non-toxic.

Organic beauty products, once rare, are now easier to find. Their effectiveness is on par with, or sometimes superior to, conventional commercial beauty products. If you can't find an organic product that suits you, look for ones that offer organic ingredients combined with all-natural ingredients.

We've determined leaf awards based on the percentage of all the brands sold containing either:

- all certified organic ingredients
- a mix of certified organic ingredients and natural ingredients
- all natural ingredients, or mostly natural ingredients, and that do not contain any of the following ten most unsafe ingredients: *mercury, thimerosol, lead acetate, formaldehyde, toluene, petroleum distillates, ethylacrylate, coal tar, dibutyl phthalate, potassium dichromate.*

at least 25% of the brands sold meet the above criteria.
at least 50% of the brands sold meet the above criteria.
at least 75% of the brands sold meet the above criteria.
90% or more of the brands sold meet the above criteria.

AVEDA
1846 Fourth St. Berkeley 94710 510-849-0992
1708 Redwood Hwy. Space A35 Corte Madera 94925 415-927-2594
2230 Chestnut St. SF (Marina) 94123 415-674-1405
3938 24th St. SF (Noe Valley) 94114 415-647-0565
Stonestown Galleria 3251 20th Ave. Space 211 SF (Sunset) 94132 415-566-7550
225 Hillsdale Shopping Center San Mateo 94403 650-378-8300
Hours vary by location www.aveda.com
Hair and skin care products, essential oils, and body care products made from plant-based, organics, or sustainable ingredients.

BARE NECESSITIES
421 Castro St. SF (Castro) 94114 415-626-5859
Mon-Sat 10-9 Sun 11-8
Cosmetics, bath, body, skin care, and hair care products made from natural and organic ingredients.

BEAUTY CENTER
2973 College Ave. Berkeley 94705 510-845-2485
1821 Solano Ave. Berkeley 94707 510-526-5066
252 Main St. Los Altos 94022 650-559-9004
2034 Mountain Blvd. Oakland (Montclair) 94611 510-339-9763
3264 Lakeshore Ave. Oakland (Lake Merritt/Downtown) 94610 510-835-8347
3976 Piedmont Ave. Piedmont 94611 510-653-7837
501 14th St. Oakland (City Center Plaza) 94612 510-419-0404
Hours vary by location www.beautycenteronline.com
Beauty supply store chain; several natural and organic product lines.

BEAUTY COMPANY ✍

2259 Polk St. SF (Russian Hill) 94109 415-567-8740
Mon-Fri 10-8 Sat-Sun 10-6
Beauty supply store and salon; carries some organic and vegan product lines.

BODY SHOP, THE ✍

1818 Redwood Hwy. Corte Madera 94925 415-924-1285
112 Serramonte Center Daly City 94015 650-755-4198
5637 Bay St. Emeryville 94608 510-547-8007
11A Stanford Shopping Center Palo Alto 94304 650-323-1951
Hilltop Mall 2430 Hilltop Mall Rd. Richmond 94806 510-222-5102
SF International Airport North Terminal SF (SFO) 94128 650-794-9160
506 Castro St. SF (Castro) 94114 415-431-8860
16 California St. SF (Financial District) 94111 415-397-7455
2106 Chestnut St. SF (Marina) 94123 415-202-0112
Stonestown Galleria 3251 20th Ave. SF (Sunset) 94132 415-682-7894
100 Powell St. SF (Union Square) 94101 415-399-1802
SF Shopping Center 865 Market St. SF (Union Square) 94103 415-538-7913
166 Hillsdale Shopping Center San Mateo 94403 650-572-4708
Hours vary by location www.thebodyshop.com
Beauty supplies, skin care, aromatherapy, fragrances and essential oils.
Hair care and bath products. Some all natural items.

BODY TIME ✍

2509 Telegraph Ave. Berkeley 94704 510-548-3686
1942 Shattuck Ave. Berkeley 94704 510-841-5818
2911 College Ave. Berkeley 94705 510-845-2101
5521 College Ave. Oakland (College Ave.) 94618 510-547-4116
611 San Anselmo Ave. San Anselmo 94960 415-459-5806
1465 Haight St. SF (Haight) 94117 415-551-1070
Hours vary by location www.bodytime.com
All-natural beauty products and cosmetics; aromatherapy.

CAT MURPHY'S SKIN CARE SALON ✍

561 Bridgeway St. Suite 2 Sausalito 94965 415-332-4296
Wed-Sat by appt. only www.catmurphy.com
Skin treatment center; house-made, paraben-free products;
mineral-based make-up.

CHURCH STREET APOTHECARY ✍✍✍

1767 Church St. SF (Noe Valley) 94131 415-970-9828
Mon-Sat 11-7 Sun 11-5 www.churchapothecary.com
Holistic, organic health and beauty products including bath, beauty,
and fragrances.

ELEPHANT PHARMACY ✍✍✍

1607 Shattuck Ave. Berkeley 94709 510-549-9200
4470 El Camino Real Los Altos 94022 650-472-6800
909 Grand Ave. San Rafael 94901 415-462-6000
Hours vary by location www.elephantpharmacy.com
Full service homeopathic pharmacy with a selection of beauty, body,
and bath supplies.

EVA CLAIBORNE SKIN INSTITUTE ✍✍✍

39 Main St. Tiburon 94920 415-497-3635
Mon-Fri 8-8 Sat by appt. www.evaclaiborne.org
Marine and plant-based natural skin care products.

EVO SPA ✍✍

216 Strawberry Village Mill Valley 94941 415-383-3223
Mon-Sat 9-9 Sun 10-7 www.evo-spa.com
Beauty and wellness spa, skin care, bodywork, nutrition, cleansing treatments.
Uses some organic and natural product lines.

FRINGE SALON

371 Primrose Rd. Burlingame 94010 650-343-4409
Tue-Sun 9-7
Organic and natural shampoos, hair treatments.

HYDRA

1710 Fourth St. Berkeley 94710 510-559-9796
1919 Fillmore St. SF (Pacific Heights) 94115 415-474-9372
Hours vary by location www.hydrasoap.com
Natural, handmade bath and body products. Mostly vegan ingredients;
recyclable packaging.

JOUVENCE SKIN REJUVENATION CENTER

1375 Burlingame Ave. Burlingame 94010 650-348-3882
Tue-Sat 10-6
Organic and natural skin care; natural mineral make-up.

JURLIQUE

2136 Fillmore St. SF (Pacific Heights) 94115 415-346-7881
Mon-Sat 10-7 Sun 11-6 www.jurlique.com
Organic and biodynamic skin care products based on natural and
plant-derived ingredients.

L'OCCITANE EN PROVENCE

1618A Redwood Hwy. Corte Madera 94925 415-924-7843
660 Stanford Shopping Center #188 Palo Alto 94304 650-289-9984
Two Embarcadero Square Street Level R-2110 Suite 1 SF (Financial District) 94111
415-677-9931
2207 Fillmore St. SF (Pacific Heights) 94115 415-563-6600
Stonestown Galleria 3251 20th Ave. Suite 16 SF (Sunset) 94132 415-665-2863
865 Market St. Suite 102 SF (Union Square) 94103 415-856-0213
556 Castro St. SF (Castro) 94114 415-621-4668
1864 Union St. SF (Marina) 94123 415-614-9660
Hours vary by location www.loccitane.com
Women's and men's bath, body, hair care; perfume; home fragrance, candles.
Personal skin care consultation. Braille labelling, recycled packaging.

LUSH

2116 Union St. SF (Marina) 94123 415-921-5874
240 Powell St. SF (Financial District) 94102 415-693-9633
Hours vary by location www.lush.com
International company that makes everything by hand using natural
and organic ingredients.

MADKAT

1411 Burlingame Ave. Burlingame 94010 650-685-8448
915 Cole St. SF (Cole Valley) 94117 415-665-8448
3836 24th St. SF (Noe Valley) 94114 415-643-8448
1418 Grant St. SF (North Beach) 94133 415-391-3841
Hours vary by location
Hair, body, and nail products.

NANCY BOY

347 Hayes St. SF (Hayes Valley) 94102 888-746-2629
Mon-Fri 11-7 Sat-Sun 11-6 www.nancyboy.com
Locally produced beauty, body, and bath products specializing
in 100% natural essential plant oils.

OCCASIONS BOUTIQUE

858 Cole St. SF (Cole Valley) 94117 415-731-0153
Mon-Sat 10-7 Sun 11-5:30
Gift, bath, and body shop; natural products.

ORIGINAL SWISS AROMATICS ✐✐✐✐
602 Freitas Parkway San Rafael 94903 415-459-3998
Mon-Fri 9-5 www.originalswissaromatics.com
Organic, therapeutic-grade essential oils and accessories.

PHARMACA INTEGRATIVE PHARMACY ✐✐✐✐
1744 Solano Ave. Berkeley 94707 510-527-8929
230 East Blithedale Mill Valley 94941 415-388-7822
7514 Redwood Blvd. Novato 94945 415-892-3700
925 Cole St. SF (Cole Valley) 94117 415-661-1216
Hours vary by location www.pharmaca.com
Full-service homeopathic pharmacy with extensive beauty, body,
and bath section.

SANDRA CARON EUROPEAN SPA ✐✐✐
105 East Third Ave. San Mateo 94401 650-347-9666
Mon-Sat 10-9 Sun 10-6 www.sandracaron.com
Natural soaps, herbal and flower extracts, antioxidants, lotions,
mineral skin care.

SKIN AND BODY THERAPY ✐✐✐
2066 Broadway Redwood City 94063 650-474-0776
By appt. Tue-Sat
www.skinandbodytherapy.com
Organic and plant-based skin care products for men and women.

SKIN ENVY ✐✐✐
1110 Burlingame Ave. Suite 107 Burlingame 94010 650-558-0939
Tue-Fri 4-8 Sat 10-4:30 Sun by appt. www.skinenvyspa.com
Natural and organic facial cleansers and lotions.

SUMBODY & SUMTIME SPA ✐✐
2167 Union St. SF (Cow Hollow) 94123 415-775-6343
1350 Park St. Alameda 94501 510-523-2639
Hours vary by location www.sumbody.com
Natural bath, body, and at-home spa products.

SUSAN'S SOAP ✐✐✐✐
Allied Arts Guild 75 Arbor Rd. Menlo Park 94025 650-329-1492
Mon-Sat 11-5 (Nov-Dec open daily)
Handmade soaps; vegetable, herbal, and fruit ingredients.

WILLA HOME ✐✐✐✐
1414 Burlingame Ave. Burlingame 94010 650-375-1213
Mon-Sat 10-6 Sun 12-5
Organic, herbal lotions; flower essences; hand-molded vegetable and olive oil
soaps; Santa Maria Novella products.

**Many grocery stores also carry a wide selection of beauty products. See the
following listings under *Eating In-Grocery Stores* for further information:**

Good Earth Natural & Organic Foods	Real Food Company, The
Mollie Stone's	Thom's Natural Foods
Paradise Foods	Whole Foods Market
Rainbow Grocery	Woodlands Market

When it comes to beauty products, it can be really challenging to
separate what's good for you and the planet and what the product
label says. We've tried to identify the best eco-friendly beauty product
retailers, but we would like to hear about your experiences.
Visit www.greenopia.com and tell us about the effectiveness and
assortment of products you found.

Anyone who has ever been in, or walked near, a conventional hair and nail salon knows that the chemical vapors coming from within can be overwhelming. And many of the chemicals used in the products are potentially hazardous to the health and safety of stylists as well as customers. Improper or poor ventilation can worsen the problems. Environmentally-friendly alternatives for toxic ingredients are increasingly available so it makes sense to choose salons that are healthier for you and the workers inside.

If you already have a favorite salon, ask for least-toxic treatments and check on sanitation procedures. (The only way to effectively and naturally clean salon equipment is by using an FDA-approved autoclave, a device designed to heat solutions and the equipment they contain above their boiling point.) Also, ask your salon to carry beauty products with non-toxic or less-toxic ingredients.

For hair care, we have determined leaf awards based on the percentage of salon and grooming products (excluding hair dye) sold and used in-house that are made with:

- all certified organic ingredients;

- a mix of certified organic ingredients and natural ingredients;

- all natural ingredients; or mostly natural ingredients, and that do not contain any of the following ten most unsafe ingredients: *mercury, thimerosol, lead acetate, formaldehyde, toluene, petroleum distillates, ethylacrylate, coal tar, dibutyl phthalate, potassium dichromate.*

For a salon to be eligible for the highest leaf awards, it must also offer hair-coloring products that are non-toxic.

For nail salons, we have determined whether or not the polishes used are phthalate-, toluene-, and formaldehyde-free. Also, we looked for acetone-free polisher remover. Although we have instituted leaf-award requirements specific to nail care, if the salon sells other types of beauty products, it must meet the product-related criteria above as well as the nail care requirements.

🍃 at least 25% of salon products meet the above criteria.

🍃🍃 at least 50% of salon products meet the above criteria.

🍃🍃🍃 at least 50% of salon products meet the above criteria; and over 25% of any hair-coloring products are non-toxic; plus any nail polishes are phthalate-, toluene-, and formaldehyde-free, and polish remover is acetone-free.

🍃🍃🍃🍃 at least 75% of salon products meet the above criteria, and, over 25% of any hair-coloring products are non-toxic and any henna used is non-synthetic; plus any nail polishes are phthalate-, toluene-, and formaldehyde-free, polish remover is acetone-free, and the ventilation system allows for outdoor air exchange.

17 JEWELS 🍃🍃
4801 Telegraph Ave. Oakland (Temescal) 94610 510-653-1059
Tue-Fri 10-7 Sat 9-5 www.17jewelssalonspa.com
Hair salon, facials, and waxing; natural products.

BELLI CAPELLI 🍃🍃
1728 Divisadero St. SF (Pacific Heights) 94115 415-346-4100
Mon 12-7 Tue-Wed 10-7 Thu-Fri 10-8 Sat 9-5 www.bellicapellisalon.com
Salon and day spa; Aveda products.

CHAKRA SALONSPA 🍃🍃
256 Sutter St. 2nd Floor SF (Union Square) 94108 415-398-5173
Mon-Fri 11-7 Sat 10-6 Sun 11-5 www.chakrasalonspa.com
Hair care, waxing, cosmetics, tinting; natural products.

DARIN DAVID SALON 🍃🍃
1722 Solano Ave. Berkeley 94707 510-524-8121
Tue-Sat 10-8
Hair salon; Aveda products.

ELIXIR 🍃🍃
1599 Hopkins St. Berkeley 94707 510-526-1700
Tue-Sat 8-9 Sun-Mon By appt. www.elixirsalonspa.com
Hair and nail care, massage; Aveda products.

FACE IT BEAUTY SALON AND SPA 🍃🍃
2343 Market St. SF (Castro) 94114 415-431-7233
Mon, Wed-Fri 11-8 Sat-Sun 11-7
Hair, facial, microdermabrasion, waxing, manicure and pedicure services.
Also sells Aveda and Dermalogica products.

FRINGE SALON 🍃
371 Primrose Rd. Burlingame 94010 650-343-4409
Tue-Sun 9-7
Hair services. Organic and natural shampoos, hair treatments.

HAIR NOW SOUTH BEACH 🍃🍃
2 Townsend St. SF (SOMA) 94107 415-495-1912
Tue-Fri 11-7 Sat 9-5
Hair salon; Aveda products.

INCOGNITO 🍃🍃
Fox Mall 1419 Burlingame Ave. Suite V Burlingame 94010 650-343-0733
Wed-Fri 12-8 Sat 9-5 www.kellyodea.com
Hair, nail, and skin salon; Aveda products.

JOI NAIL SPA 🍃
1597 Solano Ave. Berkeley 94707 510-559-3500
Tue-Sat 10-7 Sun 10-6 www.joinailspa.com
Nail care, massage, facials, and waxing.

KAMALASPA 🍃🍃🍃
240 Stockton St. 7th Floor SF (Financial District) 94108 415-217-7700
Mon-Sat 9:30-8 Sun 10-7 www.kamalaspa.com
Ayurvedic spa, salon, and nail services. All natural and organic products.
Eco-friendly facilities.

NINA HOMISAK HAIR DESIGN 🍃🍃
1580 Solano Ave. Suite C Albany 94707 510-525-5563
Mon-Sat by appt.
Hair salon; organic products.

PARIS SALON AND SPA 🍃

915 Fourth St. San Rafael 94901 415-459-3600
Mon 10-6 Tue-Fri 9-8 Sat 9-7 Sun 11-5 www.parissalonspa.com
Women's and men's hair and spa services, massage; Aveda products.

PERFECT TEN NAIL SALON, THE 🍃🍃

25 West 25th Ave. Suite 2 San Mateo 94403 650-578-8152
Mon-Sat 8-7:30
Manicures and pedicures; herbal and fruit-based cleansers, lotions. "Solo salon" appts. available for chemically-sensitive people.

PIEDMONT HAIRPORT 🍃

4072 Piedmont Ave. Piedmont 94611 510-923-9300
Tue-Sat 9:30-7
Haircuts, perms, hair color, facial waxing; organic and natural products.

SALON DES ARTISTES 🍃

1001 Bridgeway Suite A2 Sausalito 94965 415-331-7993
Daily 10-7 and by appt.
Hair color and highlighting services; hand-formulated, natural products.

SHEAR BLISS 🍃🍃

275 Gough St. SF (Hayes Valley) 94102 415-255-8827
Tue-Fri 10-7 Sat 9-5 www.shearblisssalon.com
Hair care and styling, makeup; Aveda products.

SOLE SALON & SANCTUARY 🍃🍃

2980 College Ave. Suite 1 Berkeley 94705 510-848-5633
Tue-Fri 11-7 Sat 10-5 www.solesalon.com
Hair care and coloring, waxing, cosmetics.

STAR CITY SALON & DAY SPA 🍃🍃🍃🍃

349 Visitacion Ave. Brisbane 94005 650-589-9062
By appt. Mon-Fri 9-9 Sat 9-5 Sun 10-5
Hair care and styling. Natural hair color; choice of fragrance-free or aromatherapy products.

THAIRAPEUTICS 🍃🍃🍃🍃

1396-A Solano Ave. Albany 94706 510-525-3314
Mon-Thu 10-6 Fri 9-5 and Mon-Fri 7-9 by appt. Sat 9-3 and 3-6 by appt.
www.thairapeutics.com
Integrative therapies for hair, skin, body, and spirit. Reiki; wellness consulting.

TIZKA 🍃🍃

23 Ross Common Ross 94957 415-461-5515
Mon-Sat 9-6 www.tizkasalonspa.com
Hair care, styling and coloring; Aveda products.

TREAT AVEDA SALON 🍃🍃

1928 Fillmore St. SF (Pacific Heights) 94115 415-567-0166
Tue 9:30-7 Wed-Thu 9:30-8 Fri-Sat 9:30-7 Sun 11-5   www.treatsf.com
Hair and face care, waxing services; Aveda products.

VIERRA AND FRIENDS 🍃🍃

85 Carl St. SF (Cole Valley) 94117 415-665-9335
Mon-Sun 8-10
Hair and skin salon; some organic products.

There is nothing like indulging yourself with a massage, sauna, or special beauty treatment and the spas listed below can all pamper you. Best of all, you can rest easier knowing that your indulgence is truly nurturing for your body.

The day spas we've listed here have all created environments that are healthy and restful and have also committed to carrying eco-friendly, natural products.

We have determined leaf awards based on the percentage of beauty and spa products that the spa sells and uses in-house that contain:

- all certified organic ingredients;

- a mix of certified organic ingredients and natural ingredients;

- all natural ingredients, or mostly natural ingredients, and that do not contain any of the following top ten unsafe ingredients: *mercury, thimerosol, lead acetate, formaldehyde, toluene, petroleum distillates, ethylacrylate, coal tar, dibutyl phthalate, potassium dichromate.*

> ✿ at least 25% of treatments and/or brands meet the criteria.
>
> ✿✿ at least 50% of treatments and/or brands meet the criteria.
>
> ✿✿✿ at least 75% of treatments and/or brands meet the criteria.
>
> ✿✿✿✿ 90% or more of treatments and/or brands meet the criteria.

ABOUT FACE & BODY ✿✿✿
3190 College Ave. Berkeley 94705 510-428-2600
Mon-Tue 10:30-5:30 Wed-Sat 10:30-8 Sun 10:30-5:30 www.aboutfaceandbody.net
Full-service day spa. Massage, facials, waxing, nail services, spray tanning.

ALCHEMY SKIN SPA ✿✿✿
1510C Walnut St. Berkeley 94709 510-981-9881
Tue-Sat by appt. www.alchemyskinspa.com
Facials, waxing, lash and brow services. Synthetic-free, cruelty-free, mostly organic products.

ARTBEAT SALON & GALLERY ✿✿
1887 Solano Ave. Berkeley 94707 510-527-3100
Tue-Sun 10-7 www.artbeatsalon.com
Hair and skin care services; Aveda Concept Salon.

BELLI CAPELLI ✿✿
1728 Divisadero St. SF (Fillmore) 94115 415-346-4100
Mon 12-7 Tue-Wed 10-7 Thu-Fri 10-8 Sat 9-5
Aromatherapy salon, hair and skin care, waxing, massage; Aveda products.

BELLA PELLE ✿✿✿
9 Maiden Lane SF (Financial District) 94108 415-362-6384
Mon-Fri 8-8 Sat 9-5 Sun 11-5 www.bellapelle.com
Organic body and skin treatments in a New York-style skin studio.

EARTH AND SKY OASIS ✿✿

391 Sutter St. Suite 710 SF (Financial District) 94108 415-989-0014
Tue-Sat 9-5:30 by appt. www.earthandskyoasis.com
Full line of health and body care including massage, skin care, and nutritional therapy.

EVA CLAIBORNE SKIN INSTITUTE ✿✿✿

39 Main St. Tiburon 94920 415-497-3635
Mon-Fri 8-8 Sat by appt. www.evaclaiborne.org
Facial and body therapies; aromatherapy; ayurveda; marine and plant-based natural skin care products.

EVO SPA ✿✿

216 Strawberry Village Mill Valley 94941 415-383-3223
Mon-Sat 9-9 Sun 10-7 www.evo-spa.com
Beauty and wellness spa, skin care, bodywork, nutrition, cleansing treatments. Uses some organic and natural product lines.

INTERNATIONAL ORANGE ✿✿✿✿

2044 Fillmore St. 2nd Floor SF (Pacific Heights) 94115 888-894-8811
Mon-Fri 11-9 Sat-Sun 9-7 www.internationalorange.com
Full-service spa, yoga studio; redwood sundeck. Uses many organic and natural product lines.

KABUKI SPRINGS & SPA ✿✿✿

1750 Geary Blvd. SF (Japantown) 94115 415-922-6000
Daily 10-10 www.kabukisprings.com
Massage, spa services, communal baths. Corn-based, bioplastic gift cards.

KAMALASPA ✿✿✿

240 Stockton St. 7th Floor SF (Financial District) 94108 415-217-7700
Mon-Sat 9:30-8 Sun 10-7 www.kamalaspa.com
Ayurvedic spa, salon and nail services. All natural and organic skin products. Eco-friendly facilities.

MEDITRINA ✿✿

3923 Piedmont Ave. Piedmont 94611 510-601-7111
Tue-Fri 10-8 Sat 10-6 www.meditrinaspa.com
Wellness center and day spa; natural body care products.

PARIS SALON AND SPA ✿

915 Fourth St. San Rafael 94901 415-459-3600
Mon 10-6 Tue-Fri 9-8 Sat 9-7 Sun 11-5 www.parissalonspa.com
Hair and spa services, massage; Aveda products.

REBECCA SMITH SKIN CARE ✿✿✿✿

300 Poplar St. Suite 7 Mill Valley 94941 415-272-3291
By appt.
Holistic facial treatments. Dr. Hauschka products.

SANDRA CARON EUROPEAN SPA ✿✿✿

105 East Third Ave. San Mateo 94401 650-347-9666
Mon-Sat 10-9 Sun 10-6 www.sandracaron.com
Massage, mud baths, body wraps, and facials. Natural soaps, lotions; mineral skin care.

SCHIZANDRA ✿✿✿

493 Sanchez St. SF (Castro) 94114 415-553-8886
Mon 11-7 Tue 11-8 Wed 11-7 Thu 8-8 Fri 9-7 Sat 9-4 www.schizandrahealth.com
Offers acupuncture, massage, and herbal therapy services.

SEN SPA 🍃🍃🍃
1161 Gorgas Ave. SF (Presidio/Presidio Heights) 94129 415-441-1777
Tue-Fri 10-9 Sat-Sun 9-7 www.senspa.com
Day spa services; vegan, organic foods.

SIMPLY GORGEOUS 🍃🍃🍃
2064 Antioch Ct. Suite D Oakland (Montclair) 94611 510-339-1888
Mon by appt. only Tue-Sat 9-7 Sun 10-5 www.simplygorgeousdayspa.com
Natural skin and body treatments; holistic vitamins; colon hydrotherapy.

SKIN AND BODY THERAPY 🍃🍃
2066 Broadway Redwood City 94063 650-474-0776
Tue-Sat by appt. www.skinandbodytherapy.com
Organic, plant-based skin care; facial massage, skin detoxification.

SKIN ENVY 🍃🍃🍃
1110 Burlingame Ave. Suite 107 Burlingame 94010 650-558-0939
Tue-Fri 4-8 Sat 10-4:30 Sun by appt. www.skinenvyspa.com
Facials, massage, waxing, facial threading, henna tattoos. Natural and organic
facial cleansers, lotions.

SKIN THERAPY 🍃🍃🍃
736 Polhemus Rd. San Mateo 94402 650-574-5346
Tue-Sat by appt.
European natural facial treatments, massage.

SPA DE BEAUTE 🍃🍃
846 Oak Grove Ave. Menlo Park 94025 650-321-7776
Mon by appt. Tue-Sat 10-8 Sun by appt. www.spadebeaute.com
Skin care, massage, herbal and fruit body wraps, aromatherapy; no-polish
manicures and pedicures.

STAR CITY SALON & DAY SPA 🍃🍃🍃
349 Visitacion Ave. Brisbane 94005 650-589-9062
Mon-Fri 9-9 Sat 9-5 Sun 10-5
Natural hair coloring; chemical-free, organic facials. Aromatherapy and
fragrance-free appointments.

STELLAR SPA 🍃
26 Tamalpais Dr. Corte Madera 94925 415-924-7300
Tue-Fri 9-9 Sat-Sun 10-6 www.stellarspa.com
Uses their own biodynamic skin care line and Eminence organic skin care,
makeup artistry; massage therapy and variety of body treatments.

TEA GARDEN SPRINGS 🍃🍃
38 Miller Ave. Mill Valley 94941 415-389-7123
Mon-Sat 9:30-7:30 Sun 10:30-7:30 www.teagardensprings.com
Spa treatments, massage, facials.

THERAPEIA 🍃🍃🍃
1801 Bush St. SF (Pacific Heights) 94115 415-885-4450
Mon-Fri 10-9 Sat-Sun 9-8 www.therapeiaspa.com
Integrative therapeutic health and specialized treatments for the body,
including endermologie and acupuncture.

WATERCOURSE WAY 🍃🍃🍃
165 Channing Ave. Palo Alto 94301 650-462-2000
Mon-Thu 8-11 Fri Sat 8-midnight Sun 8-11 www.watercourseway.com
Massage, skin care, private hot tub rooms; organic and natural products.

Try to look for products that contain natural fragrance rather than synthetic fragrance. The latter is by far more common so you'll have to be on the lookout.

For the past 50 years, 80-90% of fragrances have been synthesized from petroleum, not from natural sources, as advertisers might like us to believe. A few of the commonly found harmful chemicals in fragranced products are acetone, benzene, phenol, toluene, benzyl acetate, and limonene. Stay away from these!

Harmful health effects of fragrance are caused not only by the chemicals mentioned above and a few thousand other individual chemicals, but each fragrance may well contain hundreds of different chemical combinations.

Since fragrance ingredients are protected under trade secret laws, the consumer is kept in the dark about many of the harmful chemicals that make up synthetic fragrances. When the label says "fragrance," watch out!

Synthetic fragrances are also harmful to marine life, and are a source of pollution. One of the EPA's top ten reasons for poor indoor air quality is the presence of artificial fragrances. Fragrance is increasingly cited as a trigger in health conditions such as asthma, allergies, and migraine headaches.

THE SEARCH FOR SAFER ALTERNATIVES

Looking for the words "natural" or "safe" won't guarantee that the beauty products you buy really are safe. But some companies are making safer products today and are striving to make even safer products in the future.

Choose products that are healthier for you now. Visit the Environmental Working Group's Skin Deep database (www.ewg.org/reports/skindeep), the world's largest searchable database of ingredients in cosmetics. Find out if your favorite products contain hazardous chemicals and find safer alternatives at this site. Also check out www.safecosmetics.org for more information about what's being done to encourage manufacturers to make their products safer.

Tell your cosmetics companies you want safe products. Call them, write them, or email them to let them know where you stand. Look on product packaging for a customer service hotline or check the company's website.

Behind the Green Label

Ecologically advanced clothing is an idea whose time has come. Organic and low-impact fibers can now be found in big-box stores and on high-fashion runways alike. As the market starts to boom (or bloom), consumers can help push the envelope by looking behind the green label to find out what's really going on. This will in turn advance the whole discussion of what eco-fashion truly is. Once we recognize that every thread, button, and dye has an ecological impact, we can focus on the individual characteristics of materials, methods, and processes.

As conscious consumers, or "end users," we need to be cognizant of the ecological benefits and costs of any given fiber, not just in the way it is made, but how it is sold, worn, and disposed of. For example, growing organic cotton rather than conventional cotton reduces the amount of chemicals released into the soil, air, and water. However, this organic cotton has likely traveled thousands of miles to be spun, knit, cut, sewed, and finally distributed to retail stores and consumers. If that garment is then worn a few times and discarded, it has taken a heavy toll on the environment, whether organic fiber or not.

Bamboo, another green textile, is a fast-growing renewable resource that requires few, if any, chemical inputs to cultivate. However, the processing of bamboo from plant to textile fiber is actually quite toxic and chemically intensive. Synthetic fibers are typically considered worse than natural fibers because they are derived from non-renewable petroleum sources. However, when we consider that synthetic fabrics can be made from recycled plastics, and that the final garment can be recycled in a cyclical, cradle-to-cradle model, synthetics take on a different significance. Also, synthetic garments often call for cold-water washing and line drying, both of which significantly reduce their lifecycle impact.

Yet there is no perfect process or product. Consuming less is the single most influential purchase decision a person can make. The green textile industry is still largely based on material substitution: replacing harmful materials or processes with less harmful ones. In the future, companies will develop systems that speak to the whole product lifecycle including creating cyclical products that never see the landfill.

LYNDA GROSE
Lynda Grose first merged fashion and ecology designing the Esprit Ecollection in 1990. Currently she directs marketing for the Sustainable Cotton Project, teaches sustainable fashion design at California College of the Arts, and designs for and consults with companies on sustainable practices.

A significant percentage of the world's pesticide, herbicide, and water usage comes from growing and processing the fibers used in our clothing. Buying clothes and fabrics made with organically grown or recycled fibers is by far the best choice. This helps reduce health risks to laborers and promotes production methods that are better for the environment. (You may also want to look for sweatshop-free and fair trade identification when you buy clothing.)

Try to find clothes that are unbleached or bleached with hydrogen peroxide only, and that use natural or low-impact dyes and no wrinkle-free treatments (these can be toxic).

Making your own clothing out of sustainably produced fabrics and knitting your own sweaters out of low-impact yarns may be the greenest way to dress of all. Fabric and yarn stores are beginning to carry more materials grown without the use of synthetic chemicals, dyed with natural or low-impact dyes, and processed without huge amounts of chemical inputs.

A note: Although we love vintage clothing stores and resale shops and find them inherently positive on the reduce/reuse/recycle level, we have not included them on our list. They are difficult to evaluate and there are many more than we are able to list.

Sustainable clothing and fabrics are areas with still emerging standards, but at this point, we're evaluating our stores based on the percentage of goods sold that are made with certified organic or low-impact fibers, or recycled or recyclable fibers.

In some cases, where stores made exceptional efforts in other areas (the use of alternative energy, good wastewater management, reduced packaging, among others), we gave that business's commitment to sustainability consideration in granting leaf awards.

---

at least 25% of clothing or fabric and/or yarn stock is made from organic or natural fibers or a blend thereof, or contains recycled content.

at least 50% of clothing or fabric and/or yarn stock is made from the materials listed above.

at least 75% of clothing or fabric and/or yarn stock is made from the materials listed above.

90% or more of clothing or fabric and/or yarn stock is made from the materials listed above.

Type of clothing/shoes:

B   Baby clothing and/or gear

C   Children's clothing/shoes

M   Men's clothing/shoes

W   Women's clothing/shoes

A HAPPY PLANET 🌱🌱🌱🌱 B C M W
4501 Irving St. SF (Sunset) 94122 415-753-8300
Wed-Sun 12-6 and by appt. www.ahappyplanet.com
Organic cotton undergarments, socks, loungewear, and baby clothing.

AMERICAN APPAREL 🌱 B C M W
2301 Telegraph Ave. Berkeley 94704 510-981-1641
2174 Union St. SF (Cow Hollow) 94123 415-440-3220
1615 Haight St. SF (Haight) 94117 415-431-4028
Hours vary by location www.americanapparel.net
Has an organic, undyed, sweatshop-free cotton line of clothing.

AUGUST 🌱🌱 M W
5410 College Ave. Oakland (College Ave.) 94618 510-652-2711
Daily 11-6 www.augustshop.com
Men's and women's premium denim; high-end knits. Focuses on sustainable,
fair trade materials.

BARE NECESSITIES CLOTHING AND SCENTS 🌱🌱🌱 W
291 Primrose Rd. Burlingame 94010 650-344-3700
Mon-Sat 11-6
Casual apparel from repurposed fabrics. Fair trade tribal sweaters;
Nepalese jewelry; natural, locally made massage oils.

BRYN WALKER 🌱🌱 W
1799B Fourth St. Berkeley 94710 510-525-9418
2111D Vine St. Berkeley 94709 510-845-1109
Mon-Sat 10-6 Sun 12-5
Natural fiber clothing. Tencel and linen products.

DHARMA TRADING COMPANY 🌱 B C M W
1604 Fourth St. San Rafael 94901 415-456-1211
Mon-Sat 10-6 www.dharmatrading.com
Blank clothing for do-it-yourself design; crafts; less-toxic fabric treatments
and fixatives.

FAT KAT SURF SHOP 🌱🌱 C M W
1906 Sir Francis Drake Blvd. Fairfax 94930 415-453-9167
Mon-Fri 11-7 Sat 10-7 Sun 10-5 (seasonal hours) www.fatkatsurfshop.com
Skate and surf shop. Decks from reclaimed wood; natural and
organic-fiber clothing.

FOOTLOOSE BIRKENSTOCK STORE 🌱🌱🌱 C M W
92 East Third Ave. San Mateo 94401 650-347-4242
Mon 10-5 Tue-Fri 10-5:30 Sat 10-5
Birkenstock shoes and repairs; also carries Mephisto, Keen, Dansko,
Ecco brands.

GIGGLE 🌱 B
2110 Chestnut St. SF (Marina) 94123 415-440-9034
Mon-Sat 10-7 Sun 11-6 www.egiggle.com
Stylish baby clothes, decor, gear, and gifts. Some organic.

GLOBAL EXCHANGE FAIR TRADE STORE 🌱🌱 B C M W
2840 College Ave. Berkeley 94705 510-548-0370
4018 24th St. SF (Noe Valley) 94114 415-648-8068
Hours vary by location www.globalexchange.org
Organic cotton tees. Hemp, bamboo, leather, and wood accessories made from
recycled materials. All items imported, fair trade. Non-profit.

HIP & ZEN 🌿🌿🌿 C M W

379 Marin Ave. Mill Valley 94941 888-447-6936
Daily 9-5 www.hipandzen.com
Hand-made, fair trade, recycled, organic, natural apparel and accessories.

LEELA 🌿 W

1314 Burlingame Ave. Burlingame 94010 650-685-8330
Mon-Sat 10-7 Sun 11-6 www.ilikeleela.com
Women's casual clothing and activewear. Organic cotton and bamboo blends.

LULULEMON 🌿🌿 M W

1111 Burlingame Ave. Burlingame 94010 650-347-5858
1981 Union St. SF (Cow Hollow) 94123 415-776-5858
Hours vary by location www.lululemon.com
Yoga-inspired athletic apparel for men and women.

MEPHISTO 🌿🌿 M W

1799C Fourth St. Berkeley 94710 510-558-7343
Daily 10-6 www.mephistoberkeley.com
Ergonomic walking shoes using all natural materials vegetable tanning,
latex rubber soles.

MEYER BUNJE 🌿🌿🌿 W

308 Lorton Ave. Burlingame 94010 650-347-4626
Mon-Sat 10-5
Art-inspired women's clothing and accessories; local artist-made jewelry.

MIRANDA CAROLIGNE 🌿🌿🌿 M W

485 14th St. SF (Mission) 94103 415-355-1900
Tue-Sun 1-7 www.mirandacaroligne.com
One-of-a-kind reconstructed and recycled clothing.

MOLLUSK, THE 🌿🌿 M W

4500 Irving St. SF (Sunset) 94122 415-564-6300
Daily 10-6:30 www.mollusksurfshop.com
Surf shop. Organic fiber shirts; wooden surfboards.

ORAPA GALLERY OF WEARABLE ARTS 🌿🌿🌿🌿 W

Allied Arts Guild 75 Arbor Rd. Suite D Menlo Park 94025 650-321-2197
Mon-Sat 10-5 www.orapagallery.com
Local, artist-made, women's natural-fiber clothing and accessories;
repurposed antique kimonos.

PATAGONIA 🌿🌿🌿 B C M W

770 North Point St. SF (Fisherman's Wharf) 94109 415-771-2050
Mon-Wed 10-6 Thu 10-7 Fri 10-6 Sun 10-5 www.patagonia.com
Clothing made from recycled fibers and organic cotton.

PENDLETON 🌿🌿 M W

Strawberry Village 800 Redwood Hwy. Suite 121 Mill Valley 94941 415-389-9396
Town and Country Village Suite 40 Palo Alto 94301 650-329-9755
Mon-Sat 10-6 Sun 12-5 www.pendleton-usa.com
Wool clothing for men and women; tribal trading blankets designed by
contemporary Native American artists.

P-KOK 🌿🌿🌿 M W

791 Haight St. SF (Haight) 94117 415-861-7565
Tue-Fri 12-6:30 Sat-Sun 11-7
Natural bohemian clothes for urban living.

RABAT SHOES 🍃 M W
1825 Fourth St. Berkeley 94710 510-549-9195
1440 Burlingame Ave. Burlingame 94010 650-558-0175
2080 Chestnut St. SF (Marina) 94123 415-929-8868
4001 24th St. SF (Noe Valley) 94114 415-282-7861
Hours vary by location www.rabatshoes.com
Hand-made shoes, leather belts, accessories.

REI 🍃 C M W
1338 San Pablo Ave. Berkeley 94702 510-527-4140
213 Corte Madera Town Center Corte Madera 94925 415-927-1938
1119 Industrial Rd. Suite IB San Carlos 94070 650-508-2330
840 Brannan St. SF (SOMA) 94103 415-934-1938
Hours vary by location www.rei.com
Outdoor clothing and gear using some natural fibers.
SF green certified business.

RESIDENTS APPAREL GALLERY 🍃 M W
541 Octavia St. SF (Civic Center) 94102 415-621-7718
Mon-Sat 12-7 Sun 12-5:30 www.ragsf.com
Locally-made clothing and accessories using natural and organic materials,
including hemp, organic cotton, bamboo, recycled, and vintage fabrics.

RUBY2 🍃🍃 B C M W
1431 Haight St. SF (Haight) 94117 415-554-0555
3602 20th St. SF (Mission) 94110 415-550-8052
Hours vary by location www.rubygallery.com
Deconstructed and recycled clothing and jewelry; organic cotton
children's clothing.

SEE JANE RUN SPORTS 🍃🍃 W
5817 College Ave. Oakland (College Ave.) 94618 510-428-2681
3910 24th St. SF (Noe Valley) 94114 415-401-8338
Mon-Fri 11-7 Sat 10-6 Sun 11-6 www.seejanerunsports.com
Women's athletic apparel and accessories; some organic cotton and wool.

TELA D 🍃🍃 M W
51 Bolinas Rd. Fairfax 94930 415-455-9410
Daily 11:30-6 www.teladorganics.com
Eco-friendly clothing; organic cotton, hemp, bamboo.

TWENTY TWO 🍃🍃 M W
5856 College Ave. Oakland (College Ave.) 94618 510-594-2201
Mon-Thu 11-6 Fri-Sat 11-7 Sun 11-6 www.shop22shoes.com
Original, vegetable-dyed leather shoes for men and women.

WADDLE AND SWADDLE 🍃🍃 B W
1677 Shattuck Ave. Berkeley 94709 510-540-7210
Mon-Sat 11-7 Sun 11-5 www.waddleandswaddle.com
Eco-friendly gifts and clothing for infants and moms.

WORLD CENTRIC 🍃🍃🍃🍃 M W
195C Page Mill Rd. Palo Alto 94306 650-283-3797
Mon-Fri 10-6 for pre-ordered item pick-up www.worldcentric.org
Organic fair trade undyed cotton tee shirts and camisoles. Order on website or
phone and pick up 1-2 days later. Hosts fair trade film and speaker series.

YOGA OF SAUSALITO 🍃🍃 W
110 Caledonia St. Sausalito 94965 415-332-9642
Daily 10-7 www.yogaofsausalito.com
Retail store adjacent to yoga studio; some organic cotton clothing and gifts.

YOGA STUDIO ✑ C W
2207 Larkspur Landing Circle Larkspur 94939 415-318-7666
650 East Blithedale Ave. Mill Valley 94941 415-380-8800
1823 Divisadero Street SF (Pacific Heights) 94115 415-292-5600
Hours vary by location www.yogastudiomillvalley.com
Yoga studio and retail store. Non-toxic yoga mats; organic cotton and bamboo
fiber clothing.

FABRIC/YARN STORES

AMAZING YARNS ✑✑
2559 Woodland Pl. Emerald Hills 94062 650-306-9218
Mon-Tue, Sat-Sun 11-6 www.amazingyarn.com
Hand-painted, natural-dyed, and undyed yarns. Original pattern designs;
custom buttons.

AMBATALIA FABRICS ✑✑
1 El Paseo Mill Valley 94941 415-388-6278
Tue-Sat 10-5 Sun 12-5 www.ambataliafabrics.com
Culturally and environmentally sustainable fabrics, yarn, sewing accessories.

ARTICLE PRACT ✑✑✑
5010 Telegraph Ave. Oakland (Temescal) 94609 510-595-7875
Tue-Thu 11-7 Fri-Sun 11-6 www.articlepract.com
Organic cotton and wool yarns; hemp; bamboo; recycled materials.

ATELIER MARIN ✑
217 San Anselmo Ave. San Anselmo 94960 415-256-9618
Tue-Fri 11-6 Sat 12-5 Sun 12-4 www.ateliermarinyarn.com
Yarn, knitting patterns, accessories; classes for all levels. Some organic,
natural-dyed yarns.

IMAGIKNIT ✑
3897 18th St. SF (Castro) 94114 415-621-6642
Mon-Sat 11-6:30 Sun 11-4 www.imagiknit.com
Yarn, knitting supplies, patterns. Bamboo needles; instruction for all skill levels.

KNITTER'S STUDIO, THE ✑✑✑
725 Santa Cruz Ave. Menlo Park 94025 650-322-9200
Tue-Wed, Fri-Sat 11-6 Thu 11-8 Sun 12-4 www.knittersstudio.com
Plant-dyed and undyed natural-fiber and vegan yarns. Yak, alpaca yarns;
bamboo knitting and crochet supplies; natural buttons; classes.

MARIN FIBER ARTS ✑
1026 Court St. San Rafael 94901 415-459-4600
Tue-Sat 10-6 Sun 12-4 www.marinfiberarts.com
Knitting supplies and classes; organic, natural-fiber yarns.

STASH YARN + INSPIRATION ✑✑✑✑
1820 Solano Ave. Berkeley 94707 510-558-9276
Tue-Sat 10-6 Sun 12-5 www.stashyarn.com
Supplies and classes for knitting and crocheting; natural-dyed yarns. Stock
from local artisans and worker cooperatives.

STUDIO KNIT ✑✑
320 Miller Ave. Mill Valley 94941 415-389-9994
Tue-Sat 11-6 www.studio-knit.com
Untreated and recycled yarn products; knitting supplies; classes.

YARN PAPER SCISSORS ✂ ✂

1410B Burlingame Ave. Burlingame 94010 650-348-1425
Tue-Fri 12-5 Sat 11-5 www.yarnpaperscissors.com
Children's yarn and paper supplies. Natural, local yarn and eco-wool; knitting studio; repurposing events.

GIFTS, ACCESSORIES, AND BABY PRODUCTS

Getting Goods

Before you make your next gift purchase, think about all aspects of the item: where it came from, how it was made, who made it, and its impact on the environment and human health.

The shops listed here, offering items such as candles, picture frames, lotions, baby products, toys, and much more, do take these considerations into account.

Although it's a bonus if the items are also made by local artisans, this was not part of our criteria.

To make it into the guide, 25% of items sold must be made from organic, natural, renewable, or recycled materials, and use less-toxic glues, paints, and finishes.

ARTISAN SHOP

Allied Arts Guild 75 Arbor Rd. Menlo Park 94025 650-325-2450
Mon-Sat 10-5 www.alliedartsguild.org
Non-profit artists' co-op. Gifts, home decor, and accessories from recycled and repurposed materials.

BELL AND TRUNK

1411 18th St. SF (Potrero Hill) 94107 415-648-0519
Mon-Fri 11-6 Sat-Sun 10-3
Eco-friendly accessories; organic bags; recycled fabrics; recycled cards.

BODY WISE MASSAGE

1566 Fourth St. San Rafael 94901 415-459-6333
Mon-Sat 10:30-6:30
Low-cost massage clinic and retail store. Natural-fiber clothing; non-toxic massage and yoga accessories; some organic oils.

BRILLIANT EARTH

SF (Nob Hill) 800-691-0952
By appt. www.brilliantearth.com
Conflict-free diamond jewelry and recycled gold and platinum merchandise.

CHEEKY MONKEY TOYS

714 Santa Cruz Ave. Menlo Park 94025 650-328-7975
Mon-Sat 10-6 www.cheekymonkeytoys.com
Educational and science games and toys. Wooden trains; traditional wagons; tricycles. Play area.

COMMON SCENTS

3920A 24th St. SF (Noe Valley) 94114 415-826-1019
Mon-Fri 10-7 Sat 10-6 Sun 11-5
Personal care products and fragrances.

DAY ONE-THE CENTER FOR NEW AND EXPECTANT PARENTS

Town & Country Village 855 El Camino Real Palo Alto 94303 650-322-3291
3490 California St. Suite 203 SF (Western Addition) 94118 415-440-3291
Hours vary by location www.dayonecenter.com
Products and support for babies and new parents. Natural, vegetarian vitamin supplements; homeopathic treatments; lending library; classes.

DHARMA TRADING COMPANY

1604 Fourth St. San Rafael 94901 415-456-1211
Mon-Sat 10-6 www.dharmatrading.com
Blank clothing for do-it-yourself design; crafts; less-toxic fabric treatments and fixatives.

EARTHSAKE

1772 Fourth St. Berkeley 94710 510-559-8440
Mon-Thu 10-6 Fri-Sat 10-7 Sun 11-6 www.earthsake.com
Natural and eco-friendly bedding, furniture, mattresses, linens, body care, and yoga products.

EARTHSONG

1701 Haight St. SF (Haight) 94117 415-751-0127
Daily 11-7 www.earthsongoutlet.com
Handmade paper journals, paper-free greeting cards, handcrafted gifts, and natural body products.

ECOEXPRESS

85 Galli Dr. Suite E Novato 94949 800-733-3495
Mon-Fri 9-6 www.ecoexpress.com
Gift shop and online gift basket service featuring a wide selection of fair trade, sweatshop free, and organic or natural gifts, wine, gift baskets, bath and body products, chocolate, coffee and tea, kitchen decor, and baby products. Local courier delivery available in the San Francisco Bay Area.

FAT KAT SURF SHOP

1906 Sir Francis Drake Blvd. Fairfax 94930 415-453-9167
Mon-Fri 11-7 Sat 10-7 Sun 10-5 (seasonal hours) www.fatkatsurfshop.com
Skate and surf shop. Decks from reclaimed wood; natural and organic-fiber clothing.

GIGGLE

2110 Chestnut St. SF (Marina) 94123 415-440-9034
Mon-Sat 10-7 Sun 11-6 www.egiggle.com
Stylish and eco-friendly baby clothes, decor, gear, toys, and cleaning products. Also has full on-line store.

GLOBAL EXCHANGE FAIR TRADE STORE

2840 College Ave. Berkeley 94705 510-548-0370
4018 24th St. SF (Noe Valley) 94114 415-648-8068
Hours vary by location www.globalexchange.org
Coffee, tea, books, clothing, toys, games, jewelry, home and garden, bath and body, stationery, musical instruments. All items imported, fair trade. Non-profit.

GOLDEN GATE AUDUBON NATURE STORE

2530 San Pablo Ave. Suite G Berkeley 94702 510-843-2222
Mon-Fri 9-5 www.goldengateaudubon.org
Wild birdseed, books, field guides, environmental education toys and games.

GOLDEN GATE SCHOOL OF FENG SHUI

1165 Magnolia Ave. Larkspur 94939 415-945-8899
Mon-Fri 10-5 Sat by appt. www.fengshuischool.com
Natural-fiber home accessories, fair trade gifts, organic essential oils.

Getting Goods

HIP & ZEN
379 Marin Ave. Mill Valley 94941 888-447-6936
Daily 9-5 www.hipandzen.com
Natural apparel and accessories; handmade, fair trade, recycled, organic.

JUNIPER TREE SUPPLIES
2520 San Pablo Ave. Berkeley 94702 510-647-3697
Mon-Sat 11-6:30 Sun 11-6 www.junipertreesupplies.com
Ready-made and do-it-yourself crafts, gifts.

LEARNING EXPRESS
850 Emmett Ave. Belmont 94002 650-654-4644
2710 Mowry Ave. Fremont 94538 510-791-9990
Hours vary by location www.learningexpress.com
Children's educational toys. Science kits and building sets; arts and crafts;
wooden toys and puzzles.

LETTER PERFECT
384 University Ave. Palo Alto 94301 650-321-3700
Mon-Sat 10-6 www.letterperfect.com
Recycled paper and 100 percent cotton greeting cards; wedding invitations;
archival journals.

MEYER BUNJE
308 Lorton Ave. Burlingame 94010 650-347-4626
Mon-Sat 10-5
Art-inspired women's clothing and accessories; local artist-made jewelry.

NATURAL RESOURCES
1367 Valencia St. SF (Mission) 94110 415-550-2611
Mon-Thu 11-7 Fri-Sat 11-6 Sun 11-5 www.naturalresources-sf.com
Pregnancy, childbirth and early parenting resource center including
eco-friendly baby clothing and products.

NATURE AT PLAY
1375 Burlingame Ave. Burlingame 94010 650-344-0440
Mon-Sat 10-6 Sun 11-5 www.natureatplay.com
Wooden toys, puzzles, games; non-toxic children's arts and crafts.

PLANETWEAVERS
518A Castro St. SF (Castro) 94114 415-575-0240
Sun-Thu 10-9:30 Fri-Sat 10-10:30 www.planetweavers.com
Gift store devoted to unique and exploratory shopping. Committed to
global fair trade.

PLAY STORE, THE
508 University Ave. Palo Alto 94301 877-876-1111
Tue-Sat 10:30-5:30 Sun 1-5 www.playstoretoys.com
Wood toys and games; beeswax crayons; natural arts and crafts kits.
Organic cotton toys, linens.

RENAISSANCE SPIRIT
Allied Arts Guild 75 Arbor Rd. Suite W Menlo Park 94025 650-329-1492
Mon-Sat 11-4 www.alliedartsguild.org
Artist studio and gallery behind organic garden. Jewelry made from recycled
materials and lapidary stones. Handmade, fair trade journals from Nepal.

SOAP SISTAHS
1797 Solano Ave. Berkeley 94707 510-528-0837
Mon-Fri 11-6 Sat 10-6 Sun 11-5
Eco-friendly bath and body care, gifts, crafts, loungewear.

TWIG & FIG

2110B Vine St. Berkeley 94709 510-848-5599
Tue-Sat 10-6 Sun 11-5 www.twigandfig.com
Custom and ready-made stationery; reclaimed cotton fiber paper.

WORLD CENTRIC

195C Page Mill Rd. Palo Alto 94306 650-283-3797
Mon-Fri 10-6 for pre-ordered item pick-up   www.worldcentric.org
Biodegradable, compostable food service products, recycled paper products.
Organic and fair trade chocolates, food, and clothing. Order on website or
phone and pick up 1-2 days later. Hosts fair trade film and speaker series.

YOGA OF SAUSALITO

110 Caledonia St. Sausalito 94965 415-332-9642
Daily 10-7 www.yogaofsausalito.com
Retail store adjacent to yoga studio selling handmade local jewelry, beeswax
candles, eco-friendly yoga mats and bags.

FLORISTS

Purchasing flowers may seem like a wonderful way to bring the beauty
of nature into our homes or the perfect way to acknowledge our loved
ones but often, flowers are not quite what they appear to be.

The truth is, the flower industry is one of the heaviest users of agricultural chemicals. Over 60% of the fresh-cut flowers sold in the U.S.
are imported from countries whose environmental standards are less
stringent than our own.

In some cases, chemicals banned in the U.S. are used in other
countries and find their way back here through imported agricultural
goods—on all those flowers, for instance. Luckily, organic flowers
are increasingly available, just as beautiful, and better for you and the
planet.

> To be listed, florists had to meet the minimum requirement that more
> than 25% of the total flower stock be organically grown. However,
> some of the florists listed below performed substantially higher than
> the required minimum.

CHURCH STREET FLOWERS

212 Church St. SF (Castro) 94114 415-553-7762
Mon-Fri 9-7 Sat 10-7 www.churchstreetflowers.com
Uses some organic flowers.

IXIA

2331 Market St. SF (Castro) 94114 415-431-3134
Mon-Fri 9-6 Sat 11-5 www.ixia.com
Uses some organic flowers.

OAK HILL FARM

One Ferry Building #7 SF (Embarcadero) 94111 415-399-0220
Mon-Fri 10-6 Sat 8-6 Sun 10-5 www.oakhillfarm.net
Sustainably-grown fresh-cut flowers, floral greens, and ornamental grasses
from their own state-certified organic farm in Glen Ellen. Also offers custom
floral design services and a variety of gifts and vases.

Most of us recycle our paper, try to use both sides, and read as much as we can on-line. But when we do need to buy paper and supplies, what about closing the loop and buying recycled materials? Purchasing paper with recycled content saves our forests and protects our watersheds.

You'll find different levels of recycled content in paper and other supplies—from 10% to 30%, and sometimes up to 100% post-consumer. Look for the recycled symbol (chasing arrows), and a minimum of 30% post-consumer recycled content. And while you're at it, try to find paper products bleached without harsh chemicals like chlorine.

To encourage increased availability and sales of recycled paper products in all office and paper supply stores, we have chosen not to assign variable leaf award levels in this category.

We have established a minimum threshold retailers must meet to be included in the guide. At least 25% of the paper and office supplies they offer must be sustainably produced and made from recycled, reclaimed resources.

CARDOLOGY
50 Post St. SF (Financial District) 94104 415-391-1966
Mon-Fri 9-6 Sat 10-5
Recycled greeting cards and paper goods.

ECOLOGY CENTER STORE
2530 San Pablo Ave. Berkeley 94702 510-548-3402
Tue-Sat 11-6 www.ecologycenter.org/store
Eco-friendly gardening supplies, books, household products, and recycled paper products.

GREEN EARTH OFFICE SUPPLY
1400 Coleman Ave. Suite H-16 Santa Clara 95050 800-327-8449 or 408-969-0900
Mon-Fri 11-6 www.greenearthofficesupply.com
Full line of eco-friendly office, school, and food service supplies. Showroom and on-line ordering available.

GREEN OFFICE, THE
575 Cole St. SF (Cole Valley) 94117 415-221-2400
By appt. for pickup of local orders www.thegreenoffice.com
Environmentally-friendly and sustainable office products; school and paper supplies. Phone and online orders can be picked up locally.

GREENER PRINTER
2800 Seventh St. Berkeley 94710 510-898-0000
Mon-Fri 8:30-5:30 www.greenerprinter.com
Environmentally-friendly printing service. New Leaf paper, Climate Cool shipping.

INKWORKS PRESS
2827 Seventh St. Berkeley 94710 510-845-7111
Mon-Fri 8-5 www.inkworkspress.org
Worker-collective offset printing. Recycled papers, vegetable oil inks.

KELLY PAPER

27317 Industrial Blvd. Hayward 94545 510-783-2200
296 27th St. Oakland (Lake Merritt/Downtown) 94612 510-444-6727
320 Industrial Rd. San Carlos 94070 650-592-5855
1375 Howard St. SF (SOMA) 94103 415-522-0420
1352 San Mateo Ave. South SF 94080 650-624-8645
Hours vary by location   www.kellypaper.com
Recycled paper products in small and bulk quantities; retail and commercial
printing and graphics.

MARIN IDEAL STATIONERS

1212 Strawberry Village Mill Valley 94941 415-383-2600
1727 Grant Ave. Novato 94945 415-898-7338
170 Northgate One San Rafael 94903 415-491-4123
Hours vary by location
Recycled and reclaimed office and paper supplies.

PAPER SOURCE

1925 Fillmore St. SF (Pacific Heights) 94115 415-409-7710
740 Hearst Ave. Berkeley 510-665-7800
2061 Chestnut St. SF (Marina) 415-614-1585
Hours vary by location   www.paper-source.com
Recycled cards, envelopes, and paper goods.

WALDECK'S OFFICE SUPPLIES

500 Washington St. SF (Financial District) 94111 415-981-3381
Mon-Fri 8:30-5:30   www.waldecks.com
Recycled office products. Toners, paper goods; recycling for old computers,
printers, copiers. SF green certified business.

WORLD CENTRIC

195-C Page Mill Rd. Palo Alto 94306 650-283-3797
Mon-Fri 10-6 for pick up of ordered items   www.worldcentric.org
Sugarcane fiber tableware and biodegradable picnic supplies. Phone and
online orders only that can be picked up locally.

XPEDX PAPER & GRAPHICS

330 Brush St. Oakland (Lake Merritt/Downtown) 94607 510-839-8863
Mon-Fri 7:30-6 Sat 9-4 www.xpedx.com
Recycled paper products in small and bulk quantities; retail and commercial
printing and graphics.

We urge you to support the retailers in the guide, but if
you find yourself in one of the large office supply chains,
look for post-consumer recycled content and chlorine-free
recycled paper items. Also, ask these stores to carry more
recycled products. If enough people ask, they will get
the message.

Most people think natural fibers are better for the environment than synthetic fibers. This isn't necessarily true. When considering the sustainability of fibers, it is necessary to look at the whole lifecycle: from the growing or extraction, through the processing and dyeing, to the cutting and sewing of fabric to clothing. Further, the shipping from place of manufacture to point of purchase, the washing, drying, dry cleaning and other care requirements, and ultimately the garment's disposal must also be taken into consideration. Each fiber has a different impact at each stage of its lifecycle.

FABRICS

Cotton
When it comes to cotton, look for organically grown, biologically produced, with low-impact dyes.

Wool
Look for organic, naturally scoured, un-dyed or dyed without the use of heavy metals.

Linen and Hemp
Ask for dew-retted (this is the means by which the fibers are extracted to make the fabric), organic, non-chlorine bleached.

Bamboo
Ask for a tencel process (allows fabric to be made from the plant's pulp).

Polyester
Look for recycled content and recyclable options. Ask for non-genetically modified, corn-based polyester.

FIBERS

Natural
All natural fibers are renewable and biodegradable, as long as the dyes are non-toxic.

Synthetic
Synthetic fibers are petroleum based and made from a non-renewable resource. They are not biodegradable but are readily recyclable if not blended with natural fibers.

Getting Goods

Fair trade certification strives to ensure that farmers in the developing world get a fair price for their crops and good conditions under which to work. Fair trade helps guarantee freedom of association, prohibits forced child labor, and preserves agricultural traditions by keeping farming profitable, especially for small-scale and family farmers. Developing-world farmers often lack market access and pay high premiums to dealers. By forming cooperatives, cutting out intermediaries, guaranteeing a set floor price for crops (including a bonus for organics), and setting labor and environmental standards, it is the goal of the fair trade model to create market opportunities for disadvantaged producers. TransFair, a leading fair trade certifier, currently offers certification in the U.S. for coffee, tea and herbs, cocoa and chocolate, fresh fruit, sugar, rice, and vanilla.

Although it is not widely recognized, fair trade certification also has strong ecological benefits. TransFair enforces strict environmental guidelines created by Fairtrade Labelling Organizations International (FLO), the world's main association of fair trade groups based in Bonn, Germany. Through detailed integrated farm-management practices, these standards serve to protect watersheds, virgin forests and wildlife, prevent erosion, promote natural soil fertility, conserve water, and prohibit the use of genetically modified organisms.

TransFair's long list of prohibited agro-chemicals also helps protect workers and reduce fossil fuel dependence. Trans Fair claims that its environmental standards are the most stringent in the industry, second only to the USDA's organic label. Since TransFair guarantees growers a premium for organic crops, this also creates an incentive to go organic and helps pay for ongoing certification fees.

The Rainforest Alliance is another third-party certifier of sustainable agricultural products and also has programs for sustainable forestry and tourism. Through their labeling program, a product can be certified if it meets their high standards of land conservation, integrated farm management practices, and fair labor conditions. The Rainforest Alliance's agricultural program currently covers bananas, citrus, cocoa, coffee, and flowers.

For more information, visit www.transfairusa.org and www.rainforest-alliance.org.

Animal Family Values

Dogs, cats, fish, birds, chinchillas—the list of animals we regard as part of our family keeps growing. Although like most people we refer to our animals as pets, we like to think of them as our "kids." Like you, we have chosen to bring our companion animals into our homes. And just like our human kids, our animals need and deserve an environment and a lifestyle that is good for their health and well-being. Those of us in the Bay Area are fortunate to be where there is a range of eco-friendly ways to meet the needs of our animal family members.

When you are shopping for pet products, we urge you to shop like you're shopping for yourself. Everything we do affects our environment and our health in some manner. The same is true for our pets. When considering products for your pet, consider whether or not you would feed this food to your children or wash their hair with this shampoo. Look at the list of ingredients. If it is full of stuff you can't pronounce, look around to see if another product is available. Educate yourself as to what "human grade," "all-natural," and "organic" really mean when it comes to pet food The government does not regulate all these claims on pet food labels. Be extra careful with flea and tick repellents. Obviously they contain compounds designed to harm something (heck, their job is to rid pets of fleas and ticks!) so make sure you use them sparingly and according to package directions. If you don't absolutely need to use a flea or tick product—don't! If a regular shampoo will do the job use that instead.

Try to support pet product and service businesses that strive to create a healthy environment—both for your pet and for all of us. If you have the option to use a green business, do so. These businesses, in addition to selling eco-friendly products, have committed to operating in an eco-friendly manner. Businesses that offer eco-friendly products and services have made a commitment to be better environmental stewards. And some have been subject to a range of inspections to demonstrate that commitment. Making smart purchasing and spending decisions is good for your pet and you!

VIRGINIA DONOHUE AND MARK KLAIMAN
Virginia Donohue and Mark Klaiman founded Pet Camp® in 1997 in San Francisco. Pet Camp is certified by the City and County of San Francisco as a Green Business and is the only overnight dog and cat care facility in the country certified as a Green Business.

As with humans, natural, organic food, free from unnecessary additives, is best for pets. All too often, commercial pet food is chock-full of ingredients that may not be conducive to optimal health for dogs, cats, and other friends.

We have evaluated pet food purveyors based on the percentage of products sold that contain all certified organic; a mix of certified organic and natural; or all natural ingredients.

When it comes to pet care and grooming we feel it is best to minimize the use of products containing harsh chemicals and potentially toxic treatments. Not only is your pet exposed, you and other household members are as well—every time you touch, scratch, pat, or hold your animal. In fact, some pet treatments can be very harmful, so it is important to review your options.

We took a look at pet care products (such as flea/tick treatments, shampoos, and other grooming products) with an eye toward their content. Our listings reflect the percentage of products sold and, in the case of grooming establishments, the percentage of products used that contain non-toxic, natural, and/or organic ingredients.

To be included in the guide, businesses must meet our minimum requirement that 25% of their products comply with the standards outlined above.

> �🌿 at least 25% of products meet the above criteria.
> ✍🌿🌿 at least 50% of products meet the above criteria.
> 🌿🌿🌿 at least 75% of products meet the above criteria.
> 🌿🌿🌿🌿 90% or more of products meet the above criteria.

ALPHA PET SUPPLY 🌿🌿🌿
960 San Pablo Ave. Albany 94706 510-525-7361
Mon-Fri 10-6:30 Sat 9:30-6 Sun 10-5
Conventional, raw, and holistic pet care; organic, fair trade coffee for humans.

ANIMAL COMPANY, THE 🌿🌿
4298 24th St. SF (Noe Valley) 94114 415-647-8755
Mon-Sat 10-6 Sun 12-5 www.theanimalcompany.com
Organic, natural, and holistic products; exotic birds.

BELLA AND DAISY'S DOG BAKERY & BOUTIQUE 🌿🌿🌿🌿
1750 Union St. SF (Cow Hollow) 94123 415-440-7007
Mon-Fri 11-7 Sat-Sun 11-6 www.bellaanddaisys.com
Homemade treats and organic dog and cat food. Also has a Friday night "Yappy Hour" where pets and owners can mingle and snack on organic treats.

BERNAL BEAST, THE 🌿🌿🌿
509 Cortland Ave. SF (Bernal Heights) 94110 415-643-7800
Mon-Fri 11-7 Sat 10-6 Sun 11-5 www.bernalbeast.com
Natural pet supplies; self-service dog wash; directory of groomers and walkers.

BEST IN SHOW ✐✐✐✐
545 Castro St. SF (Castro) 94114 415-864-7387
300 Sanchez St. SF (Castro) 94114 415-863-7387
Hours vary by location   www.bestinshowsf.com
Food, toys, clothing, treats, collars, leashes, tags, carriers, and
pet sitting services.

BIRDERS' GARDEN ✐✐✐✐
926 El Camino Real San Carlos 94070 650-595-0300
Tue-Sat 10-6 Sun 12-5
Organic seed formulated for native Bay Area birds; bird feeders and houses;
natural pesticides.

BOWWOWMEOW ✐
737 Laurel St. San Carlos 94070 650-802-2845
2150 Polk St. SF (Russian Hill) 94109 415-440-2845
Hours vary by location   www.bowwowmeow.net
Organic dog food, treats, toys; organic kitty litter; hemp collars; recycled
rubber products. Grooming with herbal shampoo.

DOG BONE ALLEY ✐✐✐✐
1342 Park St. Alameda 94501 510-521-5800
Mon-Thu 10-7 Fri-Sat 10-8 Sun 10-7   www.dogbonealley.com
Organic and natural pet food, supplies, and pet care products.

DOG SPA, THE ✐✐
169 West Portal Ave. SF (West Portal) 94127 415-661-8333
Daily 10-5   www.thedogspasf.com
Dog boutique and grooming service; many all-natural products.

DOLLY'S TREASURES ✐✐✐
1021 Alameda de las Pulgas Belmont 94002 650-592-5002
Mon-Fri 10-7 Sat 11-6
Organic and natural pet food, toys, accessories, flea/tick treatments, and
grooming products.

FOR PAWS ✐✐✐✐
69 Bolinas Rd. Suite B Fairfax 94930 415-456-4685
Tue-Fri 11-6:30 Sat 10-6 Sun 12-5   www.forpaws-online.com
Pet grocery and boutique. Organic food and treats; non-toxic pet care.

GEORGE ✐✐✐✐
1844 Fourth St. Berkeley 94710 510-644-1033
2411 California St. SF (Pacific Heights) 94115 415-441-0564
Hours vary by location   www.georgesf.com
Supplies for dogs and cats. Organic food, hemp bed covers, jute collars.

GROOMING WITH TLC ✐✐✐✐
2070 Broadway Redwood City 94063 650-299-0860
Tue-Sat 8-6
Organic and natural shampoo, flea treatments, dog treats; cotton leashes.

HAPPY PET ✐✐✐✐
709 Taraval St. SF (Sunset) 94116 415-566-2952
Mon-Sat 11-6   www.canineconfections.com
Holistic pet shop and organic canine bakery.

HEALTHWIZE FOR PETS ✐✐✐✐
157 Fillmore St. SF (Haight) 94117 415-552-0233
Mon-Fri 11-7:30 Sat-Sun 10:30-6:45   www.healthwizeforpets.com
Natural food and accessories for dogs, cats, fish, and small pets.

Caring for Critters

HOLISTIC HOUND 🍃🍃🍃🍃

1510 Walnut St. Suites A & B Berkeley 94709 510-843-2133
Mon-Sat 10-6 Sun 11-5 www.holistichound.com
Natural and holistic pet care and supplies.

JEFFREY'S NATURAL PET FOODS 🍃🍃🍃🍃

3809 18th St. SF (Castro) 94114 415-864-1414
Daily 10-9
Fresh, organic, vet-approved dog food, all-natural, homeopathic remedies,
accessories, and toys.

NOE VALLEY PET COMPANY 🍃🍃🍃

1451 Church St. SF (Noe Valley) 94131 415-282-7385
Mon- Fri 10-8 Sat 10-6 Sun 10-5 www.noevalleypet.com
Natural food, beds, accessories; dog walking service.

PAWSITIVELY GROOMED PET SALON 🍃🍃

1427 Broadway Burlingame 94010 650-342-0012
Tue-Sat 9-5:30
Dog grooming; organic pet food, treats, and pet care products.

PAWTRERO HILL BATHHOUSE & FEED CO. 🍃🍃🍃🍃

199 Mississippi St. SF (Potrero Hill) 94107 415-863-7297
Mon-Fri 11-7 Sat 11-6 Sun 12-5 www.pawtrero.com
Self-service pet wash; anesthesia-free teeth cleaning; pet photography;
accessories from natural and recycled materials.

PET CAMP 🍃🍃🍃🍃

525 Phelps St. SF (Bayview/Hunter's Point) 94124 415-282-0700
Mon-Fri 7-6 Sat 8 a.m.-11 a.m. Sun 3-6 www.petcamp.com
Overnight and daycare for dogs and cats. SF certified green business.

PET CLUB 🍃

508 Tamalpais Dr. Corte Madera 94925 415-927-2862
Mon-Fri 9-8 Sat 9-7 Sun 10-7
Natural canned and dried pet food.

PET FOOD EXPRESS 🍃🍃

1101 University Ave. Berkeley 94702 510-540-7777
6925 Mission St. Daly City 94015 650-997-3333
2220 Mountain Blvd. Oakland (Montclair) 94611 510-530-5300
6398 Telegraph Ave. Oakland (North Oakland) 94609 510-923-9500
5144 Broadway Oakland (Rockridge) 94611 510-654-8888
1975 Market St. SF (Castro) 94103 415-431-4567
Stonestown Galleria 3160 20th Ave. SF (Sunset) 94132 415-759-7777
1933 Davis St. San Leandro 94577 510-562-2222
Hours vary by location   www.petfoodexpress.com
Organic and natural pet food, supplies.

PET PLACE, THE 🍃🍃

777 Santa Cruz Ave. Menlo Park 94025 650-325-PETS (7387)
Mon-Fri 10-6 Thu 10-8 Sat 10-5
Holistic and homeopathic remedies; certified dog masseuse; formaldehyde-free
scratching posts; natural pet care books and lending library.

PETS ARE US 🍃🍃🍃

449 Broadway Millbrae 94030 650-697-3258
Mon-Sat 10-6 Sun 11-5
Natural, organic, and raw foods; supplies for dogs, cats, birds, reptiles,
rodents; self-service dog wash.

PLAZA DE PAWS ✑✑✑✑
1429 Burlingame Ave. Burlingame 94010 650-579-3647
Mon-Sat 10-6 Sun 12-5 www.plazadepaws.net
Organic dog and cat food; natural grooming products.

PUPPY HAVEN ✑✑✑✑
772 Stanyan St. SF (Haight) 94117 415-751-PETS
Daily 10-7
Natural food, treats, and accessories; raw food for canines; pet wash.

REDHOUND ✑✑✑✑
5523 College Ave. Oakland (College Ave.) 94618 510-428-2785
Mon-Fri 10-7 Sat 10-6 Sun 11-5 www.redhoundpets.com
Natural and organic dog and cat supplies; puppy training classes.

SCRUB A PUP DOG WASH ✑✑✑✑
119 West 25th Ave. San Mateo 94403 650-577-9665
Tue-Fri 9:30-5:30 Wed 9:30-8 Sat 9-5 Sun 10-4 www.scrubapupdogwash.com
Do-it-yourself and full-service dog wash. Natural shampoos and herbal
treatments; natural rubber biters; organic treats.

SOUTH PAW BATHHOUSE & FEED CO. ✑✑✑✑
199 Brannan St. SF (SOMA) 94107 415-882-7297
Mon-Fri 11-7 Sat 11-6 Sun 12-5 www.pawtrero.com
Self-service pet wash; anesthesia-free teeth cleaning; pet photography;
accessories from natural and recycled materials.

SUNSET PET SUPPLY ✑✑✑✑
2226 Taraval St. SF (Sunset) 94116 415-661-4236
Mon-Fri 10-7 Sat 9:30-6:30 Sun 11-6 www.sunsetpetsupply.com
Holistic and natural pet food; eco-friendly supplies.

TOP PAWS ✑✑✑✑
1001 Bridgeway C2 Sausalito 94965 415-331-PAWS
Mon-Sat 10-7 Sun 10-6 www.top-paws.com
Mostly organic, additive-free pet food and treats; non-toxic pet toys.

VILLAGE DOG, THE ✑✑✑✑
632 San Pablo Ave. Albany 94706 510-525-9925
Tue-Wed 10-6 Thu 11-7 Fri 10-6 Sat 11-5 Sun 12-4 www.thevillagedog.com
Organic pet food, treats, and supplements; personalized training services.

WHO DOES YOUR DOG? ✑
6090 Redwood Blvd. Suite A Novato 94945 415-897-0405
All pets are taken between 8-10 a.m. www.whodoesyourdog.com
Grooming services; botanical shampoo. Full grooming comes with
complimentary all-day boarding.

WOODLANDS PET FOOD & TREATS ✑✑✑
701 Strawberry Village Mill Valley 94941 415-388-PETS
Daily 10-8 www.woodlandspet.com
Natural, preservative-free pet care.

We were excited to find many local merchants and service
providers with eco-friendly options. Share your findings with
other pet owners on www.greenopia.com: How was the grooming?
Did your pets like the food? Did the flea treatment work? How
was the staff's rapport with your pet?

For many people, pets make life better. Some basic "green" knowledge can help make for a happier pet, a healthier household, and a greener world.

Look for natural and organic pet food. This will not only be good for your pet's health, but buying organic products helps support good land management and sustainable practices.

Pets are good for kids. Certain studies have shown that children who grow up with at least two pets are more than 75% less likely to develop allergies later in life.

Pesticides aren't good for pets or the people who pet them. Be very cautious with pet products that contain toxic pesticides like organophosphates. These chemicals are potentially harmful to your pet, you, and especially children. The EPA estimates that on the day a product containing organophosphates is used, a child can be exposed to 500 to 50,000 times the safe levels of the toxic substance.

Although you don't want to douse your pet in toxins, it is also important to keep the bugs in check. Ticks can carry Lyme disease, a serious and poorly understood disease that attacks the nervous system. If you live in an area where Lyme disease is a risk, be very cautious and seek sound advice on keeping ticks off you and your furry friends.

Pet waste doesn't just smell bad, it can represent a major source of bacterial pollution when rain washes it into waterways and on to beaches. Always clean up after your pet. And why not try to use biodegradable, non-petroleum-based bags for this purpose?

Because pet waste is produced in such quantity, San Francisco has become the first city in America to launch a pilot program to turn it into methane fuel gas. Using bacteria to "digest" the pet waste, the City of San Francisco is hoping it can turn this polluting nuisance into a clean fuel.

If you are ready to add a new family member, remember that your local shelter is the best place to adopt.

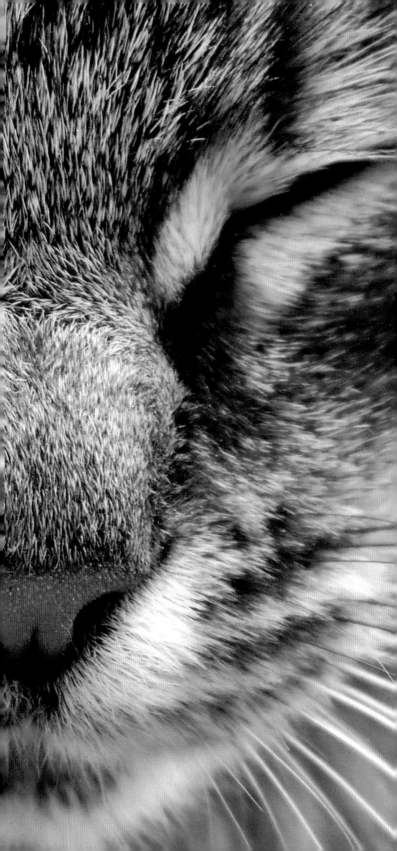

A new generation of travel

A new generation of travel is being born—hotels, restaurants, destinations, and transportation options that are green from the inside out. And it's happening without sacrificing style, fine design, comfort, service, and fun.

The whole notion of what constitutes comfortable accommodations is changing. No longer is "greenwashing" adequate. Rather, this new generation of hotels begins its commitment to environmental sustainability when construction starts. Built to the standards set by the U.S. Green Building Council, these hotels are constructed with green building techniques, including the use of recycled materials, resource efficiency, and other practices that are sustainable environmentally and beneficial to guests.

Tobacco-free environments and water conservation placards are yesterday's way of signaling a commitment to preserving and providing clean environments. The industry has moved far beyond such attempts. Today's truly green buildings install wood certified by the Forest Stewardship Council as harvested in a sustainable manner. Guests walk on specially designed carpets that include recycled content and have low chemical emissions. Hotel guest room bedding fabrics are made with recycled polyester and other textiles, so they can be machine washed to avoid dry cleaning chemicals. And guest room electrical systems are managed with a single key card for maximum energy efficiency.

Moreover, green travel not only benefits visitors and the environment, it also benefits employees. For example, when harsh cleaning products are replaced with citrus-based cleansers that work just as effectively, the health risks associated with chemical use are greatly reduced.

Travelers looking for a truly environmentally-sensitive experience should begin by checking for the coveted certifications from the San Francisco Green Business Program and Leadership in Energy and Environmental Design (LEED). These awards mean your destination—whether a hotel, a restaurant, or a new shoe shop—has made a real commitment to providing a clean, sustainable structure, thereby moving all of us toward a cleaner, more sustainable environment.

STEFAN MÜHLE
Stefan Mühle is general manager of San Francisco's Orchard Hotel and the Orchard Garden Hotel. The Orchard Hotel is certified by the San Francisco Green Business program. The Orchard Garden Hotel will be the first hotel in California to earn a LEED-NC rating.

We live in a world in which travel has become increasingly essential and complex. We, as travelers, are faced with a myriad of choices—the form of transport, the type of accommodation, or the planning of an itinerary. Eco-tourism offers some exciting new opportunities to experience the world without leaving a heavy footprint. Work with an agency that specializes in that kind of travel if you'd like to see faraway places in an environmentally-friendly way. Bon voyage!

Although many travel agencies are familiar with eco-tourism and might be able to help you find eco-tour packages or hotels, to be listed here, businesses must focus primarily on eco-travel and actively promote it. Because this is an emerging field, we chose not to award leaves.

GLOBAL EXCHANGE REALITY TOURS
2017 Mission St. Suite 303 SF (Mission) 94110 415-255-7296
Mon-Fri 9-5 www.globalexchange.org
Responsible, socially-just, international tours.

GREEN TORTOISE ADVENTURE TRAVEL
494 Broadway St. SF (North Beach) 94133 415-956-7500
Mon-Fri 9-7 Sat 12-6 www.greentortoise.com
Eco-friendly tours. Mexico, Belize, Guatemala, U.S. national parks.

HIMALAYAN HIGH TREKS
241 Dolores St. SF (Mission) 94103 415-551-1005
By appt. www.hightreks.com
Responsible, low-impact tours to Buddhist areas around the world.

NATURE TRIP
493 Vermont St. SF (Potrero Hill) 94107 415-355-0450
By appt. www.naturetrip.com
Eco-friendly, natural history adventures. Bird watching, conservancy, and wildlife behavior. SF green certified business.

SIERRA CLUB OUTINGS
85 Second St. 2nd Floor SF (SOMA) 94105 415-977-5522
Mon-Fri 8:30-5 www.sierraclub.org/outings
Provides outdoor educational and travel adventures around the world for people of all ages, abilities, and interests. Strong emphasis on ecological sustainability.

SEACOLOGY
1623 Solano Ave. Berkeley 94707 510-559-3505
Mon-Fri 9-5 www.seacology.org
Combines land- and sea-based activities for participants in many of Seacology's island project sites in such locations as Tanzania, Fiji, and Indonesia. A $1,000 donation to Seacology is requested from all participants.

WILDERNESS TRAVEL
1102 Ninth St. Berkeley 94710 510-558-2488
Mon-Fri 8:30-5 www.wildernesstravel.com
Low-impact, responsible wildlife, cultural, and hiking tours.

Whether you are planning a family vacation, welcoming family or friends into town, or going away on business, the hotel you choose matters. Next time, when selecting a hotel, take into account factors that will affect your personal health and the health of the planet.

We have evaluated hotels based on a number of areas, all of which directly impact both the hotel guest and/or the environment. Our criteria is extensive and includes the following:

- Environmentally-sound purchasing practices (including toiletries)

- Non-toxic or low-toxic maintenance and cleaning products and practices

- "Green" landscaping

- Earth-friendly restaurant services

- Sustainable building materials

- Efficient resource management including energy, water, and waste systems

- Good ventilation and fresh air exchange

- Linens, bedding, and furnishings made of natural materials

> Performed at an overall average of at least 25% on actions in the areas listed above.
>
> Performed at an overall average of at least 50% on actions in the areas listed above.
>
> Performed at an overall average of at least 75% on actions in the areas listed above.
>
> Performed at an overall average of at least 90% on actions in the areas listed above.

Average room price:

$	$175 or less
$$	$176 - $250
$$$	$251 - $325
$$$$	$326 and up

ARGONAUT HOTEL $$$
495 Jefferson St. SF (Fisherman's Wharf) 94109 415-563-0800
www.argonauthotel.com
Boutique hotel at Fisherman's Wharf. Original 1907 style architecture and elements of the nautical history of San Francisco. Part of the eco-friendly Kimpton Hotel & Restaurant Group.*

COURTYARD BY MARRIOTT, DOWNTOWN OAKLAND $$
988 Broadway Oakland (Lake Merritt/Downtown) 94607 510-625-8282
www.marriott.com
Full-service hotel. Alameda County certified green business.

CROWNE PLAZA HOTEL CABANA 🍃🍃🍃 $$
4290 El Camino Real Palo Alto 94306 650-857-0787
www.cppaloalto.crowneplaza.com
Hotel with a Mediterranean-inspired setting, is the only hotel in California powered by solar energy.

DOUBLETREE HOTEL & EMC BERKELEY MARINA 🍃🍃 $$
200 Marina Blvd. Berkeley 94710 510-548-7920
www.berkeleymarina.doubletree.com
Pet-friendly waterside setting along the Berkeley marina.

EMBASSY SUITES HOTEL, SAN RAFAEL/MARIN 🍃🍃 $$
101 McInnis Parkway San Rafael 94903 415-499-9222
www.embassy.com
Suburban hotel. Two-room suites, complimentary breakfast. Host hotel for the annual Bioneers conference.

FAIRMONT, SAN FRANCISCO, THE 🍃🍃 $$$$
950 Mason St. SF (Nob Hill) 94108 415-772-5000
www.fairmont.com
Fully restored historic hotel in Nob Hill.

HARBOR COURT HOTEL 🍃🍃 $$$
165 Steuart St. SF (Financial District) 94105 415-882-1300
www.harborcourthotel.com
Waterfront boutique hotel near the Financial District and South of Market. Part of the eco-friendly Kimpton Hotel & Restaurant Group.*

HILTON SAN FRANCISCO 🍃🍃 $$$
333 O'Farrell St. SF (Fisherman's Wharf) 94102 415-771-1400
www.hilton.com
Deluxe hotel with restaurant and spa near Fisherman's Wharf. Anti-microbial beds.

HOSTELING INTERNATIONAL MARIN HEADLANDS 🍃🍃 $
Bldg. 941 Fort Barry Sausalito 94965 415-331-2777
www.marinheadlandshostel.org
Low-cost accommodations in the Marin Headlands. Marin certified green business.

HOTEL CARLTON 🍃🍃🍃 $
1075 Sutter St. SF (Nob Hill) 94109 415-673-0242
www.hotelcarltonsf.com
Historic hotel located near Union Square. Environmentally-friendly rooms and organic restaurant (Saha). Part of the Joie de Vivré Hospitality Group. SF green certified business.

HOTEL MONACO 🍃 $$$
501 Geary St. SF (Union Square) 94102 415-292-0100
www.monaco-sf.com
Boutique hotel and spa with French-inspired architecture. Part of the eco-friendly Kimpton Hotel & Restaurant Group.* SF green certified business.

HOTEL PALOMAR 🍃 $$$
12 Fourth St. SF (SOMA) 94103 415-348-1111
www.hotelpalomar-sf.com
Urban retreat in downtown San Francisco. Part of the eco-friendly Kimpton Hotel & Restaurant Group.*

HOTEL TRITON 🍃🍃 $$$
342 Grant Ave. SF (Union Square) 94108 415-394-0500
www.hoteltriton.com
Boutique hotel. Offers a special celebrity suite. Part of the eco-friendly Kimpton Hotel & Restaurant Group.*

HYATT AT FISHERMAN'S WHARF 🍃🍃 $$$

555 North Point St. SF (Fisherman's Wharf) 94133 415-563-1234
www.fishermanswharf.hyatt.com
Full-service hotel near Fisherman's Wharf. Green focus is on recycling
and water conservation.

INN MARIN 🍃🍃 $

250 Entrada Dr. Novato 94949 415-883-5952
www.innmarin.com
Pet-friendly, family owned and operated hotel and restaurant. Marin certified
green business.

MARRIOTT, FREMONT 🍃🍃 $$

46100 Landing Parkway Fremont 94538 510-413-3700
www.marriott.com
Full-service hotel. Alameda County certified green business.

MARRIOTT, OAKLAND CITY CENTER 🍃🍃 $$

1001 Broadway Oakland (Lake Merritt/Downtown) 94607 510-451-4000
www.marriott.com
Full-service hotel. Alameda County certified green business.

MONTICELLO INN 🍃 $$$

127 Ellis St. SF (Union Square) 94102 415-392-8800
www.monticelloinn.com
Located downtown in a landmark 1906 building near Union Square, styled
along the lines of Thomas Jefferson's colonial Virginian home. Part of the
eco-friendly Kimpton Hotel & Restaurant Group.*

ORCHARD GARDEN HOTEL, THE 🍃🍃🍃🍃 $$

466 Bush St. SF (Financial District) 94108 415-399-9807
www.theorchardgardenhotel.com
First green hotel built from the ground up is a state-of-the-art, full-service
boutique hotel. LEED-certified project by the US Green Building Council.

ORCHARD HOTEL, THE 🍃🍃🍃 $$

665 Bush St SF (Nob Hill) 94108 415-362-8878
www.theorchardhotel.com
Located in the heart of San Francisco. Member of the Green Hotels
Association. SF green certified business.

PRESCOTT HOTEL 🍃🍃 $$$

545 Post St. SF (Union Square) 94102 415-563-0303
www.prescotthotel.com
Smoke-free property. Part of the eco-friendly Kimpton Hotel & Restaurant
Group. * SF green certified business.

RED VICTORIAN BED & BREAKFAST AND ART 🍃🍃🍃 $$

1665 Haight St. SF (Haight) 94117 415-864-1978
www.redvic.com
Bed and breakfast with themed rooms located on Haight St. near
Golden Gate Park.

SERRANO HOTEL 🍃 $$$

405 Taylor St. SF (Union Square) 94102 415-885-2500
www.serranohotel.com
Restored Spanish revival building near Union Square. Part of the
eco-friendly Kimpton Hotel & Restaurant Group.*

SIR FRANCIS DRAKE HOTEL 🍃🍃 $$$

450 Powell St. SF (Union Square) 94102 415-392-7755
www.sirfrancisdrake.com
Historic full-service hotel in Union Square. Part of the eco-friendly Kimpton
Hotel & Restaurant Group.*

STANFORD TERRACE INN $

531 Stanford Ave. Palo Alto 94306 650-857-0333
www.stanfordterraceinn.com
Boutique hotel near Stanford University. Santa Clara County certified green
business.

TUSCAN INN $$$

425 North Point St. SF (Fisherman's Wharf) 94133 800-648-4626
www.tuscaninn.com
Boutique hotel near Fisherman's Wharf. Italian villa decor; pet friendly.
Part of the eco-friendly Kimpton Hotel & Restaurant Group.*
SF green certified business.

VILLA HOTEL FLORENCE $$$

225 Powell St. SF (Union Square) 94102 866-823-4669
www.villaflorence.com
Boutique hotel focused on Italian-inspired fashion, food, and wine. Part of the
eco-friendly Kimpton Hotel & Restaurant Group.*

* The Kimpton Hotel & Restaurant Group donates a percentage of the room
revenue from each of its hotels to The Trust for Public Land.

Minimize your carbon emissions by traveling by train,
bus, bike, or on foot whenever possible. Ride the train
instead of taking short-hop domestic flights or driving
alone in your car—it's a great way to travel with others
and enjoy the scenery along the way!

Use a digital camera to reduce the amount of chemicals
and water needed to process regular film.

If you're traveling or attending an event and want to use
a one-time use camera for convenience, be sure to find
a processing lab that will recycle camera components.
Kodak's recycling program accepts all brands and
makes it easy for any lab to participate.

The services provided by travel agents are designed to meet the
specific needs of individual travelers. Similarly, everyone experiences
a hotel differently. Rather than staying in every hotel and taking
every trip, we developed more objective criteria. To add that
personal dimension, and to help others as they make their travel
plans, we'd like to hear from you: How knowledgeable was the
travel agent you used for booking your green trip? How well did
they serve you? What did you think of the green hotel you stayed
in? What did you think about the products they use or their décor?
Was the relationship between price and value reasonable?

The Service Sector Goes Green

Lately, the service sector has come under increased scrutiny for its environmental impacts. Although these types of companies—auto mechanics, dry cleaners, real estate agents, banks, and telecommunications companies, among others—aren't as visible a set of polluters as their industrial brethren, they can be far from benign. Service-sector businesses can be gluttonous consumers of resources and can generate vast quantities of waste, some of it quite toxic.

The good news is that many of these services are getting greener. Today, there are dry cleaners (and their wet-cleaning alternatives) that use less-toxic processes, utility programs that offer renewable energy, nontoxic pest control companies, even green real estate agents.

There is a great deal of satisfaction to be had from shopping at these merchants beyond benefiting from the good, green services they offer. For one thing, they are usually locally based firms—few big national firms offer green services—so you're supporting what's become known as "local living economies" instead of faceless chain store operators.

You'll also be inspired by the passion of the people behind the counter. Nearly all of the green service providers I've met, from natural lawn care companies to greener print shops to environmentally- and socially-minded bankers, bring their creativity, intelligence, and life spirit to work each day. In many cases, they are a wellspring of information about the environmental aspects of their companies, which they love to share. You'll be surprised at all the ways service businesses can help you go green: janitorial companies that use nontoxic, biodegradable cleaners that reduce air pollution and health impacts; office supply stores that stock recycled or tree-free papers; funeral homes that offer eco-friendly burial alternatives. The list goes on.

Sorting through
Services

If your local service providers don't offer green options, ask (or demand) that they do. Many conventional service firms aren't even aware of the alternatives, or don't believe their customers are interested. Just a handful of customer requests could tip the scales. And that would be a great service that you could offer.

JOEL MAKOWER
Joel Makower is Executive Editor of the online resource center GreenBiz.com and writes "Two Steps Forward" (www.readjoel.com), a blog on business, the environment, and the bottom line.

Pharmacies are where we go to meet health needs and sometimes to seek professional guidance. Traditionally, pharmacists mixed and dispensed medications on the orders of physicians. However, more recently, pharmacies have come to include other services related to preventative care as well as illness treatment.

When our quest is for good health, how we treat ourselves becomes paramount. Many of us consider natural remedies first, and the pharmacies listed here offer the most extensive selection of alternative medications, including homeopathic remedies, herbal tinctures, and other holistic preparations.

A few stores are solely holistic pharmacies, and others, like some larger health food stores and grocery stores, have an extensive holistic remedy and personal care department.

In determining which pharmacies to include, we looked at the percentage of homeopathic remedies, natural remedies, and the presence of organic ingredients in these remedies. Where vitamins were concerned, we checked for plant-based (vs. synthetic), natural, organic, and/or herbal ingredients.

We also evaluated a pharmacy's stock of natural alternatives to traditional personal care products and medications (for example, cough medicines, sleep aids, cold and flu treatments, skin creams, shampoos, deodorants, make-up, and soap).

> To be in the guide, at least 25% of a given store's pharmacy stock must include the type of products outlined above.

APPLE HEALTH FOODS
Sequoia Station 1011 El Camino Real Redwood City 94063 1-800-67APPLE
Mon-Fri 10-7 Sat-Sun 10-6   www.applehealth.com
Natural vitamins, herbs, snacks, and beverages; organic body care; cosmetics; books.

DAILY HEALTH
1235 Ninth Ave. SF (Sunset) 94122 415-681-7675
Mon-Fri 10-8 Sat 10-5 Sun 12-5
Health food store and restaurant. Vitamins, supplements; organic, raw, vegan food.

ELEPHANT PHARMACY
1607 Shattuck Ave. Berkeley 94709 510-549-9200
4470 El Camino Real Los Altos 94022 650-472-6800
909 Grand Ave. San Rafael 94901 415-462-6000
Hours vary by location   www.elephantpharmacy.com
Alternative and conventional pharmacy. Natural and herbal remedies; body care and cosmetics; natural foods and fair trade goods. In-store advisors.

HEALTH BY HEIDI
1212 West Hillsdale Blvd. Suite G San Mateo 94403 650-572-7100
Mon-Fri 8:30 a.m.-10:30 p.m. Sat 9-9 Sun 10-9   www.healthbyheidi.com
Vitamins, supplements, skin care products.

Sorting through Services

PHARMACA INTEGRATIVE PHARMACY

1744 Solano Ave. Berkeley 94707 510-527-8929
230 East Blithedale Mill Valley 94941 415-388-7822
7514 Redwood Blvd. Novato 94945 415-892-3700
925 Cole St. SF (Cole Valley) 94117 415-661-1216
Hours vary by location   www.pharmaca.com
Traditional and alternative pharmacy. Natural body care, cosmetics, gifts.
In-store alternative medicine specialists.

SCARLET SAGE HERB COMPANY, THE

1173 Valencia St. SF (Mission) 94110 415-821-0997
Daily 11-6:30   www.scarletsageherb.com
Organic plants; natural body care; vitamins and holistic medicine.

SHEN HERBAL PHARMACY

1385 Shattuck Ave. Berkeley 94709 510-848-4372
Mon-Fri 10-6 Sat 10-5 Sun 11-5   www.drshen.com
Chinese herbs and medicines.

TOWER OF HEALTH

352 Grand Ave. South SF 94080 650-952-3406
Mon-Fri 10-7 Sat-Sun 10-4:30
Herbal and vitamin supplements; homeopathic remedies.

WEST PORTAL NUTRITION CENTER

163 West Portal Ave. SF (West Portal) 94127 415-664-0700
Mon-Sat 9-6 Sun 11-5
Vitamins, supplements, herbs, and skin care products. Mail order available.

**Many grocery stores also have extensive alternative pharmacy and
personal care sections. See *Grocery Stores* in the *Eating In* section for
more information:**

Earthbeam Natural Foods
Food Mill, The
Fresh Organics
Good Earth Natural & Organic Foods
Rainbow Grocery
Real Food Company, The
Whole Foods Market

Over one-fifth of U.S. hospitals now offer complementary
practices and alternative medicine in conjunction with
conventional care.
   (PBS/Frontline)

Growing frustration with the U.S. healthcare system has
caused consumers to seek an integrative approach to
their well-being. Research indicates patients are visiting
alternative providers and integrating their practices with
standard medical regimens.
   (Wellness Trends - The Hartman Group)

Learning how to go green and finding green service providers is one thing. Getting help from a specialist who is versed in green living is another. We've uncovered some entrepreneurial service providers who are aiming to help people go green in their homes, their lifestyles, and even in their personal career choices.

To be included, providers must have a primary focus on sustainable living. We didn't award leaves in this category because there aren't objective measurements we could use. But we encourage you to check references and give these groundbreakers a try.

BIG VISION CAREER AND PROJECT CONSULTING
Oakland 510-757-9684
By appt. www.brittbravo.com
Career coach and consultant with background in green and socially responsible business.

DON'T AGONIZE, ORGANIZE!
379 Ridge Rd. San Carlos 94070 650-367-6313
By appt. www.handymanda.blogspot.com
Green strategies for organizing and recycling. Custom storage units and shelving; closets from reclaimed doors.

GREEN CAREER TRACKS
150 Crane Drive San Anselmo 94960 612-822-0288
By appt. www.greencareertracks.com
Green career coaching; strategy, planning, skills assessment, resume development, market research, resources.

GREEN CAREERS
126 Highland Ln. Mill Valley 94941 415-389-9803
By appt. www.geocities.com/greencareers
Guidance and coaching for environmentally-focused careers.

GREEN CHI
P.O. Box 7656 Menlo Park 94026 650-368-5532
By appt.
Green feng-shui.

GREEN LIVING HOME
3969 Cowan Rd. Lafayette 94549 925-283-3190
By appt.
A holistic approach to a green lifestyle in your home and environment.

HEALING CUISINE
SF 415-381-1735
www.healingcuisine.com
Dietary consulting, classes, and cookbooks. Serves Marin and San Francisco.

HOMEGROWN WEDDINGS & EVENTS
SF 415-531-7793
By appt.
Sustainable events consultant and designer.

SILLAPERE
1661 Tennessee St. Suite 3D SF (Potrero Hill) 94107 415-553-7846
Mon-Fri 9-6 www.sillapere.com
Nationwide event design and production service. Emphasis on sustainability.

VIBRANT EVENTS
Piedmont 415-839-9665
By appt. www.vibrantevents.net
Wedding and special events planner incorporating local, organic, and socially responsible vendors.

DRY CLEANERS AND WET CLEANERS

Conventional dry cleaning almost always uses a toxic agent called *perchloroethylene* or *perc*. Perc is a chlorinated solvent that accumulates in body fat and has been listed by the International Agency for Research on Cancer as a possible human carcinogen. As a result, the California EPA has mandated that all dry cleaners in California switch to a new system. This is why you may have seen many dry cleaning establishments advertising "eco-friendly cleaning" or "organic dry cleaning." This signage may be misleading, however, so consider your choices carefully. Of the businesses that offer a non-perc option, most use hydrocarbon-based alternatives like DF-2000 and Green Earth. Although better than perc, these create smog-forming emissions so are not ideal.

Fortunately, there are two healthy and effective alternatives and we have uncovered them for you. They are better for the environment, safer for workers, and non-toxic for the customer. These alternatives are **wet cleaning** and **carbon dioxide (CO_2) cleaning.**

Only those cleaners that meet our strict requirement of offering wet cleaning or carbon dioxide cleaning exclusively qualify for a four-leaf award. Those that offer hydrocarbon cleaning in addition to wet or CO_2 cleaning qualify for a two-leaf award.

WET AND CO_2 CLEANERS

BLUE SKY CLEANERS
33366 Alvarado Niles Rd. Union City 94587 510-471-2333
Mon-Fri 8-6:30 Sat 9-3 www.blueskycleaners.com
Wet cleaning with environmentally-safe soaps; CO_2 dry cleaning. Pickup and delivery throughout the Bay Area.

BOB'S CLEANERS
777 23rd St. Richmond 94804 510-236-3471
Mon-Fri 8-6 Sat 9-5
Dedicated wet cleaners.

WET AND HYDROCARBON CLEANING (However, some also provide perc cleaning, so be sure to ask.)

ALEX'S CLEANERS
628 Lindaro St. San Rafael 94901 415-458-8180

CALIFORNIA OAK CLEANERS
4721 Geary Blvd. SF (Richmond District) 94118 415-386-6766

MEADER'S CLEANERS 🍃🍃
1877 Geary Blvd. SF (Japantown) 94115 415-922-3300
1515 North Point St. SF (Fisherman's Wharf) 94123 415-922-5790
2671 Ocean Ave. SF (West Portal) 94132 415-334-0400
1475 Sansome St. SF (Embarcadero) 94111 415-781-8200

NORGE CLEANERS 🍃🍃
398 San Pablo Ave. Albany 94706 510-526-3850

RICHARD'S DRY CLEANERS 🍃🍃
940 Old County Rd. Belmont 94002 650-591-4668

UNION FRENCH CLEANERS 🍃🍃
1718 Union St. SF (Cow Hollow) 94123 415-923-1212

VOGUE CLEANERS 🍃🍃
1530 Tiburon Blvd. Belvedere-Tiburon 94920 415-435-4545
425 Strawberry Village Shopping Ctr. Mill Valley 94941 415-388-5547
77 Miller Ave. Mill Valley 94941 415-388-3035

Our suggestions:

- Check to see if your garment can be washed by hand instead of having it professionally cleaned.

- Look for wet cleaning or CO_2 dry cleaning only. Other alternatives, although non-perc, contain a potentially toxic chemical called Siloxane D5. The manufacturing of Siloxane D5 involves chlorine. Dioxin, a waste product of chlorine, is currently one of the most toxic substances on the planet.

- If neither wet cleaning nor CO_2 dry cleaning is available in your area, and you are not highly chemically sensitive, then look for one of the non-perc, hydrocarbon-based cleaners.

- If something you have has been dry cleaned conventionally, remove it from its bag and hang it outdoors for two days to reduce the amount of perc vapor you bring into your home.

- No matter which cleaners you choose, try bringing your own reusable garment bag to reduce your use of plastic.

The products used by house cleaning services are generally not the same as those you might find in a supermarket. They are typically stronger and more concentrated, and potentially more toxic. When hiring a cleaning company, ask for a list of ingredients in all products and Material Safety Data Sheets.

Because professional cleaning products may be different from those found in stores, and because much depends upon the proper use of even non-toxic cleaning materials, it is difficult to establish firm criteria for granting leaf awards. But the companies listed here meet a minimum requirement of using natural or mostly chemical-free cleaning supplies.

At least 25% of the products used regularly by the following cleaning services are as close to 100% chemical-free as possible. Note, however, that many of the cleaning services listed below significantly out-performed this minimum requirement.

Material Safety Data Sheet (MSDS): *A compilation of information on a given product's chemicals, health and physical hazards, exposure limits, and necessary precautions for use.*

ECO-FRIENDLY CLEANING
5821 Santa Cruz Ave. Richmond 98404 510-527-8569
By appt. www.eco-friendly-cleaning.com
Residential and office cleaning. Uses environmentally safe cleaning products. Serves the East Bay.

ECO-SAFE CLEANING
P.O. Box 928 Berkeley 94701 510-845-1365
By appt.
Eco-friendly cleaning service. Serves the East Bay.

ELBOW-GREASE CLEANING
144 Highland Blvd. Kensington 94708 510-409-8885
By appt.
Non-toxic, biodegradable products. Alameda County certified green business. Serves the East Bay.

EMMA'S ECO-CLEAN
1155 Broadway St. Suite 110 Redwood City 94063 650-261-1788
By appt. Office hours Mon-Fri 8-4 www.wagescooperatives.org/emmas.html
Environmentally safe residential and commercial cleaning services. Serves the Peninsula and South Bay areas.

GREENWAY MAID
3053 Fillmore St. Suite 118 SF (Pacific Heights) 94123 415-673-3266
Mon-Fri 9-5 www.greenwaymaid.com
Worker-owned, eco-friendly home and office cleaning. Serves Peninsula and San Francisco.

HEALTHY CHOICE CARPET CLEANERS
58 West Portal Ave. SF (West Portal) 94127 415-681-5172
By appt. www.healthychoicecarpetcleaners.com
Flooring and air ducts cleaned with non-toxic, non-allergen products. Truck runs on biodiesel from vegetable oil. Serves San Francisco and North, South, and East Bays.

HOUSE SHINING

2569 Sheldon Dr. Richmond 94803 510-222-4475
By appt. www.houseshining.com
Homeopathic housecleaning. HEPA-filter vacuums and hypo-allergenic products. Serves the East Bay.

NATURAL CARE FOR CARPETS

5843 Bayview Ave. Richmond 94804 510-237-3777
By appt.
Non-toxic carpet and rug cleaning. Serves East Bay, San Francisco, and Marin.

NATURAL HOME CLEANING PROFESSIONALS

2647 International Blvd. Suite 200 Oakland 94601 510-532-6645
By appt. www.naturalhomecleaning.com
House cleaning service. Non- and less-toxic cleaning products; worker-owned cooperative. Serves areas from San Leandro to southern Richmond.

NATURAL WAY

1448 Cornell Ave. Berkeley 94702 510-524-6953
By appt.
Non-toxic, natural products. Serves the East Bay.

ORGANIC CHOICE CARPET CLEANING

1480 Drake Way San Pablo 94806 510-484-5634
By appt. www.organic-choice.com
Carpet, upholstery, and hardwood floor cleaning, restoration, maintenance. Earth-friendly techniques; residential and commercial services. Certified Green Business by Contra Costa County. Serves East Bay, San Francisco, and Marin.

OZ CLEANING COMPANY

P.O. Box 852 Fairfax 94978 510-758-7300
By appt. www.ozcleaningco.com
All non-toxic products. Serves Alameda, West Contra Costa, Marin, and Sonoma Counties.

SF EARTHLY HOUSEKEEPING

1902 Folsom St. SF (Mission) 94103 415-412-1135
By appt.
Residential and commercial cleaning. All organic and sustainable products. Serves the East Bay and San Francisco.

SUNCLEAN CARPET CARE

2021 San Antonio Ave. Unit C Alameda 94501 510-263-0321
By appt. www.suncleancarpetcare.com
Non-toxic carpet and upholstery cleaning. Serves the East Bay.

VERDE GREEN CLEANING

SF (Western Addition) 94115 415-561-9920
By appt. www.verdeclean.com
Eco-friendly cleaning service. Same cleaning team every visit. Serves San Francisco.

For more information on green cleaning, go to www.greencleaningnetwork.org.

Visit www.greenopia.com to share your findings and experiences with the businesses we've listed in the guide or any new ones you discover.

Conventional pest control operators typically use poison. As such, it's a good idea to look for alternative pest control services that use non-toxic or least-toxic methods, an approach referred to as Integrated Pest Management or IPM.

Despite what you might hear from mainstream providers, alternative, non-toxic pest control can be as effective as traditional methods, if not more so. Be very specific about how you want your home or garden treated.

Because we cannot truly measure the efficacy of the various alternative pest control methods, we have chosen not to assign leaf awards to these businesses. They do, however, meet our minimum requirement of using IPM techniques and offering non-toxic or less-toxic alternatives to traditional pest control practices.

Integrated Pest Management (IPM): *A pest management strategy that includes using traps to monitor infestations, using better sanitation practices and beneficial insects to control the identified pests, and applying pesticides so that they pose the least possible hazard, and are used only as a last resort when other control methods have failed.*

AAA ANIMAL REMOVAL
500 Laurel St. San Carlos 94070 650-594-1114
By appt.
Humane, chemical-free removal of raccoons, skunks, possums, and squirrels; pest proofing. Serves Peninsula and East Bay.

A-NON-TOXIC LIVE BEE REMOVAL
1115 Center St. Oakland (West Oakland) 94607 510-763-2009
By appt.
Non-toxic bee swarm and hive removal by professional beekeeper, operating out of a community garden. Serves San Francisco, East Bay, Peninsula, and Marin.

ASHFORD PEST CONTROL
181 Yachtsman Dr. Vallejo 94591 415-218-3002
By appt.
Pest control service providing monitoring, exclusion, sanitation, baits, and least toxic pesticides as a last resort. Serves San Francisco, San Mateo, Marin, Solano, Contra Costa, and Alameda counties.

BIO INTEGRAL RESOURCE CENTER
P.O. Box 7414 Berkeley 94707 510-524-2567
By appt. www.birc.org
Education and referral center for low- and non-toxic pest control. Publisher of two IPM journals: *IPM Practitioner* and *Common Sense Pest Control Quarterly*.

BIO-PEST
Petaluma 94952 800-246-7231
Mon-Fri 8-5 www.bio-pest.com
Organic, non-toxic pest control, elimination, exclusion, trapping and thermal treatment. All methods meet organic certification requirements. Serves Sonoma, Marin, and parts of Mendocino counties.

Sorting through Services

119

BZZ BEES

P.O. Box 2275 Berkeley 94702 510-395-3271
By appt.   www.bzzbees.com
Live honeybee removal. All-natural, non-toxic methods. Serves Oakland and San Francisco areas.

DONOVAN'S PEST CONTROL INC.

P.O. Box 6277 San Mateo 94403 650-365-1900
By appt. www.controlpests.com
Comprehensive pest control service including traditional and alternative services. Develops safest strategy after extensive investigation. Serves San Mateo, Santa Clara, Alameda, and San Francisco counties.

HUNGRY OWL PROJECT

Marin 415-454-4587
By appt. www.hungryowl.org
Sustainable pest management tools and education. Encourages natural predators through habitat conservation.

JOE'S WILDLIFE ANIMAL DAMAGE CONTROL

2508 Downer Ave. Richmond 94804 510-776-4068
By appt.
Live animal removal. Serves Marin and Contra Costa counties.

NATIONAL PESTICIDE TELECOMMUNICATIONS NETWORK

800-858-7378 www.nptn.orst.edu
A resource to call to speak directly to a toxicologist about pesticide questions, emergencies, and referrals.

PESTEC EXTERMINATOR COMPANY

4221 Mission St. SF (Mission) 94112 415-587-6817
By appt. www.pestec.com
Least-toxic pest management emphasizing prevention by pest-proofing buildings and residences, sealing entry-points, improving sanitation, exclusion devices and education. Serves greater San Francisco area.

SAN FRANCISCO DEPARTMENT OF THE ENVIRONMENT

11 Grove St. SF (Civic Center) 94102 415-355-3700
Mon-Fri 9-5 www.sfenvironment.org
A resource providing copies of SF IPM ordinances, approved pesticide list, and pest fact sheets.

Sorting through Services

We recommend that during the initial inspection of the infested area you ask for the brand and product names proposed for treatment. Then ask your provider if this is the least toxic choice you can make that will still be effective. If you can, do some research on the chemicals involved by checking the Pesticide Action Network's database at www.panna.org. Armed with this information, you can make the decisions that best meet your needs and match your comfort level.

Most people do not connect banking and finance with environmentalism but direct links can be made through investment and lending practices. For example, an investment firm may offer ways in which potential investors can screen companies on both financial and environmental criteria. These realms are not mutually exclusive. There are companies that respect the environment and are robust financial performers.

You have the right to know if a bank's lending practices require potential clients to meet certain environmental standards or if they are directly providing funding for green projects. Dig into your financial institution's fine print. Find out what your dollars are being used for.

There are financial institutions that are making a concerted effort toward making the world greener by ensuring that, for example, their larger-scale loaning practices support sustainable projects (through initiatives such as the Equator Principles), or that they offer clients the option of making socially-responsible investments (SRIs) or investments in green funds.

Listed below are firms that offer "green" banking options, socially-responsible investments with an environmental focus, and/or green funds. We expect the number of banking and finance institutions providing these services to continue to grow. We will continue to seek out new ones and add them to our list.

Equator Principles: *A financial industry benchmark for determining, assessing, and managing social and environmental risk in project financing. See www.equator-principles.com/principles.shtml for more information.*

AEGIS CAPITAL MANAGEMENT, INC. (MARJORIE A. BENNETT, CFA)
P.O. Box 99348 Emeryville 94662 510-655-9333
By appt. www.aegiscapital.com
Financial consulting and service management firm with socially responsible focus.

CALVERT SOCIAL INVESTMENT FOUNDATION
7 Elizabeth St. SF (Mission) 94110 415-824-2948
Mon-Fri 9-5 www.calvertfoundation.org
Community investments focused on creating jobs and affordable housing.

CAMBRIDGE INVESTMENT GROUP (LINDA JACOBS)
1510 Walnut St. Suite E Berkeley 94709 510-549-8777
Mon-Fri 9-5
Financial planning; SRI funds.

CATHEDRAL FINANCIAL GROUP, INC.
8080 Capwell Dr. Suite 202 Oakland (Oakland International Airport) 94621
510-638-6331
Mon-Fri 8:30-5 www.cathedralfinancial.com
Socially and environmentally responsible financial advisory practice focusing mainly on SRI funds.

CATHERINE WOODMAN, FINANCIAL ADVISOR (PROTECTED INVESTORS OF AMERICA)
900 Colusa Ave. Suite 201 Berkeley 94707 510-528-5823
By appt.   www.protectedinvestors.com
Sustainable, socially responsible investment planning and money management.

DAVID M. DOBKIN, CFP®, AIF®
1510 Walnut St. Suite E Berkeley 94709 510-549-8275
By appt.
Socially-concious financial planning.

EFFECTIVE ASSETS (LINCOLN PAYNE)
1510 Walnut St. Suite E Berkeley 94709 510-549-8780
Mon-Fri 9-5
SRI portfolio management, financial planning, investment consulting.

ESTATE CONSERVATION ASSOCIATES
P.O. Box 6881 San Rafael 94903 415-491-4762
By appt.   www.ecafinan.com
Socially and environmentally-responsible investing. Financial planning.

FORWARD FUNDS / SIERRA CLUB STOCK FUND
433 California St. SF (Financial District) 94104 415-869-6319
www.forwardfunds.com/perf-scflx.htm
Green mutual funds; Sierra Club approved.

GIRTON CAPITAL MANAGEMENT, INC.
7 La Rosa Way Larkspur 94939 415-927-4484
By appt.   www.girtoncapital.com
Socially and environmentally-responsible investment portfolio management group.

MORTGAGEGREEN
700 Larkspur Landing Circle Suite 275 Larkspur 94939 415-461-8080
www.mortgagegreen.com
Green real estate financing. Supports social and environmental causes.

NEW RESOURCE BANK
405 Howard St. Suite 110 SF (SOMA) 94105 415-995-8100
Mon-Fri 9-5   www.newresourcebank.com
Community-oriented, full-service bank focused on green and sustainable investments and lending to green businesses.

NORTH BERKELEY INVESTMENT PARTNERS
900 Colusa Ave. Suite 201 Berkeley 94707 510-528-5820
www.northberkeleyinvestment.com
Financial planning and investment services. SRI focus.

PARNASSUS INVESTMENTS
1 Market, Steuart Tower Suite 1600 SF (Financial District) 94105 415-778-0200
www.parnassus.com
Socially responsible investment firm.

PEOPLES COMMUNITY PARTNERSHIP FEDERAL CREDIT UNION
1432 Seventh St. Oakland (West Oakland) 94607 510-267-0450
Mon-Thu 11-5 Fri 11-6, 1st and 3rd Sat 9-1   www.pcpfcu.org
Community-development financial institution. Loans, financial education, savings accounts, certificates, CDs.

PRINCIPLED SOLUTIONS
865 El Camino Real Menlo Park 94025 650-462-1725
Mon-Thu 9-4 Fri 9-2   www.principledbucks.com
Financial and retirement planning; focuses on corporate responsibility, environmental sensitivity, and social justice.

PROGRESSIVE ASSET MANAGMENT (ERIC LEENSON)
520 Third St. Suite 204 Oakland (Lake Merritt/Downtown) 94607 510-622-0202
www.progressive-asset.com
Environmentally and socially-responsible investment services.

RBC DAIN RAUSCHER, SRI WEALTH MANAGEMENT GROUP (THOMAS VAN DYCK)
345 California St. 29th Floor SF (Financial District) 94104 415-445-8304
Mon-Fri 8-5
Social and environmental investment consulting and portfolio management.

RSF SOCIAL FINANCE
1002A O'Reilly Ave. SF (Presidio/Presidio Heights) 94129 415-561-3900
Mon-Fri 8-5 www.rsfsocialfinance.org
Provides innovative financial services committed to creating social benefit
and environmental sustainability.

SKBA CAPITAL MANAGEMENT
44 Montgomery St. Suite 3500 SF (Financial District) 94104 415-989-7852
Mon-Fri 6-5 www.skba.com
Investment advisory firm. Socially responsible value investing.

SOCIAL EQUITY GROUP, THE
2550 Ninth St. Suite 204A Berkeley 94710 510-644-9484
Mon-Fri 9-6 and by appt. www.socialequity.com
Investment advisory firm. Specializes in socially responsible investing.

TRILLIUM ASSET MANAGEMENT
369 Pine St. Suite 711 SF (Financial District) 94104 415-392-4806
Mon-Fri 6:30-5:30 www.trilliuminvest.com
Socially responsible investment firm.

VALENCIA GREEN
655 Montgomery St. Suite 540 SF (Financial District) 94111 415-644-9900 ext. 3
www.valenciagreensf.com
Financing for green building purchases.

VISION CAPITAL INVESTMENT MANAGEMENT
3450 Geary Blvd. Suite 203 SF (Richmond) 94118 415-731-7270
www.visioncapitalinvestment.com
Socially-responsible investment portfolio and management services.

WOMEN'S EQUITY FUND
12 Geary St. Suite 601 SF (Financial District) 94108 415-434-4495
Mon-Fri 8-4 www.womens-equity.com
SRI firm. Invests in companies that support women's issues and
environmental sustainability.

YOUR MONEY & YOUR LIFE (JAMES FRAZIN, CFP®, AIF®)
P.O. Box 78261 SF 94107 415-337-4566
Fee-only financial planning. Specializes in middle-income and LGBT families.

"The cost of a thing is the amount of what I will call life
which is required to be exchanged for it, immediately or in
the long run."
— Henry David Thoreau

In addition to turning our green lens toward the world of banks, we have started to compile a list of real estate agencies and agents who help buyers and sellers find and sell green, sustainably designed homes. It is becoming more common for real estate agents to obtain training in the features of eco-friendly properties. For instance, Ecobroker offers on-line courses for brokers to earn a green certification (www.ecobroker.com). Ask at your favorite real estate office if they have a green certified agent.

Real estate agencies and providers who help buyers and sellers find and sell green, sustainably designed homes are identified below.

AT HOME IN MARIN
1601 Second St. Suite 100 San Rafael 94901 415-451-8111
Mon-Fri 8-5 www.athomeinmarin.com
Residential real estate service focused on green homes in the San Francisco Bay Area.

ECOLOGY HOUSE
375 Catalina Blvd. San Rafael 94901 415-456-4453
Please call for visitors' schedule. No drop-ins.
Environmentally sensitive apartment building; HUD funded. Eleven-unit apartment development designed for persons with environmental illness/multiple chemical sensitivities (MCS).

GREEN KEY REAL ESTATE
SF 415-750-1120 Marin 415-999-6363
By appt. www.greenkeyrealestate.com
Green realtors specializing in sustainably designed properties.

GREENER MARIN AT KELLER WILLIAMS SAN FRANCISCO
P.O. Box 580 Forest Knolls 94933 415-259-7082
By appt. www.greenermarin.com
Eco-friendly brokerage using green products and service providers to reduce energy usage and recycle consumer waste.

MORTGAGEGREEN
700 Larkspur Landing Circle Suite 275 Larkspur 94939 415-461-8080
www.mortgagegreen.com
Green real estate financing and investments. Supports social and environmental causes.

MY MARIN HOMES/LINDA TULL
189 Sir Francis Drake Blvd. Greenbrae 94904 415-233-0125
By appt. www.mymarinhomes.com
Marin-focused green real estate agent.

Sorting through Services

Unplug chargers (for cell phones and iPods and other such devices) when not in use. Only 5% of the power drawn by a cell phone charger is used to charge the phone. The other 95% is wasted when it is left plugged into the wall.

No, there is nothing particular in the telecommunications industry that makes it more or less green, except for how the companies choose to allocate their profits. Just as you choose where to make charitable donations, so too do phone and internet service providers. Since they all offer substantially the same services, why not support a company that puts your money to work for the environment?

Because this isn't an appropriate area in which to award leaves, we offer these businesses as a reference only. But we thought you might want to help support those organizations that are, in turn, helping support the planet. The telecommunications companies listed below have chosen to donate a significant part of their profits or a percentage of your purchases to environmental causes.

Note: In some cases, these companies identify their donations as a percentage of total revenue, in other cases as a percentage of profit so the amounts donated will vary considerably. Look carefully when comparing plans and companies.

BETTER WORLD TELECOM
11951 Freedom Dr. 13th Floor Reston VA 20190 866-567-2273
Mon-Fri 9-5 (EST) www.betterworldtelecom.com
Nationwide voice and data service provider. Donates 3 percent of revenue to educational and environmental organizations.

COME FROM THE HEART
798 Verdun St. Clarksburg WV 26301 888-622-0957
www.comefromtheheart.com
Discounted long distance telephone and internet service. Donates a portion of revenue to environmental and other non-profit organizations.

EARTH TONES
1107 Ninth St. Suite 601 Sacramento 95814 888-327-8486
www.earthtones.com
Long distance, wireless phone and internet services. Donates 100% of profits to grassroots environmental organizations.

MAKANA TECHNOLOGIES
1202 Plaza del Monte Santa Barbara 93101 808-573-6702
www.makanatechnologies.com
Voice and data service provider. Donates a portion of purchases to charitable organization of the customer's choice.

RED JELLYFISH
P.O. Box 1570 Mountain View 94042 888-222-5008
www.redjellyfish.com
Internet service, cell phone recycling, e-cards. Donates 8 percent of profits to environmental organizations.

WORKING ASSETS
101 Market St. Suite 700 SF (Financial District) 94105 800-668-9253
www.workingassets.com
Wireless, long distance, and credit card services. A portion of customer charges are donated to nonprofit groups, at no extra cost.

Sorting through Services

There are more burial and cremation options than most people are aware of. With cremation, ashes can be buried, spread over a chosen area, preserved in an urn, or used to create eternal ocean reefs. Similarly, there are a variety of burial options for uncremated remains, including ones that are more sustainable than traditional practices.

For example, one form of green burial entails placing a body in a grave in either a shroud or a biodegradable wooden box. (Conversely, an embalmed body goes into the ground with toxic formaldehyde and mercuric chloride in it.) Very few burial services promote themselves as green; however, some religious traditions require burial techniques that happen to be environmentally friendly. For example, traditional Jewish burials require the unembalmed, shrouded body to be simply buried in the ground.

Because there have been very few advertised "green burials" to date, there is no clear way to create criteria upon which to base a leaf award. The centers listed here, however, all have a conservation area where remains are buried in a way that is ecologically-sound and sustainable. Also, they offer non-toxic embalming fluids and burial in a simple shroud, often made from cotton or hemp.

A FAMILY FAREWELL
P.O. Box 2726 El Granada 94018 650-726-5255
Mon-Fri 8-6
Helps families understand green burials, how to care for loved ones themselves, and to organize their final resting place.

COLORFUL COFFINS
P.O. Box 2726 El Granada 94018 650-726-5255
Mon-Fri 8-6 Emergency Hours 6 p.m.-11 p.m.
Offers biodegradable coffins, green burial, and home funerals.

ETERNAL REEFS INC.
P.O. Box 2473 Decatur GA 30031 888-423-7333
www.eternalreefs.com
Concrete reefs made from cremated remains; used to create new marine habitats.

FERNWOOD CEMETERY
301 Tennessee Valley Rd. Mill Valley 94941 415-383-7100
Mon-Fri 8:30-5 Sat 10-4 www.foreverfernwood.com
Cremation service, no embalming; biodegradable caskets and shrouds; natural rocks, plants, and trees as grave markers.

LIFEGEM
836 Arlington Heights Rd. Suite 311 Elk Grove Village IL 60007 866-543-3436
www.lifegem.com
Diamond tribute made from pressurized cremated remains.

Sorting through Services

NEPTUNE SOCIETY OF NORTHERN CALIFORNIA, THE

One Loraine Ct. SF 94118 415-771-0717
Cremated remains will be returned to the family or scattered at sea.

SEA-URN

523 Route 112 Port Jefferson Station NY 11776 800-727-1875
Water burial service. Biodegradable interment vessels made from sea salt.

We've done our best to establish how green the providers are for the services we've identified. Now, we would like your feedback: How was your experience? How effective was the service? Was the price right? Was the provider on time and available when you needed her/him? How was the customer service? Would you recommend them to a friend or use them again? Share your findings and experiences at www.greenopia.com.

Greening Your Space

Building in Sustainability

This is a unique and critical moment in human history. From consumers to corporations, all are taking on the mantle of environmental responsibility. Our global media have interconnected us such that we understand how the actions in one part of the world affect those in other parts. We now accept the Earth as a single and precious entity. At last, human beings realize the negative impact of our behavior. Though we may not have all of the answers as to how we will fix them, the problems we are facing are not insurmountable and we are finding the will to address them.

In the last few years, we environmentalists learned how to adapt. Rather than change others, we changed ourselves. We learned to speak the language of sustainability and this has made all of the difference. We now speak of solar panels as an "investment," of healthy materials as "best practices," and of energy efficiency as a "bottom line benefit." Following this example, the world took notice and green building reached the tipping point we all knew would be inevitable.

Architecture, as an industry, has a bigger environmental impact than any other. Buildings of the world consume 40% of the Earth's energy and materials. Although cars produce 30% of the carbon emissions in our air, buildings beat that with a whopping 45%. So you see, architects, engineers, contractors, and developers are in a position to affect great change. This is why you see such movement in green building; we are to blame!

Now that we understand this reality, we can affect it. In the future, this period will be regarded as the most exciting time in human history. Each day, new materials are being introduced, advancements in energy technologies are being funded, and people are asking the important questions: "Where did this come from?" and "How healthy is it?" Your role in all this is critical. Thank you for taking this all-important step to move us all towards this inevitable and sustainable future.

Greening
Your Space

ERIC COREY FREED

Eric Corey Freed founded organicARCHITECT in 1997 as an alternative to traditional design practice. organicARCHITECT unites high end design and environmental responsibility toward a future where all buildings will be green.

What you choose to buy for your home has a direct effect on both your personal health and the health of the planet. Many conventional pieces of furniture use formaldehyde as a binder, are coated with toxic finishes, use synthetic fillers, and can off-gas harmful chemicals. But there are a growing number of alternatives available that are more sustainably produced.

To avoid chemicals from new materials and save money, shop at unfinished wood furniture stores and finish the items with plant-based, natural finishes. Look for wood products that have the Forest Stewardship Council (FSC) seal indicating they come from sustainably managed forests. Consider buying used furniture items but avoid all pieces containing vinyl (PVC) and polyurethane foam, and pieces that may contain lead-based paint.

Wall-to-wall carpeting may look and feel pretty but the nylon variety is made from a chemical stew that takes a long time to fully off-gas. This can cause irritation to babies, children, and anyone who is chemically sensitive. When possible, look for all-wool carpeting with natural fiber backing made of jute or latex.

Check into other flooring alternatives too—recycled-content tile, cork, sustainably harvested wood, real linoleum, and area rugs made with natural materials. Many companies offer alternatives to standard fibers: jute, sisal, bamboo, and seagrass are among the most common.

The stores listed here are evaluated based on the percentage of furniture, flooring, carpeting, and/or décor sold that is sustainably made.

> at least 25% of products sold are manufactured in a sustainable way.
>
> at least 50% of products sold are manufactured in a sustainable way.
>
> at least 75% of products sold are manufactured in a sustainable way.
>
> 90% or more of products sold are manufactured in a sustainable way.

Forest Stewardship Council (FSC): *An international network promoting responsible management of the world's forests. Through consultative processes, it sets international standards for responsible forest management. The FSC label provides assurance to the consumer that the wood has been sustainably harvested.*

ABBEY CARPET 🌿

2750 Junipero Serra Daly City 94015 650-755-9915
10351 San Pablo Ave. El Cerrito 94530 510-527-4262
905 El Camino Real Menlo Park 94025 650-462-0800
990 Industrial Rd. San Carlos 94070 650-593-0631
3301 Geary Blvd. SF (Western Addition) 94118 415-752-6620
563 Harlan St. San Leandro 94577 510-352-4450
One North Amphlett Blvd. Suite F San Mateo 94401 650-347-0800
822 Francisco Blvd. West San Rafael 94901 415-456-3656
Hours vary by location www.abbeycarpet.com
National carpet and flooring company; wool, hemp, sisal.

AMBER FLOORING 🌿🌿🌿

409 Sycamore Valley Rd. Danville 94526 925-820-5110
5652 San Pablo Ave. Emeryville 94608 510-486-1750
Hours vary by location www.amberflooring.com
Wood flooring dealer; custom design and installation; EcoTimber
and sustainable woods; hardwood sanding and dust containment.

BLACK'S FARMWOOD 🌿🌿🌿🌿

P.O. Box 2836 San Rafael 94912 877-321-9663
By appt. Mon-Fri 9-5
Reclaimed wood: redwood, hand-hewn barn beams, barn siding,
wide plank flooring.

CERAMIC TILE DESIGN 🌿

189 13th St. SF (SOMA) 94103 415-575-3785
846 West Francisco Blvd. San Rafael 94901 415-485-5180
Hours vary by location www.ceramictiledesign.net
Sustainable tile and counter materials in recycled glass, metal, wood,
and more. USGBC Member.

EARTHSOURCE FOREST PRODUCTS 🌿🌿🌿🌿

1618 28th St. Oakland (West Oakland) 94608 510-208-7257
2035 Newcomb Ave. SF (Bayview/Hunter's Point) 94124 415-648-7257
Mon-Fri 8-4:30 Sat 8-2 www.earthsourcewood.com
Sustainably harvested and reclaimed wood products; FSC certified.
New garden furniture line.

ECO DESIGN RESOURCES 🌿🌿🌿🌿

633 Quarry Rd. Suite A San Carlos 94070 650-591-1123
Mon-Fri 10-5 Sat 11-4 www.ecodesignresources.com
Green residential design services; building materials including area rugs,
carpeting, cork, bamboo, and reclaimed woods.

ECO TIMBER 🌿🌿🌿🌿

1611 Fourth St. San Rafael 94901 415-258-8454
Mon-Fri 9-5 www.ecotimber.com
Sustainably harvested and reclaimed wood flooring; non-toxic glues for
manufacturing and installation; green internal business practices; FSC certified.

ECOHOME IMPROVEMENT 🌿🌿🌿🌿

2619 San Pablo Ave. Berkeley 94702 510-644-3500
Tue-Fri 10-6 Sat 9-4 Sun 11-4 www.ecohomeimprovement.com
Eco-friendly flooring including certified wood, bamboo, cork, linoleum,
natural wool, terrazzo, and eco tiles.

ECO-TERRIC 🌿🌿🌿🌿

1401 16th St. 2nd Floor SF (Potrero Hill) 94103 415-558-8700
Mon-Fri 9-5 Sat 10-4 www.eco-terric.com
Green and healthy home furnishings. Also offers design and
consultation services.

FINDECOR 🌿

258 Noe St. SF (Castro) 94114 415-437-6789
Tue-Fri 12-7 Sat 11-7 Sun 11-6 www.findecor.com
Recycled and reclaimed furniture, home décor, lighting; resin products.

FLOORING ALTERNATIVES 🌿🌿🌿

758 Gilman St. Berkeley 94710 877-639-1345
Mon, Wed, Fri-Sat 10-4 Tue, Thu 10-6 www.flooringalternatives.com
Flooring supplier; bamboo, cork, reclaimed and FSC certified sustainable
hardwoods; natural linoleum.

GREEN FUSION DESIGN CENTER 🌿🌿🌿🌿

20 Greenfield Ave. San Anselmo 94960 415-454-0174
Mon-Sat 10-6 Sun by appt. www.greenfusiondesigncenter.com
Sustainable design. Structures, bedding, home décor, gardening, and
landscaping; consultation and education.

GREENSAGE 🌿🌿🌿🌿

P.O. Box 460753 SF (Civic Center) 94146 415-453-7915
Mon-Fri 9-5 www.greensage.com
Green design, consulting and products since 1988. Total focus is on sustainable
and environmentally healthy products and home.

HABITATS (FORMERLY ASIANTIQUES) 🌿🌿🌿

Store: 801 Delaware St. Berkeley 94710 510-540-5440
Warehouse/Open to Public: 1036 Ashby Ave. Berkeley 94710 510-540-5440
Daily 11-6 www.asiantiqueweb.com
Specializes in handcrafted furniture and décor from reclaimed and sustainable
woods. Asian antique dealer.

HIGH COTTON LIVING 🌿

1820 Solano Ave. Berkeley 94707 510-526-4770
Mon-Sat 10-6 www.highcottonliving.com
Luxury bedding, bath, and home furnishings.

HOOT JUDKINS 🌿🌿🌿

1400 El Camino Real San Bruno 94066 650-952-5600
1269 Veterans Blvd. Redwood City 94063 650-367-8181
Mon-Fri 9-6 Sat 9-5 Sun 11-5 www.hootjudkins.com
Finished and unfinished wood furniture; beeswax, milk paint, oils. Custom wood
finishing and delivery service.

LUXANT 🌿

416 Ninth St. SF (SOMA) 94103 415-863-1098
11 37th Ave. San Mateo 94403 650-573-1098
Daily 10-6 www.luxantusa.com
Home furniture and décor; pre-owned; refurbished; plantation wood.

MADERA 🌿🌿🌿🌿

1587 Sir Francis Drake Blvd. Fairfax 94930 415-516-3567
Daily 9-5
Recycled wood furniture using non-toxic finishes. Cabinetry, indoor and outdoor
furniture.

MAISON REVE 🌿🌿

11 Throckmorton Ave. Mill Valley 94941 415-383-9700
Mon-Sat 10-6 Sun 11-5 www.maisonreve.com
Home and garden store offering interior decorator services, garden design,
container parties, wish list shopping, workshops, and bridal registry.

MARIN OUTDOOR LIVING 🌿🌿

2100 Redwood Hwy. Greenbrae 94904 415-924-8811
Mon-Fri 10-6 Sat 10-5 Sun 11-4 www.marinoutdoorliving.com
Retail store and design services; chlorine-free hot tub systems; non-toxic and
non-wood fiber furniture; eco-smart fuel.

MILL VALLEY BAMBOO ✐✐✐✐
14 East Sir Francis Drake Blvd. Larkspur 94939 415-925-1188
101 Roblar Dr. Novato 94949 415-883-6888
Hours vary by location www.mvbamboo.com
Certified sustainably harvested bamboo flooring products, installation
and maintenance. Customers can choose from a range of patterns and
customized styles.

PROPELLER ✐✐
555 Hayes St. SF (Civic Center) 94102 415-701-7767
Mon-Sat 11-7 Sun 12-5 www.propellermodern.com
Modern furniture using environmentally friendly materials.

RUBY LIVINGDESIGN ✐✐✐
180 Townsend St. SF (SOMA) 94107 415-541-9206
Mon-Fri 10-6:30 Sat 10-6 Sun 12-5 www.rubyliving.com
High-end home furniture; emphasis on natural and recycled material;
organic fiber bedding and beds.

SKYSIDE STUDIOS ✐✐✐✐
Bldg. 20C Pimentel Ct. Suite 8 Novato 94949 415-883-9455
Mon-Fri 9-5 www.skysidestudios.com
Sustainable cabinetry using the latest in technology, materials, and
environmentally friendly processes.

SMITH & HAWKEN ✐✐
1330 10th St. Berkeley 94710 510-527-1076
1208 Donnelly Ave. Burlingame 94010 650-558-0052
800 Redwood Hwy. Strawberry Village Shopping Ctr. Mill Valley 94941
415-381-1800
705 Stanford Center Palo Alto 94304 650-321-0403
2040 Fillmore St. SF (Pacific Heights) 94115 415-776-3424
Hours vary by location www.smithandhawken.com
Natural and organic gardening supplies; sustainable home and garden décor;
outdoor solar lighting.

TOUCH, THE ✐
956 Valencia St. SF (Mission) 94110 415-550-2640
Mon-Sat 11-6 Sun 2-6
Recycled, refurbished vintage furniture.

WOODEN DUCK, THE ✐✐
2919 Seventh St. Berkeley 94710 510-848-3575
Mon-Sat 10-6 Sun 12-5 www.thewoodenduck.com
Restored, recycled wood furniture.

Greening
Your Space

About that new carpet smell… and the smell of fresh
paint. That smell indicates the presence of VOCs,
volatile organic compounds. VOCs are emitted as gases
from certain solids or liquids. VOCs include a variety of
chemicals, some which may have short- and long-term
adverse health effects. VOCs are especially hazardous
indoors where concentrations may be up to ten times
higher than outdoors. Look for natural products and finishes
to avoid exposure to these dangerous chemicals.

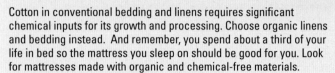

BEDS, BEDDING, AND LINENS

Cotton in conventional bedding and linens requires significant chemical inputs for its growth and processing. Choose organic linens and bedding instead. And remember, you spend about a third of your life in bed so the mattress you sleep on should be good for you. Look for mattresses made with organic and chemical-free materials.

Businesses that offer bedding and linens are evaluated based on the percentage of products sold that are characterized by one or more of the following:

• produced with non-toxic or low-toxic materials;

• made with renewable, natural, organic or recycled materials;

• are sustainably manufactured;

• are locally produced with sustainable materials.

If the establishment sells mattresses, to be included in the guide, all mattress stock must be made with 100% certified organic and chemical-free materials.

---

     at least 25% of products meet the above criteria.

     at least 50% of products meet the above criteria.

     at least 75% of products meet the above criteria.

     90% or more of products meet the above criteria.

A HAPPY PLANET
4501 Irving St. SF (Sunset) 94122 415-753-8300
Wed-Sun 12-6 and by appt. www.ahappyplanet.com
Organic bedding, beds, frames, mattresses, linens, non-toxic wood furniture, hemp bath sheets, home products, and onesies.

DOWN ETC...
228 Townsend St. SF (SOMA) 94107 415-348-0084
Mon-Fri 9-6 www.downetc.com
Feather and down sleeping pillows, comforters, and duvets.

EARTHSAKE
1772 Fourth St. Berkeley 94710 510-559-8440
Mon-Thu 10-6 Fri-Sat 10-7 Sun 11-6 www.earthsake.com
Natural bedding, body care, and yoga products.

EUROPEAN SLEEPWORKS
2966 Adeline St. Berkeley 94703 510-841-5340
Mon-Sat 10-6 Sun 12-5 www.sleepworks.com
European-style, latex-core and wood-slat mattresses. Pillows, bedding, and furniture.

FOAM STORE OF MARIN, THE
813 A St. San Rafael 94901 415-453-3626
Mon-Fri 11-6 Sat 10-5 www.myfoam.com
Sustainable upholstery and eco-friendly latex mattresses. Retail store with online presence as well.

Greening Your Space

FOAMORDER.COM ✿✿

1325 Howard St. SF (SOMA) 94103 415-503-1188
Mon-Fri 10-6 Sat 10-5 Sun 11-5 www.foamorder.com
Sustainable upholstery and eco-friendly latex mattresses. Retail store with
online presence as well.

GREEN FUSION DESIGN CENTER ✿✿✿✿

20 Greenfield Ave. San Anselmo 94960 415-454-0174
Mon-Sat 10-6 and by appt. www.greenfusiondesigncenter.com
Complete sustainable design resource for structures, interiors, bedding,
home décor, gardening, landscaping; consultation, and education.

MATSU BEDDING ✿✿✿✿

1350A Park St. Alameda 94501 510-337-9923
1519 Solano Ave. Berkeley 94707 510-525-7873
1435 Fourth St. Suite B San Rafael 94901 415-482-6699
Hours vary by location www.matsu-store.com
Japanese-style bedding.

MURASAKI ✿

6050 College Ave. Oakland (College Ave.) 94618 510-547-6252
Mon-Sat 10:30-6:30 Sun 11-6 www.murasaki-oakland.com
Futon shop; bedding, gifts, home décor.

RUBY LIVINGDESIGN ✿✿✿

180 Townsend St. SF (SOMA) 94107 415-541-9206
Mon-Fri 10-6:30 Sat 10-6 Sun 12-5 www.rubyliving.com
High-end home furniture; emphasis on natural and recycled material;
organic fiber bedding and beds.

SPRING ✿✿✿✿

2162 Polk St. SF (Russion Hill) 94109 415-673-2065
Mon 11-5 Tue-Sat 10:30-7 Sun 11-5 www.astorecalledspring.com
Organic bedding and mattresses; many other eco-friendly products
for the home.

NURSERIES AND GARDEN SUPPLIES

When doing your gardening and yard work, check out the nurseries
that offer organic options. Choosing organic plants, seeds and
starts, soil, potting mixes, fertilizers, and pest control products will
promote better stewardship of the land and create a healthier home
environment for you.

At least 25% of plant inventory must be grown organically to qualify a
particular nursery for listing. For garden supplies, at least 25% of the
products carried must be chemical-free or non-toxic.

BERKELEY HORTICULTURAL NURSERY
1310 McGee Ave. Berkeley 94703 510-526-4704
Mon-Wed, Fri-Sun 8:30-5 www.berkeleyhort.com
Independent nursery; organic vegetables and edibles; non-toxic
pest management.

COMMON GROUND ORGANIC GARDEN SUPPLY
AND EDUCATION CENTER
559 College Ave. Palo Alto 94306 650-493-6072
Tue-Fri 10-5:30 Sat-Sun 10-5 www.commongroundinpaloalto.org
Non-profit, organic gardening education center and supply;
natural pest control.

FLORA GRUBB GARDENS
1074 Guerrero St. SF (Mission) 94110 415-648-2670
Mon-Sat 9-5 Sun 10-5 www.floragrubb.com
Nursery specializing in exotics, tropicals, palms, garden furnishings, and
organic soils. All edibles are organic. Also provides non-toxic
garden design services. New location will open in Third
Street Corridor of Bayview Spring 2007.

FRIENDS OF THE REGIONAL PARKS BOTANIC GARDEN
Tilden Regional Park Berkeley 94708 510-841-8732
Thu 9-11 a.m., April to December www.nativeplants.org
Sells only California native plants, some rare and endangered, that are
not usually grown horticulturally.

GARDEN SHED, THE
1136 El Camino Real San Carlos 94070 650-508-8600
Mon-Fri 11-7 Sat-Sun 12-5 www.thegardenshed.org
Organic greenhouse and gardening supplies.

GARDEN SHOP AT UC BERKELEY BOTANICAL GARDEN
200 Centennial Dr. Suite 5045 Berkeley 94720 510-642-3343
Daily 10:30-4:30 Closed first Tue each month www.botanicalgarden.berkeley.edu
Sales of plants propagated at UC Berkeley Botanical Garden.
Botanically-inspired gifts, cards, jewelry, and pottery.

GREEN JEANS GARDEN SUPPLY
690 Redwood Hwy. Mill Valley 94941 415-389-8333
Mon-Sat 9-5:30 Sun 10-5 (seasonal hours)
Organic edibles, vegetables, and perennials; non-toxic pest management, soil
amendments, bulk organic fertilizer.

MAGIC GARDENS LANDSCAPE NURSERY
729 Heinz Ave. Berkeley 94710 510-644-2351
Tue-Fri 9-4:30 Sat 9-5 www.magicgardens.com
Organic plants, starts, and soils; educational and hands-on classes.

NATIVE HERE NURSERY
101 Golf Course Dr. Tilden Park Berkeley 94708 510-549-0211
Fri 9-12 Sat 10-1 www.ebcnps.org/nativeherehome.htm
Custom grown plants native to Contra Costa and Alameda Counties. Volunteers
are welcome to help with seed collecting, sowing, watering, potting, sales,
maintenance, and more. A project of California Native Plant Society.

O'DONNELL'S ORGANIC NURSERY & HABITAT RESTORATION
1700 Sir Francis Drake Blvd. Fairfax 94930 415-453-0372
Daily 9-5:30
Fully organic nursery; gardening, landscaping, habitat consultations;
native plants.

SLOAT GARDEN CENTER
700 Sir Francis Drake Blvd. Kentfield 94904 415-454-0262
657 East Blithedale Ave. Mill Valley 94941 415-388-0102
401 Miller Ave. Mill Valley 94941 415-388-0365
2000 Novato Blvd. Novato 94947 415-897-2169
675 El Camino Real San Bruno 94066 650-869-6000
3237 Pierce St. SF (Marina) 94123 415-440-1000
327 Third Ave. SF (Richmond) 94118 415-752-1614
1580 Lincoln Ave. San Rafael 94901 415-453-3977
2700 Sloat Blvd. SF (Sunset) 94116 415-566-4415
Daily 8:30-5:30 www.sloatgardens.com
Expansive garden supply with certified organic amendments, plant starts,
low-spray and locally produced ornamentals. Educational programs
related to gardening, soil, water, and insect management also available.

SMITH & HAWKEN
1330 10th St. Berkeley 94710 510-527-1076
1208 Donnelly Ave. Burlingame 94010 650-558-0052
800 Redwood Hwy. Strawberry Village Shopping Ctr. Mill Valley 94941
415-381-1800
705 Stanford Center Palo Alto 94304 650-321-0403
2040 Fillmore St. SF (Pacific Heights) 94115 415-776-3424
Hours vary by location www.smithandhawken.com
Natural and organic gardening supplies; sustainable home and garden
decor; outdoor solar lighting.

SUBURBAN HABITAT
866 Grant Ave. Novato 94945 415-898-7678
Mon-Sat 10-5:30 Sun 11-2 www.suburbanhabitat.com
Healthy backyard ecosystems; native plants, organic fertilizers and starts;
beneficial insects.

URBAN FARMER STORE, THE
653 East Blithedale Ave. Mill Valley 94941 415-380-3840
2121 San Joaquin St. Richmond 94804 510-524-1604
2833 Vicente St. SF (Sunset) 94116 415-661-2204
Hours vary by location www.urbanfarmerstore.com
Drip irrigation systems and organic fertilizers; free classes.

URBAN FOREST HOME
1880 Solano Ave. Berkeley 94707 510-525-2500
Tue-Thu 11-6 Fri 11-8 Sat 10-8 Sun 12-6 www.urbanforest.com
Fresh, preserved, and artificial flowers, plants, trees; eco-friendly home
decor and gifts.

WESTBRAE NURSERY
1272 Gilman St. Albany 94706 510-526-7606
Mon-Sat 8:30-5 Sun 9-4:30 www.westbraegarden.com
Organic herbs, vegetables, edibles.

WILDHEART GARDENS
2135 East 28th St. Oakland (East Oakland) 94606 510-368-2811
By appt. www.wildheartgardens.com
Edible, medicinal, native, and drought-resistant plants; fruit and nut trees.

YABUSAKI'S DWIGHT WAY NURSERY
1001 Dwight Way Berkeley 94710 510-845-6261
Mon-Wed, Fri-Sat 9-5 Sun 9-4
Family-owned, independent nursery. Bonsai, Japanese maple trees,
bamboo, perennial plants, and flowers.

YERBA BUENA CALIFORNIA NATIVE PLANT NURSERY
19500 Skyline Blvd. Woodside 94062 650-851-1668
Tue-Sat 9-5 www.yerbabuenanursery.com
Organic native plants; garden consultation and design;
demonstration gardens.

Tired of mowing that lawn? Does your water bill make you
see red instead of green? Maybe it's time for xeriscaping,
an environmentally-conscious form of landscaping that
uses indigenous and drought-tolerant plants, drip
irrigation systems, and mulch to conserve as much water
as possible.

Still hungry for change? Why not apply the principles of
permaculture to your yard? Permaculture adopts methods
and practices from ecology, appropriate technology,
and sustainable agriculture providing the techniques to
establish productive environments to supply food, energy,
shelter, and other material and non-material needs.

GARDENING AND LANDSCAPING

Well-planned landscaping can conserve water, attract and protect
wildlife, keep your house cooler in summer, save you money, and even
feed you! And land that is cared for naturally feels better and can
actually take less maintenance in the long run. In contrast, a yard that
is maintained with pesticides and other chemicals can pose a threat to
your family and pets, while artificially keeping plants alive with
soil-depleting chemical fertilizers.

Our list consists of garden designers, landscape architects, and arborists
whose main or sole purpose is creating environmentally-friendly
gardens, planting and maintaining native and drought-tolerant species,
using Integrated Pest Management (IPM) techniques, and/or designing
water conservation or reclamation systems into garden plans.

To be listed, at least 25% of time and/or projects in a given year must
be devoted to environmentally-sound landscaping and gardening
practices. Note that some of these businesses may also be LEED
(Leadership in Energy and Environmental Design) accredited.

ALLEN LAND DESIGN
1478 Olivet Rd. Santa Rosa 95401 707-526-3177
Mon-Fri 8-5 www.allenlanddesign.com
Master planning, hardscape and landscape design; specializes in olive
grove installation. On-site organic olive nursery; olive oils.

EQUINOX LANDSCAPE CONSTRUCTION CORPS
1811 Grand Ave. Suite B San Rafael 94901 415-456-6480
By appt. www.equinox-landscape.com
Landscape design, installation and maintenance of organic gardens,
permaculture plantings, irrigation, water features, building. Serves Marin
and Sonoma counties.

FLORA GRUBB GARDENS
1074 Guerrero St. SF (Mission) 94110 415-648-2670
Mon-Sat 9-5 Sun 10-5 www.floragrubbgardens.com
Unique, non-toxic landscaping and garden design using plants from
their nursery.

GARDENER'S GUILD
2143 East Francisco Blvd. San Rafael 94901 415-457-0400
Mon-Fri 7-5 www.gardenersguild.com
Garden design, installation, and maintenance; integrated pest
management, interior, and exterior plant care.

GREEN FUSION DESIGN CENTER
20 Greenfield Ave. San Anselmo 94960 415-454-0174
Mon-Sat 10-6 Sun by appt. www.greenfusiondesigncenter.com
Complete sustainable design resource; structures, interiors, decor,
gardening, landscaping; consultation and education.

JENNIFER HALL
40 Merrill St. SF (Bernal Heights) 94134 415-305-1589
Mon-Fri 9-5 www.jenniferhallgardens.com
Gardening and landscape design, installation, and maintenance;
English-style perennial and natural landscaping. Serves San Francisco.

MAGIC GARDENS LANDSCAPE NURSERY
729 Heinz Ave. Berkeley 94710 510-644-2351
Tue-Fri 9-4:30 Sat 9-5 www.magicgardens.com
Unique gardens from consultation to implementation. Lush plantings,
custom stonework. Serves East Bay and Marin.

O'DONNELL'S ORGANIC NURSERY & HABITAT RESTORATION
1700 Sir Francis Drake Blvd. Fairfax 94930 415-453-0372
Daily 9-5:30
Sustainable landscaping. On-site analysis to identify natives and
competitive non-natives.

SECOND NATURE DESIGN
SF (Glen Park) 94131 415-586-6578
Mon-Fri 9-5 and by appt.
Restores native plant communities; reuses building materials.

SLOAT GARDEN CENTER, CUSTOM GARDEN DESIGN
401 Miller Ave. Mill Valley 94941 415-388-3754
Daily 9-5 www.sloatgardens.com
Located within the Sloat Garden Center, expert consultants provide
landscape and garden design, as well as educational programs related
to gardening, soil, water, and insect management.

SUBURBAN HABITAT
866 Grant Ave. Novato 94945 415-898-7678
Mon-Sat 10-5:30 Sun 11-2 www.suburbanhabitat.com
Healthy backyard ecosystems: native plants, organic fertilizers and starts,
beneficial insects.

WILDHEART GARDENS
2135 28th St. Oakland (Lake Merritt/Downtown) 94606 510-368-2811
www.wildheartgardens.com
Permaculture garden and landscape design; classes in permaculture
through Merritt College.

YERBA BUENA CALIFORNIA NATIVE PLANT NURSERY
19500 Skyline Blvd. Woodside 94062 650-851-1668
Tue-Sat 9-5 www.yerbabuenanursery.com
Native plants garden consultation and design.

Greening
Your Space

More professionals are "going green" thanks to increased consumer demand and their own research into, and awareness of, the impact they can have on the planet. However, not all green building and design professionals are experienced in all areas, so check into their primary focus and field of expertise. Look for those who specialize in your need—water use and reclamation, chemical-free environments, solar energy installation, use of green materials, and so on.

Be aware that with a few exceptions, most professionals and tradespeople listed here offer conventional as well as green services so be clear about your wishes.

The professionals listed here were chosen because of their experience in sustainable or green building design and/or construction. At least 50% of their annual projects must have a green, environmentally-oriented approach. Because these businesses couldn't be measured against a single objective standard, we did not grant leaf awards in this category. *

The Green Media Group LLC is not responsible for the outcome or performance of the work/service/products/materials of any company or individual listed in this guide. When hiring a professional or trade listed below, it is up to you to verify the experience and skills of the listed practitioners. For California, you can check on the status of a contractor's license by going to www.cslb.ca.gov.

Build It Green: *A non-profit membership organization that promotes healthy, energy- and resource-efficient buildings in California. Offers Certified Green Building Professional Training in residential design and construction for building, real estate and other professionals.*

USGBC (U.S. Green Building Council): *A non-profit membership organization made up of leaders from all sectors of the building industry working to promote buildings that are environmentally responsible and healthy places to live and work.*

LEED (Leadership in Energy and Environmental Design): *LEED's Green Building Rating System™ is the national benchmark for the design, construction, and operation of high performance green buildings. LEED also offers a professional accreditation exam for building professionals.*

You can also look for LEED-accredited or certified green builders at www.builditgreen.org. Build It Green also offers green home tours. Check their website for locations and times.

Greening Your Space

ARCHITECTS

ALB DESIGNS
10 G St. San Rafael 94901 415-457-2545
By appt. www.albdesigns.com
Sustainable architecture, interior design.

ARCHITECTURE STUDIO

1001 Bridgeway Suite C Sausalito 94965 415-332-3438
By appt. www.architecturestudioonline.com
Architecture, interior, and furniture design services; passive solar design.
Build It Green certified.

ARKIN TILT ARCHITECTS

1101 Eighth St. Suite 180 Berkeley 94710 510-528-9830
By appt. www.arkintilt.com
Ecological planning and design; specialists in energy and resource efficiency,
and alternative construction systems. LEED accredited, Build It Green certified.

BRIDGET BREWER ASSOCIATES

10 G St. San Rafael 94901 415-457-9046
Mon-Fri 9-5
Independent architect and landscaper; specializes in remodels and cooperative
housing developments; native plant design.

DAN SMITH & ASSOCIATES

1107 Virginia St. Berkeley 94702 510-526-1935
By appt. www.dsaarch.com
Site-responsive, ecological design using a range of sustainable design
practices, from passive solar basics to comprehensive green design.
LEED accredited.

DEBOER ARCHITECTS

1835 Pacific Ave. Alameda 94501 510-865-3669
By appt. www.deboerarchitects.com
Full-service custom residential design using natural, sustainable materials;
specializes in bamboo, creating custom furniture and fixtures.

FULL CIRCLE DESIGN GROUP

329 Bryant St. Suite 3A SF (SOMA) 94107 415-357-0110
By appt. www.fullcirclearchitecture.com
Architectural design and project management; interior design, custom
cabinetry, carpentry. LEED accredited, Build It Green certified, and
USGBC member.

GELFAND PARTNERS ARCHITECTS

450 Geary St. Suite 100 SF (Financial District) 94102 415-346-4040
By appt. www.gelfand-partners.com
Master planning and architectural services; focuses on sustainability and
community responsibility. LEED accredited, USGBC member.

GETTMAN SCHOW ARCHITECTURE

52 DeLuca Pl. San Rafael 94901 415-721-7123
By appt. www.gsarchitecture.com
Residential design, new construction, remodels, and additions. Build It Green
certified.

GHA/GEOFFREY HOLTON & ASSOCIATES

339 15th St. Suite 212 Oakland (Lake Merritt/Downtown) 94612 510-663-9797
By appt. www.ghadesign.net
Residential architect; custom furniture and fixture design; site restoration and
landscape schematics. Specializes in net-zero energy and carbon-neutral
designs. Build It Green certified, USGBC member.

GREEN BUILDING EXCHANGE

305 Main St. Redwood City 94063 650-369-4900
Daily 10-8 www.greenbuildingexchange.com
Resource for finding green architects in the Bay Area.

HEALTHY HOME PLANS

316 Miller Ave. Suite H Mill Valley 94941 415-383-5105
Mon-Fri 9-6 www.healthyhomeplans.com
Architect designed home plans; residential solar design; alternative energy
efficiency planning; new and remodeled homes.

HUBBELL DAILY ARCHITECTURE + DESIGN

159 Ethel Ave. Mill Valley 94941 415-383-8884
By appt. www.hdarch.us
Architectural and design services. Build It Green certified.

INKMOON ARCHITECTS

1654 San Anselmo Ave. San Anselmo 94960 415-455-0179
By appt. www.inkmoon.com
Sustainably-minded design studio; residential and commercial services.
LEED accredited, Build It Green certified, and USGBC member.

JACKSON LILES ARCHITECTURE

290 Division St. Suite 311 SF (SOMA) 94103 415-233-4036
By appt. www.jacksonliles.com
Architecture firm; sustainable design for residential and commercial spaces;
interior design; environmental hazard assessment. Build It Green certified,
USGBC member.

LEDDY MAYTUM STACY ARCHITECTS

677 Harrison St. SF (SOMA) 94107 415-495-1700
By appt. www.lmsarch.com
High-performance, environmentally-sensitive architecture; focus on
sustainable design, community engagement, design that matters.
USGBC member.

MERCEDES CORBELL DESIGN + ARCHITECTURE

800 Pine St. Studio 12 Oakland (West Oakland) 94607 510-832-8970
By appt. www.mercedescorbelldesign.com
Green architectural design; residential and small commercial projects.
Build It Green certified.

MICHELLE KAUFMANN DESIGNS

580 Second St. Suite 245 Oakland (West Oakland) 94607
By appt. www.michellekaufmann.com
Full-service firm; specializes in modern, sustainable design and prefabricated,
modular construction. LEED accredited, USGBC member.

NEWLAND + WINNEN DESIGN STUDIO

1441 Casa Buena Dr. Suite 306 Corte Madera 94925 415-924-4951
By appt. www.newwindesign.com
Architecture and interior design studio; specializes in custom residential and
small structure design. Build It Green certified.

ORGANICARCHITECT

716 Montgomery St. Studio Two SF (Financial District) 94111 415-474-7777
By appt. www.organicarchitect.com
Sustainable design; expertise in passive solar, green materials, natural building
methods. LEED accredited, Build It Green certified, and USGBC member.
SF green certified business.

PALTER/DONZELLI DESIGN

50-B Hancock St. SF (Castro) 94114 415-552-0802
By appt.
Architectural design; specializes in residential remodeling and
new construction. Build It Green certified.

PFAU ARCHITECTURE
630 Third St. Suite 200 SF (SOMA) 94107 415-908-6408
By appt. www.pfauarchitecture.com
Architecture firm; green building for residential, commercial, institutional
projects. LEED accredited, Build It Green certified, and USGBC member.

SIEGEL & STRAIN ARCHITECTS
1295 59th St. Emeryville 94608 510-547-8092
By appt. www.siegelstrain.com
Environmentally sustainable design; focus on climate-responsive buildings,
ecologically-sound materials, and minimal site impact. LEED accredited,
Build It Green certified, and USGBC member.

SOLUTIONS
1806 Belles St. SF (Presidio/Presidio Heights) 94129 415-386-4600
By appt.
Green architecture and planning. AIA member, Build It Green certified,
LEED accredited.

SUSTAINABLE ARCHITECTURE & CONSULTING
55 Cazneau Ave. Sausalito 94965 415-331-2858
By appt. www.sustainable-architecture.com
Boutique design and consulting firm specializing in green, sustainable design.

TAMLEY ARCHITECTURAL DESIGN
P.O. Box 554 Woodacre 94973 415-488-1698
By appt. www.tamleyarchitecture.com
Custom residential architect; specializes in straw-bale construction.
Build It Green certified.

THOMAS SAXBY ARCHITECT
403 Martin Luther King Jr. Way Oakland (West Oakland) 94607 510-451-1720
By appt. www.tsaxbyarchitect.com
Architect; specializes in preservation and restoration of historic buildings.
Build It Green certified.

TODD JERSEY ARCHITECTURE
1321 Eighth St. Suite 2 Berkeley 94710 510-528-5477
By appt. www.toddjerseyarchitecture.com
Green architecture firm; applies sustainable design principles to residential
and commercial projects.

UPWALL
1256 Howard St. SF (SOMA) 94103 415-550-0236
By appt. www.upwallarchitects.com
Sustainable, environmentally responsible architecture and design.

URBAN STRUCTURE
51 Rodgers St. SF (SOMA) 94103 415-255-3155
By appt. www.urbanstructure.biz
Boutique design firm; specializes in major residential remodels,
new construction. Build It Green certified.

VAN DER RYN ECO DESIGN COLLABORATIVE
P.O. Box 858 Inverness 94937 415-669-7005
By appt. www.vanderryn.com
Green architects, sustainability consultants, and developers of mixed-use infill
projects with a green focus.

VOX DESIGN GROUP
421 Castro St. Mountain View 94041 650-694-6200
Mon-Fri 8-5 www.voxdesigngroup.com
Green design, construction, and renovation. LEED accredited,
Build It Green certified, and USGBC member.

WAGSTAFF ARCHITECTS

275 Miller Ave. Suite 202 Mill Valley 94941 415-383-2160
Mon-Fri 9-6 www.wagstaffarchitects.com
Boutique architectural design firm; residential and small commercial projects.
Build It Green certified.

TRADESPEOPLE

BAMBOO CABINETS BY ALTERECO

Sausalito 94966 415-331-8342
By appt. www.bamboocabinets.com
Modern bamboo custom cabinetry. Build It Green certified, USGBC member.

EARTHFIRST ELECTRIC

441B 43rd Ave. SF (Richmond) 94121 415-254-5908
By appt. www.efelectric.com
Electrical service and installation. LEED accredited, USGBC member.

ECOCRAFT

1432 Carleton St. Berkeley 94702 510-665-3100
By appt. www.ecocraft.com
Eco-friendly custom cabinetry.

FLACK + KURTZ

405 Howard St. Suite 500 SF (SOMA) 94105 415-398-3833
By appt. www.flackandkurtz.com
Complete engineering services; mechanical, electrical, plumbing, fire
protection, security, information technology, and architectural lighting design.
LEED accredited, USGBC member.

MOONDANCE PAINTING

2528 Heide Ct. El Sobrante 94803 888-97-PAINT
By appt. www.moondancepainting.com
Green-friendly painting; non-toxic, low-waste washes; non-toxic interior paints;
dry-wall repair; shingle restoration.

RANDY COLOSKY DESIGN

903 Guerrero St. SF (Mission) 94110 415-370-3969
By appt. www.randycoloskydesign.com
Custom furniture, architectural carpentry, cabinetry; sustainable woods,
low-VOC finishes.

RENU: SMART SOLUTIONS FOR HEALTHY HOMES

42 Redhill Ave. San Anselmo 94960 415-462-0245
By appt. www.renuyourhome.com
Full-service contracting company; specializing in improving the health,
comfort, and efficiency of homes. Build It Green certified. Marin certified
green business.

STONELACE DESIGNS

2222 Third St. Berkeley 94710 510-665-9013
By appt. www.stonelacedesigns.com
Decorative interior painting and plastering; low-toxicity materials.
Build It Green certified.

WOODSHANTI COOPERATIVE, INC.

909 Palou Ave. SF (Bayview/Hunter's Point) 94124 415-822-8100
By appt. www.woodshanti.com
Custom cabinetry and furniture; responsibly harvested lumber, natural
finishes. Build It Green certified, FSC certified, Smart Wood certified.
SF green certified business.

A BEAUTIFUL PLACE
194 Inverness Way Alameda 94502 510-814-8910
By appt. www.abeautifulplace.com
Residential interior architecture, decoration. Build It Green certified.

ATMOSPHERA
526 Third Ave. Suite A3 San Rafael 94901 415-455-8430
By appt. www.atmospherahome.com
Non-toxic, healthy home design; signature line of home goods and furnishings.

CAROLINE DAY DESIGN
844 Elizabeth St. SF (Noe Valley) 94114 415-641-8474
By appt.
Full-service residential interior design and consultation; specializes in
feng shui, green design. Build It Green certified.

CAROLYN ROBBINS SITE DESIGN
100 Bayo Vista Way Suite 64 San Rafael 94901 415-460-0339
By appt. www.carolynrobbinsdesign.com
Residential and commercial interior design firm using green practices
and materials.

CHRISTINE REID
Albany 510-559-9710
By appt. www.christinereid.net
Interior designer, sculptor, textile designer. Build It Green certified.

ECO-TERRIC
1401 16th St. 2nd Floor SF (Potrero Hill) 94103 415-558-8700
Mon-Fri 9-5 Sat 10-4 www.eco-terric.com
Green, healthy home design and consultation.

GREEN FUSION DESIGN CENTER
14 Greenfield Ave. San Anselmo 94960 415-454-0174
Mon-Sat 10-6 Sun by appt. www.greenfusiondesigncenter.com
Complete sustainable design resource: structures, interiors, flooring,
cabinetry, home decor, consultation and education. LEED accredited,
Build It Green certified, and USGBC member.

GREENSAGE
P.O. Box 460753 SF (SOMA) 94146 415-453-7915
By appt. www.greensage.com
Green design, consulting, and products. LEED accredited, USGBC member.

PECHÉ INTERIORS
1395 San Carlos Ave. San Carlos 94070 650-591-8881
By appt.
Residential interior design specializing in green building materials and
furnishings; indoor air quality and health.

SUSTAINABLE HOME
Palo Alto 650-855-9464
By appt. www.sustainablehome.com
Interior design with a focus on environmentally sensitive materials.
Build It Green certified, USGBC member.

TRANQUIL SPACES DESIGN GROUP
P.O. Box 1637 Pacifica 94044 800-548-3344
By appt. www.tranquilspaces.com
Residential and commercial interior design following principles of feng shui
and holistic design. USGBC member.

NOTE: Many architects also offer interior design services. Please see the
Architects section.

Greening
Your Space

ENVIRONMENTAL CONSULTANTS

BUILD IT GREEN
1434 University Ave. Berkeley 94702 510-845-0472
By appt. www.BuildItGreen.org
Free information resources, including advice from green building professionals, a
green product and a supplier directory. LEED accredited members,
USGBC member.

ENERGY MANAGEMENT SERVICES
110 Second St. Sausalito 94965 415-289-0147
By appt. www.e-m-services.com
Energy efficiency and renewable energy consulting services.

GREEN LIVING HOME
3969 Cowan Rd. Lafayette 94549 925-283-3190
By appt.
A holistic approach to a green lifestyle in your home and environment.
Specializing in creating healthy living spaces for pets. Build It Green certified.
USGBC member.

NATURAL BUILDERS, THE
100 Behrens St. El Cerrito 94530 510-325-4277
By appt. www.naturalbuildersworkshop.com
Green building design, build and consultation; rammed earth, strawbale,
bamboo, and natural materials.

SIMON & ASSOCIATES, INC.
200 Brannan St. Suite 204 SF (SOMA) 94107 415-908-3757
By appt. www.greenbuild.com
Sustainable building and LEED consulting, specifications review and materials
research, workshops and trainings. LEED accredited and USGBC member.

GENERAL CONTRACTORS

BASHLAND BUILDERS
1461 Park Ave. Emeryville 94608 510-652-5795
By appt. www.bashland.com
High-end design and building contractor; custom cabinetry.
Build It Green certified.

BRENDAN UNIACKE CONSTRUCTION
332 Southcliff Dr. South SF 94080 650-794-1395
By appt.
Independent general contractor; plumbing, carpentry, plastering, painting, and
flooring installation.

COLLIER OSTROM, INC.
1395 Fairfax Ave. SF (Bayview/Hunter's Point) 94124 415-206-0803
Mon-Fri 8-5 www.collier-ostrom.com
Remodeling contractors; green building; residential and commercial remodels.
Build It Green certified.

DREW MARAN CONSTRUCTION, INC.
480 Lytton Ave. Suite 6 Palo Alto 94301 650-323-8541
By appt. www.drewmaran.com
Sustainable approach to design, demolition, renovation, and new
home building. LEED accredited, Build It Green certified, and USGBC member.

EBERSOLE BUILDERS
340 Channing Way Suite 145 San Rafael 94903 415-458-8813
By appt. www.ebersolebuilders.com
Green building; renovations and repairs to remodels and additions.
Build It Green certified, USGBC member.

FORM + FUNCTION CONSTRUCTION
429 Castro St. Mountain View 94041 650-249-1908
By appt. www.formxfunction.com
Custom green residential and commercial contracting and construction.
LEED accredited, Build It Green certified, and USGBC member.

FRYER CONSULTING
6114 LaSalle Ave. Suite 282 Oakland (Montclair) 94611 510-682-4908
By appt. www.fryerconsulting.com
Commercial and residential property inspections; construction consulting.
Build It Green certified.

GREEN BUILDERS OF MARIN
205 Montego Key Novato 94949 415-884-0700
By appt. www.greenbuildersofmarin.com
Green-focused general contractor; remodels and new additions.
Build It Green certified, USGBC member.

HAMMERSCHMIDT CONSTRUCTION
313 State St. Los Altos 94022 650-948-4200
By appt. www.hammerschmidtinc.com
Green remodeling; design, build, and remodel services. Build It Green certified.

JEFF KING & COMPANY, INC.
251 Balboa St. SF (Richmond) 94118 415-221-5012
By appt. www.jeffkingandco.com
General remodel construction. Build It Green certified.

LORAX DEVELOPMENT
P. O. Box 411494 SF 94141 415-264-4428
By appt. www.loraxdevelopment.com
Residential contractor; renewable materials, and energy-efficient systems.
Build It Green certified.

MCCUTCHEON CONSTRUCTION, INC.
1280 Sixth St. Berkeley 94710 510-558-8030
Mon-Fri 8-5 www.mcbuild.com
General contractor; residential remodeling, new construction, light
commercial projects. Build It Green certified.

MGS CONSTRUCTION, INC.
2001 Spring St. Redwood City 94063 650-369-4658
By appt. www.mgsconstructioninc.com
Employee-owned design/build firm; general contracting and craftsmen
services in all trades. Build It Green certified.

RENAISSANCE REMODELERS
144 Melville Ave. San Anselmo 94960 415-455-9442
By appt. www.renredmodel.com
Remodel and addition specialists; formaldehyde-free insulation and glues;
demolition; uses recycled and engineered lumber; FSC certified.
Build It Green certified.

SPRING FRIEDLANDER REMODELING
Oakland (Temescal) 510-652-7600
By appt.
Remodeling construction (CCL). Build It Green certified.

LANDSCAPE ARCHITECTS

BRIDGET BREWER ASSOCIATES
10 G St. San Rafael 94901 415-457-9046
Mon-Fri 9-5
Independent architect and landscaper; specializes in remodels and cooperative housing developments; native plant design.

EQUINOX LANDSCAPE CONSTRUCTION CORPS
1811 Grand Ave. Suite B San Rafael 94901 415-456-6480
By appt. www.equinox-landscape.com
Landscape design, installation, and maintenance. Organic gardens, permaculture plantings, irrigation.

ALTERNATIVE ENERGY CONTRACTORS (DESIGN, INSTALLATION, SERVICE, AND REPAIR)

You may be in a position to directly affect your energy consumption at home and/or at work by using alternative energy. The companies below specialize in alternative energy systems: design, installation, service, and/or repair. They may offer free consultation to help you decide which is the best energy alternative for you. (Also, you might check with your own utility company for a similar consultation and alternative energy plan. They may offer help in the form of rebates and tax incentives to homeowners who qualify.)

Because the work these groups do is so varied (from design to repair), they have not been leaf-awarded. To be included, alternative energy must be their main focus and they have to offer alternatives to conventional energy consumption.*

*The Green Media Group, LLC is not responsible for the outcome or performance of the work service/products/materials of any company or individual listed in this guide. When hiring a professional or trade listed below, it is up to you to verify the experience and skills of the listed practitioners. For California, you can check on the status of a contractor's license by going to www.cslb.ca.gov.

BAY SOLAR POWER DESIGN
1359 Linda Mar Shopping Center Pacifica 94044 877-738-8355
Daily 9-5 www.baysolarpower.com
Photovoltaic installation and design; consultation and education.

BORREGO SOLAR
727 Allston Way Berkeley 94710 510-843-1113
Mon-Fri 8:30-5:30 www.borregosolar.com
Designers and installers of solar electric systems.

COOPERATIVE COMMUNITY ENERGY
534 Fourth St. Suite C San Rafael 94901 415-457-0215
Mon-Fri 9-6 www.ccenergy.com
Alternative energy cooperative; design and project management for residential and commercial systems.

GREEN BUILDING EXCHANGE
305 Main St. Redwood City 94063 650-369-4900
Daily 10-8 www.greenbuildingexchange.com
Green building resource center with connections to alternative energy
contractors and other green building professionals.

GREENLIGHT SOLAR
150 Shoreline Hwy. Suite 1A Mill Valley 94941 415-381-2400
By appt. www.greenlightsolar.com
Solar-powered systems; project management, design, and permitting.

GRID ALTERNATIVES
995 Market St. Suite 801 SF (Civic Center) 94103 415-839-8437
Mon-Fri 9-5 www.gridalternatives.org
Low- and no-cost solar electric generation systems for low-income Bay Area
homeowners; non-profit.

HEALTHY HOME PLANS
316 Miller Ave. Suite H Mill Valley 94941 415-383-5105
Mon-Fri 9-6 www.healthyhomeplans.com
Sustainable home design; energy efficient solutions.

MARIN SOLAR
1163 Francisco Blvd. E. San Rafael 94901 888-56-SOLAR
By appt. www.marinsolar.com
PV installation and design; residential and commercial projects.

MC SOLAR ENGINEERING
2362 Walsh Ave. Santa Clara 95051 408-496-6226
Mon-Fri 8-4 www.mcsolar.com
Solar electric installation, solar hot water, and solar pool heating.

OCCIDENTAL POWER
3629 Taraval St. SF (Sunset) 94116 888-49-SOLAR
By appt. www.oxypower.com
Solar contractor offering design, installation, maintenance, and service of solar
PV, thermal, and natural gas, cogeneration systems.

OWENS ELECTRIC AND SOLAR
279 North Amphlett Blvd. San Mateo 94401 650-373-2953
By appt. www.owenselectricinc.com
Energy consulting, solar systems design, installation, and repair.

RENU: SMART SOLUTIONS FOR HEALTHY HOMES
42 Redhill Ave. San Anselmo 94960 415-462-0245
By appt. www.renuyourhome.com
Healthy home and energy efficiency testing (home performance testing). Heating
and cooling general contractor. Build It Green certified. Marin certified
green business.

SOLAR CITY
1153 Triton Dr. Suite D Foster City 94404 650-683-1028
By appt. www.solarcity.com
Solar power systems; design, installation, maintenance.

SOLARCRAFT
285-D Bel Marin Keys Blvd. Novato 94949 415-382-7717
By appt. www.solarcraft.com
Solar installer of both thermal and electric systems.

SPG SOLAR, INC.
863 East Francisco Blvd. Suite A San Rafael 94901 415-459-4201
Mon-Fri 8-5 www.spgsolar.com
Solar PV systems integrator; residential and commercial design and
installation services.

Greening
Your Space

SUN FIRST

3060 Kerner Blvd. Suite W San Rafael 94901 415-458-5870
Mon-Fri 7:30-5 www.sunfirstsolar.com
Solar design and installation; solar electric, hot water, pool heating systems.

SUN LIGHT AND POWER

1035 Folger Ave. Berkeley 94710 510-845-2997
Mon-Fri 8-5 www.sunlightandpower.com
Designs and builds solar electric, thermal, and radiant heat systems; services
and repairs existing solar hot water systems.

SUNLIGHT ELECTRIC, LLC

2001 Pierce St. SF (Pacific Heights) 94115 415-831-3300
By appt. www.sunlightelectric.com
Design, engineering, sourcing, and project management of PV systems.

SUSTAINABLE SPACES

221 14th St. SF (Mission) 94103 415-294-5380
Mon-Fri 9-5 www.sustainablespaces.com
Energy efficiency and air quality testing, evaluation, consulting.
SF green certified business.

BUILDING MATERIALS AND SUPPLIES

Almost every part of home building and furnishing can be made
environmentally sound. It may take more effort to find green building
materials but they are available and using them is worth the effort.
Green building materials save water, energy, and natural resources.
They offer better indoor air quality due to the presence of less-toxic
paints and finishes. Green products include materials using recycled
content such as glass or metal, as well as sustainably harvested wood,
or easily replenished materials like bamboo.

Of the products and materials sold by these companies, at least 25%
must be sustainably manufactured, non-toxic or low-toxic, and/or
made with renewable, natural, or recycled materials.

> $\mathcal{D}$ at least 25% of products/materials meet the above criteria.
> $\mathcal{D}\mathcal{D}$ at least 50% of products/materials meet the above criteria.
> $\mathcal{D}\mathcal{D}\mathcal{D}$ at least 75% of products/materials meet the above criteria.
> $\mathcal{D}\mathcal{D}\mathcal{D}\mathcal{D}$ 90% or more of products/materials meet the above criteria.

Greening
Your Space

BLACK'S FARMWOOD $\mathcal{D}\mathcal{D}\mathcal{D}\mathcal{D}$

P.O. Box 2836 San Rafael 94912 877-321-9663
By appt. www.blacksfarmwood.com
Reclaimed wood: redwood, hand-hewn barn beams, barn siding,
wide plank flooring.

BOFINGS ELMWOOD HARDWARE $\mathcal{D}$

2951 College Ave. Berkeley 94705 510-843-3794
Mon-Sat 8:30-5:30 Sun 10-3 www.elmwoodhardware.com
Plan-it Hardware section within store carries green alternatives in tools,
hardware, garden, plumbing, heating, electrical, paints, and cleaners.

CERAMIC TILE & DESIGN ✐

189 13th St. SF (SOMA) 94103 415-575-3785
846 West Francisco Blvd. San Rafael 94901 415-485-5180
Hours vary by location www.ceramictiledesign.net
Sustainable tile and counter materials in recycled glass, metal, wood,
and more. USGBC Member.

CLIFF'S VARIETY ✐

479 Castro St. SF (Castro) 94114 415-431-5365
Mon-Fri 8:30-8 Sat 9:30-8 Sun 11-6 www.cliffsvariety.com
Plan-it Hardware section within store carries green alternatives in tools,
hardware, garden, plumbing, heating, electrical, paints, and cleaners.

EARTHSOURCE FOREST PRODUCTS ✐✐✐✐

1618 28th St. Oakland (West Oakland) 94608 510-208-7257
2035 Newcomb Ave. SF (Bayview/Hunter's Point) 94124 415-648-7257
Mon-Fri 8-4:30 Sat 8-2 www.earthsourcewood.com
Sustainably harvested and reclaimed wood products; FSC certified.

ECO DESIGN RESOURCES ✐✐✐✐

633 Quarry Rd. Suite A San Carlos 94070 650-591-1123
Mon-Fri 10-5 Sat 11-4 www.ecodesignresources.com
Green residential design services; building materials. Non-toxic paint, tiles,
sealers, plasters, cleaners; in-house Feng Shui consultations.

ECOHOME IMPROVEMENT ✐✐✐✐

2619 San Pablo Ave. Berkeley 94702 510-644-3500
Tue-Fri 10-6 Sat 9-4 Sun 11-4 www.ecohomeimprovement.com
Eco-friendly flooring, cabinetry, countertops, tile, paint; kitchen and bath design
services; educational workshops.

FAIRFAX LUMBER & HARDWARE ✐

109 Broadway Fairfax 94930 415-453-4410
Mon-Fri 7:30-6 Sat-Sun 8:30-5 www.fairfaxlumber.com
Eco-friendly building materials; FSC certified wood; low- and no-VOC paint;
non-toxic cleaning supplies; energy-efficient plumbing supplies; native plant
nursery; non-toxic pest management.

GREEN BUILDING EXCHANGE ✐✐✐✐

305 Main St. Redwood City 94063 650-369-4900
Daily 10-8 www.greenbuildingexchange.com
Public showroom offering sustainable products, building professionals,
educational services and seminars.

GREEN FUSION DESIGN CENTER ✐✐✐✐

20 Greenfield Ave. San Anselmo 94960 415-454-0174
Mon-Sat 10-6 Sun by appt. www.greenfusiondesigncenter.com
Sustainable design. Structures, bedding, home decor, gardening, and
landscaping; consultation and education.

GREENSAGE ✐✐✐✐

P.O. Box 46053 SF (SOMA) 94146 415-453-7915
Mon-Fri 9-5 www.greensage.com
Green design, consulting and products since 1988.

MILL VALLEY BAMBOO FLOORING ✐✐✐✐

14 East Sir Francis Drake Blvd. Larkspur 94939 415-925-1188
Daily 7:30-5 www.mvbamboo.com
Certified, sustainably-harvested bamboo products; flooring, cabinets, shingles.

SPRING

2162 Polk St. SF (Russian Hill) 94109 415-673-2065
Mon 11-5 Tue-Sat 10:30-7 Sun 11-5 www.astorecalledspring.com
"Solutions for a healthy home" include: non-VOC paints, air purifiers, steam
cleaners, furnace filters, encasements, HEPA vacuum cleaners, natural
cleaning products, organic bedding and mattresses, natural personal care
products, and home accessories.

RECYCLING CENTERS/ RECYCLING SERVICES/SALVAGE YARDS

"Reduce, reuse, recycle" is still the most logical and powerful protocol
for material use. Tossing goods into the recycling bin should be what
we do after reducing our consumption and reusing existing materials.
But when it comes time to recycle something, there are many avenues
from which to choose. You can bring your recyclables to city-operated
or privately-owned recycling centers or salvage yards. Depending
on the type of salvage yard, you'll find everything from architectural
design elements to building supplies for your home remodel.

There are also recycling services that come to you, either by directly
picking up your recyclables or by providing boxes or envelopes for
mailing in such things as toner cartridges, computers, and other
electronics. Follow their directions for sorting, sending, and/or setting
out materials.

The recycling centers and salvage yards below are listed here as
resources. You can drop off recyclables or purchase salvaged building
materials at these locations. We have also listed recycling service
providers. However, because there is no objective means of awarding
any of these businesses leaves, we have not done so. Let us know
your experiences at www.greenopia.com.

RECYCLING CENTERS/RECYCLING SERVICES

ALAMEDA COUNTY WASTE MANAGEMENT AUTHORITY
777 Davis St. Suite 100 San Leandro 94577 510-614-1699
Mon-Fri 8-5 www.stopwaste.org
Curbside recycling collection as well as auto waste, yard waste,
and Christmas trees.

ALLIED WASTE OF SAN MATEO COUNTY CURBSIDE PROGRAM
225 Shoreway Rd. San Carlos 94070 650-592-2411
Mon-Fri 8-5 www.alliedwastesanmateocounty.com
Curbside recycling collection, as well as for auto waste, wood, and yard waste.

ALLIED WASTE SERVICES OF DALY CITY
1680 Edgeworth Ave. Daly City 94015 650-756-1130
Mon-Fri 8-5 www.bfidalycity.com
Curbside recycling as well as auto waste.

BERKELEY ECOLOGY CENTER CURBSIDE RECYCLING PROGRAM
2530 San Pablo Ave. Berkeley 94702 510-527-5555
Mon-Fri 7-3 www.ecologycenter.org
Curbside recycling. Glass, metal, paper, plastic.

Greening
Your Space

CITY OF EL CERRITO RECYCLING
7501 Schmidt Lane El Cerrito 94530 510-215-4350
Mon-Fri 8-5 www.ecrecycling.org
Drop off and curbside recycling. Glass, metal, yard waste, paper, plastic, and Christmas trees.

CITY OF NOVATO CURBSIDE RECYCLING PROGRAM
P.O. Box 1916 Santa Rosa 95402 415-897-4177
Mon-Fri 7-6 www.novatodisposal.com
Curbside recycling. Glass, metal, paper, plastic, and yard waste.

CITY OF PALO ALTO RECYCLING PROGRAM
P.O. Box 10250 Palo Alto 94303 650-496-5910
Daily 8-5 www.cityofpaloalto.org/public-works
Curbside recycling. Auto waste, batteries, and yard waste.

CITY OF SAUSALITO RECYCLING – BAY CITIES REFUSE
565 Jacoby St. San Rafael 94901 415-332-3646
Mon-Fri 8-3 www.ci.sausalito.ca.us/res-info/recycle.htm
Curbside recycling. Glass, cans, paper, plastic, yard waste, and Christmas trees.

COMMUNITY CONSERVATION CENTERS – BERKELEY RECYCLING CENTER
669 Gilman St. Berkeley 94710 510-524-0113
Drop off: Daily 9-4 Buy-back: Tue-Sun 9-4 www.berkeleyrecycling.org
Operates the Community Conservation Centers and Ecology Center to provide buy-back and drop-off recycling programs and a residential curbside pick-up program for the City of Berkeley.

COUNTY OF SAN MATEO RECYCLEWORKS
555 County Center 5th Floor Redwood City 94063 888-442-2666
Mon-Fri 9-5 www.recycleworks.org
Online resource for recycling information and reuse opportunities.

ECOFINDERRR
11 Grove St. SF (Civic Center) 94102 415-355-3700
Mon-Fri 9-5 www.sfenvironment.com
Recycling resource for SF residents including curbside recycling, composting, hazardous waste disposal, and used motor oil recycling drop off locations.

GREEN CITIZEN
591 Howard St. SF (SOMA) 94105 415-287-0000
Mon-Sat 10-6 Sun 11-5 www.greencitizen.com
Consumer electronics recycling.

LOS ALTOS GARBAGE COMPANY CURBSIDE PROGRAM
650 Martin Ave. Santa Clara 95050 650-961-8040
Mon-Fri 7:30-4:30 www.losaltosgarbage.com
Curbside recycling. Auto waste and yard waste.

MARIN CITY COMMUNITY SERVICES DISTRICT
630 Drake Ave. Marin City 94965 415-332-1441
Mon-Fri 9-5 www.marincity.org
Recycling service.

MARIN RECYCLING SERVICE
565 Jacoby St. San Rafael 94901 415-453-1404
Hours vary by division www.marinsanitary.com
Residential recycling collection, auto dismantling, hazardous waste collection; outreach and education.

MILL VALLEY REFUSE SERVICE

112 Front St. San Rafael 94901 415-457-9760
Mon-Fri 6-4 www.millvalleyrefuse.com
Curbside recycling.

NOVATO DISPOSAL SERVICE

3417 Standish Ave. Santa Rosa 95407 415-897-4177
Mon-Fri 7-6 Sat-Sun 7-3 www.novatodisposal.com
Green waste, curbside, and recycling center for Novato.

SOUTH SAN FRANCISCO SCAVENGER

500 East Jamie Ct. South SF 94080 650-589-4020
Mon-Fri 7-4:30 www.ssfscavenger.com
Curbside recycling. Auto waste and batteries.

USEDCARDBOARDBOXES.COM

720 S. Vail Ave. Unit B-1 Montebello 90640 888-BOXES-88
Mon-Fri 8-5 www.usedcardboardboxes.com
Reseller of high quality used cardboard boxes; moving kits. Serves
San Francisco Bay Area.

WEST CONTRA COSTA INTEGRATED WASTE MANAGEMENT AUTHORITY

1 Alvarado Square San Pablo 94806 510-215-3125
Mon-Fri 8:30-5 www.recyclemore.com
Bi-monthly curbside recycling. Auto waste, Christmas trees, and yard waste.

SALVAGE YARDS

BUILDING RESOURCES

701 Amador St. SF (Bayview/Hunter's Point) 94124 415-285-7814
Daily 9-4:30 www.buildingresources.org
Salvaged building materials and architectural elements. Wood, tile, glass,
fixtures, and hardware.

C&K SALVAGE

718 Douglas Ave. Oakland (East Oakland) 94603 510-569-2074
Mon-Fri 9-5
Salvaged building materials: lumber, timber, siding, flooring, bricks,
doors, plumbing.

CALDWELL BUILDING WRECKERS

195 Bayshore Blvd. SF (Bayview/Hunter's Point) 94124 415-550-6777
Mon-Fri 8-5 Sat 9-5 www.caldwells.com
Salvaged building materials: wood, flooring, bricks, marble, plumbing.

EAST BAY DEPOT FOR CREATIVE REUSE

6713 San Pablo Ave. Berkeley 94710 510-547-6470
Daily 11-6 www.creativereuse.org
Salvaged materials for community redistribution. Specializes in art materials,
books, small furniture, frames, and garden artifacts. Non-profit.

GILMAN TRADING COMPANY, INC.

808 Gilman St. Berkeley 94710 510-524-5500
Mon, Wed-Sun 11-6 www.gilmantradingco.com
Salvaged building materials and home décor; antiques, fine art, collectibles.

MAISON RÊVE

11 Throckmorton Ave. Mill Valley 94941 415-383-9700
Mon-Sat 10-6 Sun 11-5 www.maisonreve.com
French-influenced home and garden store. Selection includes wide
range of indoor and outdoor furniture and accessories from distressed
reclaimed materials.

OHMEGA SALVAGE

2400 San Pablo Ave. Berkeley 94710 510-204-0767
2407 San Pable Ave. Berkeley 94710 510-843-7368
Mon-Sat 9-5 Sun 12-5 www.ohmegasalvage.com
Salvaged building materials and architectural elements.

OMEGA TOO

2204 San Pablo Ave. Berkeley 94710 510-843-3636
Mon-Sat 10-6 Sun 12-5 www.omegatoo.com
Salvaged building materials and architectural elements.

RESTORE STORE, THE

9235 San Leandro St. Oakland (East Oakland) 94603 510-777-1447
Mon-Sat 9-5 www.habiteb.org/restore
East Bay Habitat for Humanity's salvaged building material warehouse.

REUSE PEOPLE, THE

9235 San Leandro St. Oakland (East Oakland) 94603 510-383-1983
Mon-Fri 10-6 Sat-Sun 10-4 www.thereusepeople.org
Salvaged building materials and architectural elements.

RUIZ ANTIQUE LIGHTING

2333 Clement Ave. Alameda 94501 510-769-6082
Tue-Sat 10-6 www.ruizlamp.com
Salvaged building materials and architectural elements, specializing in
lighting fixtures.

SCRAP - SCROUNGERS' CENTER FOR RE-USABLE ART PARTS

801 Toland St. SF (Bayview/Hunter's Point) 94124 415-647-1746
Tue-Sat 9-5 www.scrap-sf.org
Creative reuse center, store, and workshop. Reusable material donations
distributed to art and educational groups.

SINK FACTORY, THE

2140 San Pablo Ave. Berkeley 94710 510-540-8193
Tue-Sat 9-6 www.sinkfactory.com
Repairs and rebuilds new and salvaged sinks.

THIS & THAT

1701 Rumrill Blvd. San Pablo 94806 510-232-1273
Mon-Sat 8-5
Salvaged building materials and architectural elements.

URBAN ORE

900 Murray St. Berkeley 94710 510-841-7283
Mon-Sat 8:30-7 Sun 10-7 http://urbanore.citysearch.com
Salvaged building materials and architectural elements.

WHOLE HOUSE BUILDING SUPPLY

1955 Pulgas Ave. East Palo Alto 94303 650-328-8731
Mon-Fri 10-5 Sat 8-5 Sun 11-4 www.driftwoodsalvage.com
Salvaged building materials and architectural elements.

Households are no longer allowed to put certain wastes in the trash, including:

- all household batteries
- toxic cleaning supplies
- fluorescent and other mercury-containing light bulbs and lamps
- aerosols
- mercury thermometers and thermostats
- hobby and pool chemicals
- toxic gardening products (fertilizer, herbicides, pesticides)
- fire extinguishers
- oil-based paints, thinners, and stains

Public hazardous waste programs collect these wastes from households and small businesses. Sometimes appointments and proof of residency are required to participate. These programs provide safe disposal options, but remember that the best way to keep the planet healthy is to reduce your use of toxic materials in the first place.

Electronic waste (E-waste) consists of any broken or unwanted electrical or electronic appliance. This includes computers, entertainment electronics, mobile phones, and other items. Many components of such equipment are considered toxic and are not biodegradable.

Electronics are generally not accepted at hazardous waste drop-off sites but there are a number of electronics recycling centers and E-waste drop-off centers in the area. If the item is under five years old, it can often be donated to an electronics refurbishing/reuse program. For practical purposes, it is illegal to throw out all electronics. They must either be donated for refurbishment or recycled at an appropriate location. The below listings offer a number of options.

ALAMEDA COUNTY DROP-OFF
510-670-6460 (All locations)
2091 West Winton Ave. Hayward 94545
5584 La Ribera St. Livermore 94550
2100 East Seventh St. Oakland (West Oakland) 94606
Hours vary by location www.stopwaste.org
Drop-off center for batteries, cleaners, solvents, fluorescent lights, paint products, automotive fluids, and toxic garden products.

MARIN COUNTY HOUSEHOLD HAZARDOUS WASTE FACILITY
565 Jacoby St. San Rafael 94901 415-485-6806
Mon-Sat 8-4 www.marinrecycles.org
Drop-off household hazardous waste center. Batteries, paint, solvents, electronics, fuels, asbestos.

NOVATO HOUSEHOLD HAZARDOUS WASTE FACILITY
7576 Redwood Blvd. Novato 94945 415-892-7344
By appt. only www.novatodisposal.com
Household hazardous waste facilities for Novato residents.
Call for roundup dates.

SAN FRANCISCO RECYCLING AND DISPOSAL

501 Tunnel Ave. Brisbane 94134 415-330-1405
Thu-Sat 8-4 www.sfrecycliing.com/sfhww
Listing of household hazardous waste drop-off locations around SF and main
HHW facility for SF residents only.

SAN MATEO COUNTY HOUSEHOLD HAZARDOUS WASTE
PROGRAM/RECYCLEWORKS

555 County Center 5th Floor Redwood City 94063 650-363-4718
Fri 1-5 Sat 8-12 www.smhealth.org/hhw
County of San Mateo resources for Household Hazardous Waste collection
events and centers.

WALGREENS

Hours vary by location www.walgreens.com
All Bay Area locations now accept used batteries. See website
for nearest store.

WEST CONTRA COSTA INTEGRATED WASTE
MANAGEMENT AUTHORITY

1 Alvarado Square San Pablo 94806 510-215-3125
Thu-Fri 9-4, 1st Sat of month 9-4 www.recyclemore.com
Household hazardous waste disposal. Batteries, electronic waste, toxic
household items, medical supplies, oils.

To find out where to reduce, reuse, and recycle
in three easy steps, check out ecofindeRRR
(www.sfenvironment.com). Simply select a category
and size and type in your Zip Code (or use the
advanced search features) to find an environmentally
responsible disposal option at a location near you.

Many people begin their journey to green living by changing
their home environment. You can provide a great benefit to others
by sharing your insights and experiences on www.greenopia.com:
What did you think about the options and choices you were
given, or the quality of the products and services? How was
your experience with these providers? Was the cost in line with
what you were getting? Let us know!

REDUCE

- Use cloth bags or boxes for lunches instead of paper bags.

- Use washable cloth towels and napkins instead of paper towels and paper napkins.

- Bring reusable bags to the grocery store.

- Use an erasable note board instead of paper notes.

- Buy products that come without boxes or excess packaging.

- Send holiday greetings electronically over the internet.

- Take advantage of public and school libraries.

REUSE

- Reuse large and/or padded envelopes and boxes for mailings.

- Reuse paper that has been printed on one side as scratch paper.

RECYCLE

- Much of your daily waste can be recycled at the curb.

- Make sure old phone books and directories get into the recycle bin.

- Some programs now accept plastic bags.

BUYING RECYCLED PRODUCTS

Some of the benefits...

- Saves natural resources—conserves land, reduces the need to drill for oil, mine for minerals, and desecrate forests.

- Saves energy—for example, producing aluminum by recycling takes 95% less energy than producing new aluminum from bauxite ore.

- Saves clean air and water—reduces amount of pollutants emitted during resource extraction, processing, and manufacturing.

- Saves landfill space—materials go into new products, not the landfill.

- Saves money and creates jobs—creates more jobs than landfills or incinerators; is often the least expensive waste management method for cities and towns.

What can be recycled curbside varies by municipality so check your city's or county's website for specifics. You can also log on to **www.earth911.org**, type in your zip code, and get all the local recycling information you need. Be sure to rinse all bottles, cans, containers, and foil food trays before placing them in the bin.

PAPER
- White, colored, shredded (unsoiled; no paper towels)
- Newspaper
- Magazines
- Catalogs
- Paperback books
- Paperboard (cereal boxes, etc.)
- Egg cartons
- Cardboard (flattened)
- Junk mail
- Non-metallic wrapping paper
  (Note: staples, paperclips, labels, and tape are allowed)

CANS AND FOIL
- Steel
- Aluminum cans
- Metal food trays

GLASS
- Bottles, jars

PLASTIC
- #1 and #2 containers (beverage, milk, soda, water, detergent, shampoo, yogurt, margarine, etc.)

KNOW YOUR PLASTIC NUMBERS

The plastics industry has developed a series of markers, usually seen on the bottom of plastic containers. **These markers do not mean the plastic can be recycled, nor do they mean the container uses recycled plastic.** Despite the confusing use of the chasing arrow symbol, these markers **only identify the plastic type, that is, 1-PETE, 2-HDPE, 3-Vinyl, 4-LDPE, 5-PP, 6-PS, 7-Other.**

Virtually everything made of plastic is marked with a code. Not all types can actually be recycled. **Types 1 and 2 are widely accepted in container form, and type 4 is sometimes accepted in bag form. Code 6 and 7 are for polystyrene and mixed or layered plastic and has virtually no recycling potential.** You should place in your bin only those types of plastic authorized by your local recycling agency.

Greening
Your Space

DO NOT PUT THESE ITEMS CURBSIDE:
- TVs (take to an electronics recycling center)
- Computer monitors (take to an electronics recycling center)
- Auto batteries (many service stations and city- or county-operated recycling centers will accept these)
- Plastic bags (often not recyclable; check with your local waste hauler or on your county's recycling website)

Spinning Our Wheels

The biggest environmental choice we make is how we get from one place to another. Making smart transportation choices can help protect local air quality as well as the health of the planet.

Our vehicles, from cars to trucks to trains to planes, are responsible for over 40% of California's greenhouse gases and smog-forming pollution. Wildlife and their habitats are threatened by our ever-expanding roads and highways that encroach into sensitive ecosystems. But the concerns don't end there: our growing thirst for gasoline and diesel makes us reliant on foreign sources of oil from politically unstable regions of the world.

Luckily there are choices each of us can make to help the environment. When possible, walk or bike—not only is it good for the environment, it is good for us. When looking for a car to rent or buy, choose the most fuel-efficient, low-emitting vehicle available. Alternative fuels can provide even more options to help kick the oil habit. Whenever practical, take public transportation—Cal Train, BART, or the bus. And if you really want to make a difference, figure out ways to reduce your travel overall. You can also get involved with organizations that are working to improve transportation and land use decisions at the local, state, or national level.

The future is now. We don't need to wait for radical new technologies. We can make a significant reduction in the environmental impact of transportation by taking advantage of technologies available today.

PATRICIA MONAHAN
Patricia Monahan is the Deputy Director of the Union of Concerned Scientists' Clean Vehicles Program. Patricia has published numerous reports promoting cleaner transportation choices.

Perhaps the best way to start helping the planet and reversing global climate change is by getting out of your car. If that isn't a feasible option, why not consider a hybrid vehicle or one that runs on biodiesel?

One of the most exciting areas of alternative energy use is the new crop of eco-friendly vehicles. After a century of reliance on gas-powered cars and trucks, there are a growing number of dealers dedicated to providing you with low-emission, fuel-efficient alternatives to yesterday's gas guzzler.

Check out the diverse group below. We've found everything from green car brokers who can hook you up with biofuel vehicles to conventional car manufacturers with some super fuel-efficient and alternative fuel car models. (We have not listed individual dealerships because there are so many, but the manufacturers listed below sell one or more alternative fuel or hybrid models.)

The businesses listed below are not recognized by varying numbers of leaves but are included as a resource for you. If you are looking for a way to create a major change in your own energy consumption, this is a key place to start.

BIG KID TOYS
476 Soscol Ave. Napa 94559 707-256-3300
Mon-Fri 10-5 Sat 11-4 and by appt.   www.bigkidtoys.com
Smart cars, electric Zap Zebra, T-Rex, electric ATVs.

COMMUTER CARS
715 East Sprague Suite 70 Spokane WA 99202 509-624-0762
www.commutercars.com
Tango electric commuter vehicles.

ECOMOTORS
1270 Petaluma Blvd. North Petaluma 94952 707-778-2055
By appt. www.ecomotors.biz
Pre-owned, alternative-fuel vehicles. Biodiesel, hybrids.

ELECTRIC MOTORSPORT
2400 Mandela Parkway Oakland (West Oakland) 94607 510-839-9376
Mon-Fri 10-5 www.electricmotorsport.com
Electric motorcycles and scooters.

ELECTRIC VEHICLE REPAIRS & CONVERSIONS
415-550-8585
By appt.
Mechanic; electric vehicles and electric conversion. House calls only.

FORD MOTOR COMPANY
www.ford.com
Manufactures hybrid Escape SUV.

GENERAL MOTORS
www.livegreengoyellow.com
Proponents of ethanol technology.

HONDA

www.honda.com
Manufacturer of the hybrid Civic and Accord as well as some natural gas vehicles.

LEXUS

www.lexus.com
Makers of the RX400h hybrid SUV and GS450h hybrid luxury sedan.

MERCURY

www.mercuryvehicles.com
Makers of the Mariner hybrid SUV.

SAN FRANCISCO CHRYSLER JEEP

475 South Van Ness Ave. SF (Mission) 94103 415-431-3892
Mon-Fri 9-8 Sat 9-6 Sun 10-6 www.alberabros.com
Distributor of GEM electric vehicles.

SEGWAY OF OAKLAND

212 International Blvd. Oakland (Lake Merritt/Downtown) 94606 510-832-2429
Daily 9-6 www.segwayofoakland.com
Battery-powered transportation device. Sales and rentals.

TESLA MOTORS

1050 Bing St. San Carlos 94070 650-413-4000
By appt.
Offers high-performance electric vehicles.

TOYOTA

www.toyota.com
Makers of the hybrid Prius, Camry and Highlander.

VOLTAGE VEHICLE

3362 Fulton Rd. Fulton 95439 707-568-3333
Mon-Fri 9-6 Sat-Sun 10-5 www.voltagevehicle.com
Electric car dealership. Some electric trucks.

ZAP!

501 Fourth St. Santa Rosa 95401 707-525-8658
Mon-Fri 8:30-5 www.zapworld.com
Eco-friendly transportation. Electric, fuel cell, and hybrid cars; electric bicycles and scooters. Portable energy for personal electronic devices.

Walking is the most eco-friendly way to get around. Instead of shopping for that new car, consider a new pair of shoes (sustainably made, of course!).

Keep your vehicle well tuned to improve fuel economy, reduce emissions, and lengthen the life of your car. Regular maintenance should include proper tire inflation, oil changes, air filter changes, and replacement of spark plugs.

Getting Around

FUELING STATIONS

As demand for alternative fuels and alternative fuel vehicles increases, so will the fueling stations and programs. To keep up with expanding locations, visit Clean Car Maps (www.weststart.net/ccm/home) or the stations and website references listed below.

COMPRESSED NATURAL GAS (CNG)

Some stations may require membership cards for access or company-specific credit cards for payment. Refer to www.cngvc.org for the Compressed Natural Gas Vehicle Coalition's national directory of stations and their respective methods of payment.

CLEAN ENERGY
888-732-6487 (Main # for all stations)
CFN Olympian 8515 San Leandro St. Oakland (East Oakland) 94621
Oakland International Airport 7855 Earhart Rd. Oakland (East Oakland) 94621
Olympian Oil 2690 Third St. SF (Dog Patch) 94107
SF International Airport (front of United) 790 North McDonnell Rd. SF 94128
Daily 24 hours   www.cleanenergyfuels.com
Stations accept Clean Energy and major credit cards.

PG&E SERVICE CENTERS
800-684-4648 (Main # for all stations)
24300 Clawiter Rd. Hayward 94545
1100 South 27th St. Richmond 94804
1970 Industrial Way San Carlos 94002
425 Folsom St. SF (SOMA) 94105
536 Treat Ave. SF (Mission) 94110
1220 Andersen Dr. San Rafael 94901
Daily 24 hours
Stations require PG&E card payment.

TRILLIUM USA
800-920-1166 (Main # for all stations)
1101 Second St. Berkeley 94710
SF Airport 50 Old Bayshore Hwy. Millbrae 94030
Daily 24 hours   www.trilliumusa.com
Stations require Trillium access card.

ELECTRIC PLUG-IN STATIONS

CLEAN FUELING STATIONS
800-861-7759 (All locations)
43621 Pacific Commons Blvd. Fremont 94538
300 Vintage Way Novato 94945
2200 Hilltop Mall Rd. Richmond 94806
1601 Coleman Ave. Santa Clara 95050
355 McAllister St. SF (Civic Center) 94102
433 Kearny St. SF (Financial District) 94108
123 O'Farrell St. SF (Union Square) 94102
5301 Almaden Expressway San Jose 95118
2201 Senter Rd. San Jose 95112
1900 Davis St. San Leandro 94577
1077 East Arques Ave. Sunnyvale 94086
Hours vary by location   www.weststart.net/ccm/home
Stations for electric inductive small, electric inductive large, and electric conductive vehicles.

Getting Around

BIODIESEL

BERKELEY BIODIESEL COLLECTIVE
2530 San Pablo Ave. Berkeley 94702 510-594-4000 x777
www.berkeleybiodiesel.org
Biodiesel education and advocacy. See website calendar for
workshop schedule.

BIOFUEL OASIS
2465 Fourth St. Berkeley 94710 510-665-5509
Sun, Tue-Thu 4-8 Fri by appt. Sat 10-5   www.biofueloasis.com
Carboys, fuel filters, SVO supplies; bulk delivery service.

LC BIOFUELS
510-232-0416 (All locations)
116 South First St. Richmond   94804
14 Greenfield Ave. San Anselmo 94960
Hours vary by location   www.lcbiofuels.com
Biodiesel stations with B100. San Anselmo: account required for fueling;
Richmond: cash and credit cards accepted.

PEOPLE'S FUEL COOPERATIVE
4035 Judah St. Suite 402 SF (Sunset) 94122 415-747-6152
By appt.   www.peoplesfuel.org
Biodiesel delivery service. Supplies businesses, residents, co-ops.

SAN FRANCISCO BIOFUELS COOPERATIVE
521 Eighth St. SF (Civic Center) 94103 415-267-3998
Mon 6 p.m.-8 p.m. Wed 5 p.m.-7 p.m. Thu 6 p.m.-8 p.m. Sun 11 a.m.-1 p.m.
www.sfbiofuels.org
Recycled vegetable oil biodiesel.

HYDROGEN

HYDROGEN FUELING MAP
www.fuelcellpartnership.org/fuel-vehl_map.html
Map that includes all hydrogen refueling stations in the Bay Area.

Make sure your car's tires are inflated to the highest
pressure recommended in your car's manual. Under-
inflated tires cause your car to run less efficiently. If
all Americans' tires were properly inflated we could
save around 2 billion gallons of gas each year.

Idling your car for more than 10 seconds produces
emissions at almost twice the rate of normal driving.
For most cars built in the last 25 years, turning the
car off and on again doesn't use extra gas or cause
additional wear and tear.

Getting Around

The best-known auto club is also in the business of lobbying for more highways and less public transit—but we've found an alternative. There is one national auto club that is environmentally friendly. This club offers the standard roadside service, trip planning, and maps, but will also help you offset your carbon-emissions, rent hybrids, and find the best eco-resorts. What's more, they promote public transportation alternatives and other environmental causes.

We have listed the only auto club that actively works to protect the environment with their policies and revenues.

BETTER WORLD CLUB
20 NW Fifth Ave. Suite 100 Portland 97209 866-238-1137
Mon-Fri 8:30-5:30 www.betterworldclub.com
Eco-friendly auto club; discounts on membership for hybrid owners.
Eco-travel services.

Sometimes what's best for the environment is even better for you. When you have to, or just want to leave your car at home and let someone else provide the transportation, it's good to know that you have options. The taxi and limousine companies we list below offer a smooth, green ride.

Companies listed have at least part of their fleet running on an alternative fuel or hybrid system.

ECOLIMO
SF 888-432-6546
Daily 24 hours www.eco-limo.com
Chauffeured transportation in alternative-fuel vehicles. Biodiesel, electric, hybrid, CNG.

PLANETTRAN
SF 877-ECO-TAXI
Daily 24 hours www.planettran.com
Provides individuals and organizations with scheduled car service in hybrid cars to the airport or throughout the Bay Area.

YELLOW CAB CO-OP
1200 Mississippi St. SF 94107 (415) 333-3333
Daily 24 hours www.yellowcabsf.com
Hybrid or CNG taxis available. Trips must originate in SF.

Whether you have friends or family coming to town or want to test drive a hybrid or biodiesel car, check out these car rental and car share options. They are adding some gas-sipping and climate-friendly vehicles to their fleets.

All businesses listed offer rental vehicles that run on alternative fuel, hybrid engines, or are part of a car share club that offers an alternative to individual car ownership.

If you prefer two wheels to four, we have researched the Bay Area's bike rental locations. So if you like the feel of the wind in your face, your feet on the pedals, and your emissions at zero, check out our listings. Here are some places where you can rent a bike for the hour or the day. And you'll find a few other surprises in our listings to keep you on your transportation toes.

CAR RENTALS

EV RENTALS AT FOX RENT A CAR
877-EV-RENTAL (All locations)
Oakland International Airport 2600 Earhart Rd. Oakland 94621
SF International Airport 435 South Airport Blvd. SF 94128
2300 Airport Blvd. Suite 160 San Jose 95110
Hours vary by location   www.evrental.com
Rents hybrid vehicles through Fox Rent A Car locations. Be sure to ask for a hybrid when requesting a quote.

HERTZ
Oakland International Airport 7600 Earhart Rd. Oakland 94621 510-633-4300
SF International Airport 780 McDonnell Rd. SF 94125 650-624-6600
Hours vary by location   www.hertz.com
Offers hybrid cars when booking by phone.

SPECIALTY RENTALS
920 University Ave. Berkeley 94710 510-549-1580
Oakland International Airport 1 Airport Dr. Oakland 94621 800-400-8412
4218 El Camino Real Palo Alto 94306 650-856-9100
320 O'Farrell St. SF (Union Square) 94102 415-292-5300
150 Valencia St. SF (Mission) 94103 415-701-1900
SF International Airport South SF 94125 800-400-8412
10 Bellam Blvd. San Rafael 94901 415-451-1920
Hours vary by location   www.specialtyrentals.com
Offers hybrid cars in their fleet of vehicles.

CAR SHARE SERVICES

CASUAL CARPOOLING
www.ridenow.org/carpool
"Casual carpools" are informal carpools that form when drivers and passengers meet at designated locations. Casual carpools are not "run" by any organization or authority.

CITY CARSHARE
131 Steuart St. Suite 205 SF (Financial District) 94105 415-995-8588
Information and Reservations 24 hours   www.citycarshare.org
Hourly rentals of vehicles in your neighborhood. Gas and insurance included in any convertible, truck, hybrid, or SUV rental.

Getting Around

FLEXCAR

50 Fremont St. Suite 1500 SF (Financial District) 94105 877-FLEXCAR
Information & Reservations 24 hours Office Mon-Fri 8-5 www.flexcar.com
Car share service. Hybrid and standard vehicles parked around town at
convenient spaces near homes and workplaces. Pay by the hour: Gas,
insurance, and maintenance included.

ICARPOOL

www.icarpool.com
iCarpool finds carpool matches for daily commutes, long distance trips, and
scheduled events. Registration and carpool search is free with no obligation.

MATCH & GO

www.matchandgo.com
This service helps find a companion for carpooling, flights, bus rides, and more.

SPACESHARE

510-520-6175 www.spaceshare.com
Network that connects travelers heading to events and festivals with others
to share transportation and/or lodging needs.

ZIPCAR

191 Second St. SF (SOMA) 94105 415-495-7478
Mon-Fri 8:30-5:30 www.zipcar.com
Car share service. Rents hybrids, MINIs, and VWs by the hour. Gas, insurance,
and parking included. Cars parked in convenient locations.

ALTERNATIVE TRANSPORTATION

ALAMEDA BICYCLE

1522 Park St. Alameda 94501 510-522-0070
3301 East 12th St. Bldg. B, Suite 141 Oakland (East Oakland) 94602 510-536-2200
www.alamedabicycle.com
Sells and rents bicycles. Women on Wheels (WOW) offers classes on
bicycling and repair.

BAY CITY BIKE RENTALS

415-346-BIKE (All locations)
1325 Columbus Ave. SF (North Beach) 94133
2661 Taylor St. SF (North Beach) 94133
www.baycitybike.com
Broad fleet of bikes to suit all tastes, plus a full-service bicycle shop.

BIKE AND ROLL

899 Columbus Ave. SF (Fisherman's Wharf) 94133 415-229-2000
www.bikeandroll.com
Offers wide selection of bikes from comfort bikes to mountain bikes.

BIKE HUT, THE

Pier 40 SF (SOMA) 94102 415-543-4335
Daily 10-6 (Weather permitting) www.thebikehut.com
The Bike Hut started as an outpost of the Bicycle Community Project. Rent,
learn to build and repair bicycles, and buy parts and accessories.

BLAZING SADDLES BIKE RENTALS

415-202-8888 (All locations)
2715 Hyde St. SF (Fisherman's Wharf) 94109
465 Jefferson St. SF (Fisherman's Wharf) 94109
Pier 41 at the Embarcadero SF (Fisherman's Wharf) 94101
Pier 43½ SF (Fisherman's Wharf) 94133
1095 Columbus Ave. SF (North Beach) 94133
Daily from 8 a.m. www.blazingsaddles.com
Offers a wide range of bike rentals and tours. Also accessories for
those traveling with children.

LOCKSMITH MAGIC/GOLDEN GATE PARK SKATE AND BIKE
3038 Fulton St. SF (Richmond) 94118 415-668-1117
Mon-Fri 10-5 Sat 10-5:30 (weather permitting)
Bike rentals. Helmets available. Bring your own lock.

SAN FRANCISCO BIKE COALITION
995 Market St. Suite 1550 SF (Civic Center) 94103 415-431-2453
Mon-Fri 9:30-6 www.sfbike.org
Non-profit membership-based advocacy organization. Promotes the use of
bicycles for everyday transportation.

SCOOTCAR SAN FRANCISCO
431 Beach St. SF (Fisherman's Wharf) 94133 415-567-7994
Daily 9-dusk www.scootcar.net
Rents scootcars, scooters, electric cars, and motorcycles.

SOLANO AVENUE CYCLERY
1554 Solano Ave. Berkeley 94707 510-524-1094
Mon-Fri 11-7 Sat 10-6 www.solanoavenuecyclery.com
Bike rentals and sales. Accessories also available.

WALK SF
415-431-WALK www.walksf.org
Coalition that promotes safe city walking.

WHEEL FUN RENTALS
50 Stow Lake Dr. Golden Gate Park SF (Golden Gate Park) 94118 415-668-6699
Daily 10-dusk www.wheelfunrentals.com
They offer a unique fleet of cycles that can accommodate from 1 to 11 riders
(the Triple Surrey).

PUBLIC TRANSPORTATION

Perhaps the best way to start helping the planet and reversing global
climate change is by sharing a ride. It feels good and it's easy. At the
same time, you'll be reducing that commute-related stress by letting
someone else do the driving.

Check out the Bay Area's clean, safe, and reliable public transportation
systems. We have done some of the legwork for you by listing contact
numbers and web addresses for public transportation services.

Get in touch with the organizations listed below and they will set you
up with bus and train schedules and let you know the closest pick-up
spot to your home or office so you can be on your way.

511.ORG
Dial "511" www.511.org
Bay area travel guide. Links to public transit companies, estimated driving
times, public transit trip planner.

AC TRANSIT
510-891-4783 www.ACTransit.org
Operates buses in the Richmond/Berkeley, Oakland/Alameda, Hayward/San
Leandro, and Fremont/Newark areas.

BART

415-989-2278 www.bart.gov
Mass transit train serving parts of SF, East Bay, and South Bay.

BLUE AND GOLD FLEET

415-705-8200 www.blueandgoldfleet.com
Provides ferry and water excursion services to Sausalito, Tiburon, Alameda/Oakland, Vallejo, and Angel Island.

CALTRAIN

800-660-4287 www.caltrain.com
Train service between San Francisco and San Jose.

EASTBAY FERRY

510-749-5972 www.eastbayferry.com
The Alameda/Oakland ferry operates from the Clay Street (Jack London Square) ferry terminal and the Alameda (Main Street) terminal to San Francisco's Pier 39, Angel Island, and the AT&T Ball Park.

GOLDEN GATE TRANSIT

415-923-2000 www.goldengate.org
The Golden Gate buses and ferries connect to SF Municipal Railway (MUNI), Bay Area Rapid Transit (BART) and CalTrain.

NEXTBUS

510-995-3200 www.nextbus.com
Nextbus uses satellite technology and advanced computer modeling to track vehicles on their routes. Predictions are then made available on the Internet, cellphones, PDAs, and signs at bus stops.

SAMTRANS

800-660-4287 www.samtrans.org
Provides bus service throughout San Mateo county and into parts of San Francisco and Palo Alto.

SFMUNI

415-673-6864 www.sfmuni.com
SFMuni operates cable cars, trolley buses powered by electricity, streetcars, and regular buses in San Francisco.

VTA

408-321-2300 www.vta.org
The Santa Clara Valley Transportation Authority operates a 42.2 mile light rail line which starts in Santa Clara and goes to Downtown SF.

> The United States consumes almost 9 million barrels of gasoline daily — 43% of the total global daily gasoline consumption. (Alliance to Save Energy)

Getting Around

Although it's sometimes comforting to blame "industry" for all of our environmental ills, the fact is, each one of us contributes to the greenhouse gases that increase global warming. The cars we drive, the flights we take, and the energy we use in our homes and apartments directly effects what happens to our planet. This is where "carbon offsets" come into play.

The idea behind carbon offsets is to effectively mitigate the carbon emissions we produce by purchasing a carbon offset credit from a third party who, in turn, uses those funds to engage in special projects that capture and/or reduce greenhouse gases elsewhere. The goal is not only to lessen greenhouse gas emissions, but for us to recognize and take responsibility for the things we do which may have larger, or even global consequences. First and most important, reduce your carbon footprint by becoming more eco-efficient. Then, look to carbon offsets as a way to mitigate what's left.

Because this is a new and emerging field, we have not leaf-awarded these organizations but they all provide customers with the means to calculate, and the opportunity to buy, carbon offset credits.

3 PHASES
6 Funston Ave. SF (Presidio/Presidio Heights) 94129 866-476-9378
www.3phases.com
3 Phases works with utilities to offer environmentally-conscious choices for electricity consumers. SF green certified business.

BETTER WORLD CLUB
20 NW 5th Ave. Suite 100 Portland OR 97209 503-546-1137
www.betterworldclub.com
Carbon offset from air travel; travel services.

CARBON FUND
10001 Dallas Ave. Silver Spring MD 20901 240-556-1908
www.carbonfund.org
Low-cost carbon reductions; supports energy efficiency and reforestation.

CLIMATE TRUST, THE
65 SW Yamhill St. Suite 400 Portland OR 97204 503-238-1915
www.climatetrust.org
Promotes climate change solutions by providing high quality greenhouse gas offset projects and advancing sound offset policy.

COOL DRIVER
100 Market St. Suite 204 Portsmouth NH 03801 603-422-6464
www.cooldriver.org
Carbon offset from auto travel, methane capture.

DRIVE NEUTRAL
Presidio Building 36 P.O. Box 29502 SF (Presidio/Presidio Heights) 94129
415-561-1170
www.driveneutral.org
Carbon offsets and carbon calculators. Emissions reductions through Chicago Climate Exchange.

Getting Around

NATIVE ENERGY

823 Ferry Rd. P.O. Box 539 Charlotte VT 05445 800-924-6826
www.nativeenergy.com
Renewable energy projects; carbon offset fees go to build wind power on
Native American lands.

PG&E CLIMATESMART PROGRAM (LAUNCHING SPRING 2007)

245 Market St. SF (Financial District) 94105 800-743-5000
www.pge.com
Program allows customers to calculate and offset the amount of carbon their
power produces. Revenues will go towards conserving or restoring California's
forests.

RENEWABLE CHOICE ENERGY

4041 Hanover Ave. Suite 200 Boulder CO 80305 877-810-8670
www.renewablechoice.com
Promotes the development of clean alternatives to fossil fuels.

SKY ENERGY

2131 Woodruff Rd. Suite 2100 #203 Greenville SC 29607 866-759-3637
www.sky-energy.com
Carbon offsets, renewable energy credits offset emissions by
funding wind power.

SOLAR ELECTRIC LIGHT FUND

1612 K St. NW Suite 402 Washington DC 20006 202-234-7265
www.self.org
Clean, renewable energy, modern communications; serves rural, off-grid
families in developing countries.

SUSTAINABLE TRAVEL INTERNATIONAL

2060 Floral Dr. Boulder CO 80304 720-273-2975
www.my-climate.com
Travelers can help to neutralize the negative impacts of their air and ground
travel, home and hotel stays, by investing in renewable energy, biomass, and
methane capture projects.

TERRA PASS

405 El Camino Real Menlo Park 94025 650-331-0078
www.terrapass.com
Supports energy projects that balance out travel and energy use impact.

FOR MORE INFORMATION

MY FOOTPRINT.ORG

www.myfootprint.org
Assess how much land and water resources you use compared to the global
average with the Ecological Footprint Quiz.

STOP GLOBAL WARMING

15332 Antioch St. Suite 168 Pacific Palisades 90272 310-454-2561
www.stopglobalwarming.org
Personal carbon dioxide calculator; offers tips for reduction.

Every time we leave our homes, we make choices that make a
significant impact on our carbon footprint and thus on global
warming. What are your experiences with the eco-friendly
options for transportation that we've listed here? What have we
missed? Drive your comments home on www.greenopia.com.

Lots of things are going "carbon neutral" these days, but what does that really mean? Making something carbon neutral (also known as climate neutral) doesn't mean sucking up greenhouse gases or sticking a banana in the tailpipe. Carbon neutrality, or carbon offsetting, is the process by which global warming gases emitted by a certain activity, event, or process are calculated and then effectively offset by removing or preventing an equal amount of pollution elsewhere. These offsets usually involve renewable energy projects like wind power, solar, or methane; reforestation projects (trees absorb CO_2); or energy efficiency programs. Carbon offset actions can take place next door or on the other side of the world, but the desired goal is that they reduce the net amount of greenhouse gases released into the atmosphere.

If something's emissions can be calculated, then they can be offset. The list of neutralized events, companies, and products is growing fast. Music tours, restaurants, films, colleges, books (yes, *Greenopia*), web hosts, entire companies, and huge events like the Winter Olympics and the World Cup have all gone carbon neutral. But it's also something we can each do with our own actions.

The most common examples of carbon offsets for individuals are emissions from air travel, emissions from driving, and home or office energy use. There are a growing number of services out there that will help you calculate and offset your emissions if you wish to go carbon neutral, whether it's on a case-by-case basis (like air travel), or over time (like offsetting commuting or home energy use for the year). If the thing you want to offset is more complex (like an event, the production of a film, or a product) there are independent companies able to calculate the associated environmental footprint.

It should be noted that there is a certain amount of contention around the idea of carbon offsets. It is important that companies offering offsets have a reliable way of verifying their actions, such as using Green-e Certified renewable energy credits. Green-e has strict consumer and environmental safeguards. Green-e's goal is to build consumer confidence in renewable energy alternatives and provide customers with clear information about renewable energy options. Consumers can use the Green-e logo to quickly identify renewable energy options that meet Green-e's high standards.

See www.green-e.org for more information.

BIODIESEL

An alternative fuel derived from biological sources, biodiesel usually comes from recycled or virgin vegetable oils. Biodiesel is often called a carbon-neutral fuel because it releases only the quantity of carbon dioxide that was absorbed by the source from which it was derived, such as soy or canola plants.

Any diesel engine will run on biodiesel with little or no modification, and biodiesel pumps can be found in almost every state in the U.S. Biodiesel is also relatively easy to make—a process more akin to brewing beer than to refining petroleum. However, users should be aware that biodiesel acts like a solvent, so be sure to check fuel filters and hoses more often when first using biodiesel to prevent clogs. To ensure smooth usage with biodiesel, users should only use fuel meeting the ASTM (American Society for Testing & Materials) D 6751 biodiesel specification. Biodiesel is cleaner for the air than petrol diesel and releases less carbon monoxide, aromatic hydrocarbons, and particulate matter (soot).

While a 2002 EPA study indicated that a biodiesel blend of B20 increased nitrous oxides emissions (a key contributor to smog) by two percent, an October 2006 US National Renewable Energy Labs study concluded that on average B20 has no effect on nitrous oxide (NOX) emissions. (Source: City and County of San Francisco Department of the Environment)

ETHANOL

There are between five and six million ethanol-ready cars and trucks already on the road in the U.S. Many of these are "flex-fuel" vehicles that can run on ethanol or regular gasoline. Ethanol is a biofuel most commonly derived from the fermentation of corn into alcohol. New methods of transforming straw and other plant wastes into ethanol are making the production process greener.

STRAIGHT VEGETABLE OIL

While biodiesel is a refined form of vegetable oil, diesel engines can also run on unmodified, or straight vegetable oil. However this requires a modification to the engine, which heats the oil before combustion. SVO, like biodiesel, is also a clean fuel and can be free if collected from restaurants or other establishments. Straight vegetable oil is not as well studied as biodiesel, however, and there are fewer hard facts on its emissions or engine wear.

CAR SHARING

Life without a car isn't just for New Yorkers anymore. It's getting easier for everyone, thanks to new car-sharing services like Zipcar and Flexcar. These community vehicles can be checked out by the hour and include gas, insurance, and maintenance.

HYBRIDS

Part electric, part internal combustion, hybrids represent a green step forward for the automobile. Better mileage, lower emissions, better performance, and lower fuel bills make hybrids a great deal for both people and planet. Be sure to do your homework before buying a new hybrid though, and make sure you get the car you need. No need to buy a hybrid SUV if a non-hybrid compact could get better mileage and do the job. Affordable electric vehicles and plug-in electric hybrids are also expected to hit the market in the not-too-distant future.

PUBLIC TRANSPORTATION

As the number of cars in the world increases, so does the need for efficient, clean, public transport options. Many people have great public transportation systems near them and don't even know it. Consider replacing a few of your car commutes each week with a trip on the bus or train. If a stop is not within walking distance of your house, try a park-and-ride with your car or bike.

THE INCREDIBLE RIDEABLE BICYCLE

The bicycle is generally considered the single most efficient means of transportation in the world. Not only is it an elegant and effective vehicle, it is also outstanding exercise. Although in the U.S. the bike is more often thought of as a form of recreation, in Europe it is used much more commonly for daily commuting to work and school. Experiment with replacing some weekly car trips with this remarkable device.

Getting Around

Getting Plugged In

One of the most important things you can do is get plugged in to an environmental organization. Environmental groups are set up to represent you and they do important work on your behalf. When environmental groups lobby Washington, when they launch a campaign, when they act in the community, if you are involved, they are representing you. The Natural Resources Defense Council has over a million members. That's powerful. When they go into a senator's office, they bring a million concerned people with them.

There are no official rules for getting involved. You can use resources like the book you are holding right now to find organizations. Many people also get plugged in via word of mouth or searching the web. You can learn more about an organization by seeing who is on its board of directors or reading the annual report. Make sure to get involved on a level that fits your schedule and your checkbook. And I recommend being an important member of one organization rather than a low-level member at a lot of organizations. Your access and influence with that group will increase along with your effectiveness.

Government doesn't change until people demand it, and what we need now on the issue of global warming is a giant shift in attitude. To bring about big changes, we need to influence the community at the grassroots as well as the leadership at the grass tops. Environmental organizations can do both, but remember, they need you. To be effective they need resources, funding, and access. When you get involved, you bring your force as a person.

LAURIE DAVID
Laurie David is a global warming activist and founder of the Stop Global Warming Virtual March with Senator John McCain and Robert F. Kennedy, Jr., which she urges you to join. It only takes an email address. (www.stopglobalwarming.org)

It's easy to be overwhelmed by the sheer number of environmental problems that plague our cities, but the organizations listed below are making a real difference. They inform and motivate, promote environmental awareness in different areas, and provide opportunities to get involved. Engaging with any one of these groups is a great way to learn about the problems your own community faces and help find and implement the solutions to solve those problems.

All organizations in this section promote environmental preservation, conservation, education, or habitat management and have non-profit status. Many offer direct, local, community involvement through classes and/or environmental work programs.

If you know of other groups or organizations like these, please let us know. We want to include them. And check our website for the most up-to-date listings.

ACTERRA

Peninsula Conservation Center 3921 East Bayshore Rd. Palo Alto 94303
650-962-9876
Mon-Fri 9-5 www.acterra.org
"Be the Change" environmental leadership training; habitat restoration and stewardship programs; lending library; e-mail eco-calendar; and Cool It! campaign.

ACTION FOR NATURE

2269 Chestnut St. Suite 263 SF (Marina) 94123 415-421-2640
Hours vary www.actionfornature.org
Youth-oriented organization. Online environmental education games; links to other children's nature sites and activities. Sponsors local events.

ALAMEDA CREEK ALLIANCE

P.O. Box 192 Canyon 94516 510-499-9185
www.alamedacreek.org
Volunteer-based community watershed group; protects steelhead trout. Call Volunteer Coordinator at 510-794-4252 or visit website for project dates and times.

AMAZON WATCH

One Hallidie Plaza Suite 402 SF (Union Square) 94102 415-487-9600
www.amazonwatch.org
Works with indigenous and environmental organizations in the Amazon Basin to defend the environment and advance indigenous peoples' rights.

ARC ECOLOGY

4634 Third St. SF (Bayview/Hunter's Point) 94124 415-643-1190
Mon-Fri 9-4 www.arcecology.org
Provides community support with the process of closure, cleanup, and repurposing of military bases.

ARDENWOOD REGIONAL PRESERVE AND HISTORIC FARM

34600 Ardenwood Blvd. Fremont 94555 510-796-0663
www.ebparks.org/parks/arden.htm
Working nineteenth-century farm. Agriculture, history, and cultural programs for children and adults; seasonal events; produce stand. Available for weddings and special events.

AS YOU SOW
311 California St. Suite 510 SF (Financial District) 94104 415-391-3212
Hours vary www.asyousow.org
Facilitates shareholder-driven transformation of corporations toward
environmental responsibility and sustainability.

ASIAN-PACIFIC ENVIRONMENTAL NETWORK
310 Eighth St. Suite 309 Oakland (West Oakland) 94607 510-834-8920
Mon-Fri 9-5 www.apen4ej.org
Works toward environmental justice in low-income, Asian-Pacific communities.

BAY AREA COALITION FOR HEADWATERS FOREST
2530 San Pablo Ave. Berkeley 94702 510-548-3113
Hours vary www.headwaterspreserve.org
Educates and builds support for the preservation of a biologically viable
redwood forest.

BAY LOCALIZE
436 14th St. Suite 1218 Oakland (Lake Merritt/Downtown) 94612 510-834-0420
Hours vary www.baylocalize.org
A collaborative of Bay Area environmental organizations working on
localization projects.

BAY NATURE INSTITUTE
1328 Sixth Street Suite 2 Berkeley 94710 510-528-8550
Mon-Fri 9-5 www.baynature.org
Communications organization; sponsors free naturalist-led local hikes and
information programs; publishes *Bay Nature* magazine.

BAYKEEPER/SF BAY CHAPTER
785 Market St. Suite 850 SF (Financial District) 94103 415-856-0444
Mon-Fri 9-5 www.sfbaykeeper.org
Patrols Bay-Delta land and waterways; works with government agencies
to stop pollution.

BIONEERS, YOUTH & SATELLITE PROGRAM
2601 Mission St. Suite 403 SF (Mission) 94110 415-643-8633
Mon-Fri 9-5 www.bioneers.org
Forums for creative environmental education and solutions. Weekly public
radio series; annual conference of scientific and social innovators.

BLUEWATER NETWORK, A DIVISION OF FRIENDS OF THE EARTH
311 California St. Suite 510 SF (Financial District) 94104 415-544-0790
Mon-Fri 9-5 www.bluewaternetwork.org
Works to stop damage from vehicles and vessels; aims to reduce dependence
on fossil fuels.

BREAST CANCER FUND, THE
1388 Sutter St. Suite 400 SF (Civic Center) 94109 415-346-8223
Mon-Fri 9-5 www.breastcancerfund.org
Identifies and advocates for the elimination of environmental and other
preventable causes of the disease. On-line legislative tool kit, events.

CALIFORNIA ACADEMY OF SCIENCES
875 Howard St. SF (SOMA) 94103 415-321-8000
Daily 10-5 Open late third Thursday each month www.calacademy.org
Education and research institution, includes Morrison Planetarium, Natural
History Museum, and Steinhart Aquarium. Exhibits and programs relocated to
Howard Street through 2007 during Golden Gate Park site renovation.

CALIFORNIA COASTAL COMMISSION
45 Fremont St. Suite 2000 SF (Financial District) 94105 415-904-5200
Mon-Fri 8-5 See website for volunteer clean-up days and activities
www.coastal.ca.gov
Agency that regulates state-wide public access, recreation, marine health, oil
spill response, and coastal development. Resource for public education and
volunteer opportunities.

CALIFORNIA LEAGUE OF CONSERVATION VOTERS
1212 Broadway Suite 630 Oakland (Lake Merritt/Downtown) 94612
510-271-0900
Mon-Fri 8:30-5 www.ecovote.org
Non-partisan environmental political action organization, scoring representatives,
and endorsing candidates who support sustainable legislation.

CALIFORNIA NATIVE PLANT SOCIETY
916-447-2677   www.cnps.org
Native plant preservation; research, education, conservation. See their
website for Bay Area chapters' hours and activities.

CALIFORNIA STATE PARKS
800-777-0369 www.parks.ca.gov
Online directory of state nature preserves and parks; ongoing interpretive
programs at many locations. See their website for locations, days, and hours.

CALIFORNIANS FOR GE-FREE AGRICULTURE
www.calgefree.org
Promotes sustainable agriculture that is free of genetic engineering.

CALIFORNIANS FOR PESTICIDE REFORM
49 Powell St. Suite 530 SF (Union Square) 94102 415-981-3939
Mon-Fri 9-5 www.pesticidereform.org
Focus is to improve and protect public health, support sustainable agriculture,
and enhance environmental quality by building a movement across California
that changes statewide pesticide policies and practices.

CENTER FOR ENVIRONMENTAL HEALTH
528 61st St. Suite A Oakland (College Ave.) 94609 510-594-9864
Mon-Fri 9-6 www.cehca.org
Works to reduce pollution, promote alternatives to toxic chemicals.

CHEZ PANISSE FOUNDATION
1517 Shattuck Ave. Berkeley 94709 510-843-3811
Mon-Fri 9-5 www.chezpanissefoundation.org
Develops programs in public schools that use food to educate, nurture,
and empower youth. Includes the Edible School Yard and the School
Lunch Initiative.

CIRCLE OF LIFE
P.O. Box 3764 Oakland (Lake Merritt/Downtown) 94609 510-601-9790
Call for hours www.circleoflife.org
Activates people through education, inspiration, and connection to live in a way
that honors the diversity and interdependence of all life.

CITY AND COUNTY OF SAN FRANCISCO DEPARTMENT
OF THE ENVIRONMENT ECOCENTER
11 Grove St. SF (Civic Center) 94102 415-355-3700
Recycling Hotline: 415-554-7329
Mon-Fri 9-5 www.sfenvironment.com
City planning for environmental sustainability; community outreach, education,
volunteer opportunities.

CLEAN WATER ACTION
111 New Montgomery St. Suite 600 SF (SOMA) 94105 415-369-9160
Mon-Fri 10-6 www.cleanwateraction.org
Organization working for clean, safe and affordable water; prevention of health-threatening pollution; creation of environmentally-safe jobs and businesses. Organizes grassroots groups and campaigns.

COASTAL CONSERVANCY
1330 Broadway Suite 1300 Oakland (Lake Merritt/Downtown) 94612 510-286-1015
Mon-Fri 8-5 www.coastalconservancy.ca.gov
State agency funded by various state wildlife bonds. Works with local government, non-profit organizations, and landowners to protect, preserve, and restore the resources of the California coast.

COMMUNITIES FOR A BETTER ENVIRONMENT
1440 Broadway Suite 701 Oakland (Lake Merritt/Downtown) 94612 510-302-0430
Mon-Fri 9:30-5:30 www.cbecal.org
Environmental health and justice group promoting clean air, clean water and the development of toxin-free communities. Brings grassroots activism, environmental research, and legal assistance to under-served urban communities.

CRISSY FIELD CENTER
SF (Presidio/Presidio Heights) 94123 415-561-7690
Wed-Sun 9-5 www.crissyfield.org
Community environmental facility with walks, workshops, special events, café, and gift store. SF green certified business.

CULTURAL CONSERVANCY
P.O. Box 29044 SF (Presidio) 94129 415-561-6594
www.nativeland.org
Native American organization dedicated to the preservation and revitalization of indigenous cultures and their ancestral lands.

EARTHJUSTICE
426 17th St. 6th Floor Oakland (Lake Merritt/Downtown) 94612 510-550-6700
Mon-Fri 9-5 www.earthjustice.org
Public interest law firm dedicated to protecting places, natural resources, and wildlife, and to defending the right of all people to a healthy environment.

EARTH ISLAND INSTITUTE
300 Broadway Suite 28 SF (North Beach) 94133 415-788-3666
Mon-Fri 9-5 www.earthisland.org
Umbrella organization for environmental sustainability projects. Publishes *Earth Island Journal*.

EARTH SHARE OF CALIFORNIA
49 Powell St. Suite 510 SF (Civic Center) 94102 415-981-1999
Mon-Fri 9-5 www.earthshareca.org
Network of over 80 environmental organizations that promote healthy, clean, and safe communities.

ECOLOGY CENTER
2530 San Pablo Ave. Berkeley 94702 510-548-2220
Tue-Sat 11-6 www.ecologycenter.org
Environmental resource center and library. Job and volunteer listings, classes, and calendar of local events.

ELLA BAKER CENTER FOR HUMAN RIGHTS
344 40th St. Oakland (Temescal) 94609 510-428-3939
Mon-Fri 9-5 www.ellabakercenter.org
Advocacy group that encourages renewable energy, green construction, and
the creation of new jobs for urban workers. Volunteer opportunities available.

ENDANGERED SPECIES COALITION
P.O. Box 5852 Berkeley 94795 510-486-0567
Hours vary www.stopextinction.org
Utilizes public education, scientific information and citizen participation in all
decisions affecting the fate of threatened and endangered species. Citizens
can participate in grassroots organizing.

ENVIRONMENTAL JUSTICE COALITION FOR WATER
654 13th St. Preservation Park Oakland (Lake Merritt/Downtown) 94612
510-286-8400
Hours vary www.ejcw.org
Coalition of environmental justice advocates for clean water policies in California.

ETHICAL TRAVELER
P.O. Box 5883 Berkeley 94705 415-788-3666 ext. 207
Mon-Fri 9-5 www.ethicaltraveler.org
A global alliance of tourists, travelers, and travel service providers working to
leverage economic power towards improving human rights and preserving
the environment.

FOOD FIRST/INSTITUTE FOR FOOD AND DEVELOPMENT
398 60th St. Oakland (Rockridge) 94618 510-654-4400
Mon-Fri 9-5 www.foodfirst.org
Agricultural political action, conferences. Produces literature on
food-related issues.

FORESTETHICS
One Haight St. Suite B SF (Hayes Valley) 94102 415-863-4563
www.forestethics.org
Protects endangered forests through consumer engagement, corporate action
campaigns, and working with First Nations people to protect native forestland.
Volunteer opportunities available.

FRIENDS OF THE URBAN FOREST
Presidio of San Francisco Building Suite1007 P.O. Box 29456 SF (Presidio/Presidio
Heights) 94129 415-561-6890
Mon-Fri 9-5 www.fuf.net
Provides financial, technical, and practical assistance to San Franciscans
for tree planting and care. Introduces disadvantaged youth to careers in
urban forestry.

GLOBAL EXCHANGE
2017 Mission St. Suite 303 SF (Mission) 94110 415-255-7296
Mon-Fri 9-5 www.globalexchange.org
Membership-based organization promoting social, economic, and
environmental justice around the world.

GOLDEN GATE AUDUBON SOCIETY AND NATURE STORE
2530 San Pablo Ave. Berkeley 94702 510-843-2222
Mon-Fri 9-5 www.goldengateaudubon.org
Conserves and restores habitats of Bay Area birds and other wildlife. Store
sells bird seed, books, field guides, toys.

GOLDEN GATE NATIONAL PARKS CONSERVANCY
Building 201, 3rd Floor Park Headquarters at Fort Mason
SF (Marina) 94123 415-561-3000
Mon-Fri 8-5 www.parksconservancy.org
Supports and assists the Golden Gate National Parks with research,
interpretation, and conservation programs.

GREEN MUSEUM
Corte Madera   415-945-9322
www.greenmuseum.org
Online environmental art museum. Includes works from the Bay Area
and around the world.

GREEN PLANET FILMS
P.O. Box 247 Corte Madera 94976-0247 415-383-0484
www.greenplanetfilms.org
Environmental film nights and DVDs; distribution and rental to schools
and businesses.

GREENACTION FOR HEALTH AND ENVIRONMENTAL JUSTICE
1095 Market St. Suite 712 SF (Civic Center) 94103 415-248-5010
Mon-Fri 9-5 www.greenaction.org
Mobilizes community power to change government and corporate policies and
practices to protect health and promote environmental justice.

GREENBELT ALLIANCE
631 Howard St. Suite 510 SF (SOMA) 94105 415-543-6771
Mon-Fri 9-5 www.greenbelt.org
Protects Bay Area open space; promotes livable communities. See their
website for local chapters.

GREENPEACE
75 Arkansas St. Suite 1 SF (Potrero Hill) 94107 415-255-9221
Mon-Fri 9-5:30 www.greenpeace.org/usa
Uses non-violent creative confrontation to expose global environmental
problems and to force solutions.

HAYWARD SHORELINE INTERPRETIVE CENTER
4901 Breakwater Ave. Hayward   94545 510-670-7270
Sat-Sun 10-5 www.hard.dst.ca.us/hayshore.html
Environmental interpretive center built on stilts above a salt marsh.
Exhibits and programs.

HEALTH CARE WITHOUT HARM
1958 University Ave. Berkeley 94704 510-848-5343
www.noharm.org
Coalition of diverse citizen and medical industry groups working to transform
the health care industry so that it is ecologically sustainable.

HEALTHY BUILDING NETWORK
2464 West St. Berkeley 94702 510-845-5600
www.healthybuilding.net
Network of green building professionals, environmental and health activists,
and others, promoting healthier building materials as a means of improving
public health and preserving the global environment. Projects include Unity
Homes and the Pharos Project.

INTERNATIONAL HEALTHY CITIES FOUNDATION, THE
555 12th St. 10th Floor Oakland (Lake Merritt/Downtown) 94607 510-642-1715
Mon-Fri 9-3 www.healthycities.org
Links more than 7,500 Healthy Cities programs throughout the world. Programs
focus on promoting action by communities to improve their quality of life.

LITERACY FOR ENVIRONMENTAL JUSTICE
800 Innes Ave. Unit 11 SF (Bayview/Hunter's Point) 94124 415-282-6840
Mon-Fri 9-6 www.lejyouth.org
Fosters an understanding of the principles of environmental justice and
urban sustainability in young people to promote the long-term health of
their communities.

MARIN AGRICULTURAL LAND TRUST
P.O. Box 809 Corner of 5th and A St. Point Reyes Station 94956 415-663-1158
Mon-Fri 9-5 www.malt.org
Education programs, farm tours and tastings, hiking, creek
restoration programs.

MARIN AUDUBON SOCIETY
P.O. Box 599 Mill Valley 94942 415-721-4271
See website for work days and events www.marinaudubon.org
Volunteer-oriented organization to conserve and restore natural ecosystems,
focusing on birds, other wildlife, and their habitats.

MARIN COUNTY OPEN SPACE DISTRICT
Marin County Civic Center 3501 Civic Center Dr. Room 415 San Rafael 94903
415-499-6387 Office: Mon-Fri 8:30-4:30; Nature Preserves: Daily dawn to dusk
www.marinopenspace.org
Government agency which manages Marin County open space and nature
preserves. Hiking and nature trails on over 30 public lands and parks.

MARINE MAMMAL CENTER, THE
1065 Fort Cronkhite Sausalito 94965 415-289-SEAL
Marine Mammal Visitor Center adjacent from Rodeo Lagoon and Beach, Bldg. 1049
Mon-Fri 9-5 Visitor Center Daily 10-4 www.tmmc.org
Largest marine mammal facility in the world to combine animal rehabilitation
with an on-site research lab. Extensive volunteer opportunities.

NATURAL RESOURCES DEFENSE COUNCIL
111 Sutter St. 20th Floor SF (Financial District) 94104 415-875-6100
Mon-Fri 9-5:30 www.nrdc.org
Uses law, science and the support of 1.2 million members and online activists
to protect the planet's wildlife and wild places and to ensure a safe and healthy
environment for all living things.

NATURAL WORLD MUSEUM
SF 415-402-0583
See website for exhibit dates and locations www.artintoaction.org
A cultural institution dedicated to showcasing educational art exhibitions that
cultivate environmental awareness and provide new perspectives that
stimulate social engagement in conservation.

NATURE IN THE CITY
121 Parnassus Ave. SF (Cole Valley) 94117 415-564-4107
Mon-Fri 9-5 www.natureinthecity.org
Conserves and restores nature and biodiversity of San Francisco. Public
education, community organizing, conservation advocacy.

OCEAN CONSERVANCY, THE
116 New Montgomery St. Suite 810 SF (Financial District) 94105 415-979-0900
Mon-Fri 9-5 www.oceanconservancy.org
Promotes healthy and diverse ocean ecosystems and opposes practices that
threaten ocean life and human life, through research, education, and science-
based advocacy. Pacific office focuses on West Coast ocean issues.

PALO ALTO GREEN TEAM PROJECT
c/o Acterra 3921 East Bayshore Rd. Palo Alto 94303 650-962-9876
Acterra Office Mon-Fri 9-5 www.greenteamproject.org
Helps small groups of Bay Area neighbors and co-workers learn to live more
earth-friendly lifestyles. See website for meeting dates and times.

PENINSULA OPEN SPACE TRUST
222 High St. Palo Alto 94301 650-854-7696
Mon-Fri 8:30-5:30 www.openspacetrust.org
Works with private land owners to protect farmland, trails, and wildlife habitat
and offers public education programs.

PEOPLE'S GROCERY

3265 Market St. Oakland (West Oakland) 94608 510-652-7607
Office: Mon-Fri 9-5 See website for events   www.peoplesgrocery.org
The organization helps to develop self-reliant, socially just, and sustainable
food systems in West Oakland. Two of their programs include The Healthy
Snack Delivery and the Bulk Buying Program.

PERRY FAMILY FARMS AT ARDENWOOD HISTORIC FARM

34600 Ardenwood Blvd. Fremont 94555-3645 510-796-0663
Working nineteenth-century farm. Agriculture, history, and cultural programs
for children and adults; seasonal events; produce stand.

PESTICIDE ACTION NETWORK NORTH AMERICA (PANNA)

49 Powell St. Suite 500 SF (Union Square) 94102 415-981-1771
Mon-Fri 9-5 www.panna.org
Works to replace pesticide use with ecologically sound and socially just
alternatives. Links local and international consumer, labor, health, environment
and agriculture groups into an international citizens' action network.

PUBLIC HEALTH INSTITUTE

555 12th St. 10th Floor Oakland (Lake Merritt/Downtown) 94607 510-285-5500
Mon-Fri 8-5 www.phi.org
Focused on reducing indoor and outdoor environmental health risk factors for
all people in the Bay Area.

RAINFOREST ACTION NETWORK

221 Pine St. 5th Floor SF (Financial District) 94104 415-398-4404
Mon-Fri 9-5:30 www.ran.org
Protects rainforests and the rights of their inhabitants through education,
grassroots organizing, and non-violent direct action. Conducts Rainforests in
the Classroom program for students.

REGIONAL ASTHMA MANAGEMENT AND PREVENTION, BAY AREA RAMP

180 Grand Ave. Suite 750 Oakland (Lake Merritt/Downtown) 94612 510-302-3365
Mon-Fri 9-5 www.rampasthma.org
Clearinghouse of asthma information; provides technical information to asthma
coalitions and coordinates community action.

REGIONAL PARKS BOTANIC GARDEN AT TILDEN PARK

Wildcat Canyon Rd. at South Park Dr. Berkeley 94701 510-841-8732
Daily 8:30-5; Tree Tours Sat-Sun 2 p.m. www.nativeplants.org
Ten-acre California native plant display, study, and preservation garden at
Tilden Park. Flora from each region of California's 160,000 square miles.
Weekly classes. Spring plant sale. (No dogs allowed.)

RICHARDSON BAY AUDUBON CENTER SANCTUARY

376 Greenwood Beach Rd. Tiburon 94920 415-388-2524
Mon-Sat 9-5 www.tiburonaudubon.org
Four platforms with viewing scopes and educational material, Redwood Grove,
Native Plant Garden, Hummingbird Garden, pond, and a stretch of unspoiled
shore on the San Francisco Bay. Lectures, guided walks, and events.

RIVER OF WORDS

2547 Eighth St. Suite 13B Berkeley 94710 510-548-7636
Mon-Fri 9-5 www.riverofwords.org
Promoting literacy, the arts, environmental awareness, and cross-cultural
understanding in Bay Area youth.

SAN FRANCISCO BAY CONSERVATION AND DEVELOPMENT COMMISSION

50 California St. Suite 2600 SF (Financial District) 94111 415-352-3600
Mon-Fri 8-5 www.bcdc.ca.gov
An agency created to protect and enhance San Francisco Bay and encourage
the responsible use of its resources.

SAN FRANCISCO BAY NATIONAL WILDLIFE REFUGE COMPLEX

1 Marshlands Rd. Fremont 94536 510-792-0222
Visitor Center Tue-Sun 10-5; Refuge hours vary by season www.fws.gov/desfbay
National Wildlife Refuges in the San Francisco Bay Area. Public access and
education programs. See website for days and hours of tours and activities.

SAN FRANCISCO BEAUTIFUL

100 Bush St. Suite 1580 SF (Financial District) 94104 415-421-2608
www.sfbeautiful.org
Protects and enhances the city's urban environment through civic initiatives
and outreach.

SAN FRANCISCO BIKE COALITION

995 Market St. Suite 1550 SF (Civic Center) 94103 415-431-2453
Mon-Fri 9:30-6 www.sfbike.org
Transforming city streets and neighborhoods into more viable and safe places
by promoting the bicycle for everyday transportation.

SAN FRANCISCO BOTANICAL GARDEN AT THE STRYBING ARBORETUM

Golden Gate Park at Ninth Ave. at Lincoln Way SF (Sunset) 94122 415-661-1316
Garden: Mon-Fri 8-4:30 Sat-Sun and Holidays 10-4;
Free Guided Walks: Daily 1:30; Library/Bookstore: Daily 10-4; Closed major holidays
www.sfbotanicalgarden.org
Mediterranean, mild temperate and tropical cloud-forest plants displayed in
designed gardens and habitats. Horticultural library. Plant sales and bookstore.
Classes in horticulture and nature study. Sunday children's story time programs.

SAN FRANCISCO NEIGHBORHOODS PARKS COUNCIL

451 Hayes St. SF (Hayes Valley) 94102 415-621-3260
Mon-Fri 9-5:30 www.sfnpc.org
Advocates for a sustainable and equitable park system. Provides leadership
and support to park users through community programs.

SAN FRANCISCO RECREATION AND PARK DEPARTMENT, NATURAL AREAS & VOLUNTEER PROGRAMS

501 Stanyan St. McLaren Lodge SF (Haight) 94117 415-831-2700
www.parks.sfgov.org
Learn about ecology of the city's numerous parks. Restoration opportunities.

SAN FRANCISCO TOMORROW

41 Sutter St. Suite 1579 SF (Financial District) 94104 415-566-7050
By appt. www.sanfranciscotomorrow.org
Works to keep urban neighborhoods liveable, to protect and improve parks,
and to expand public transit.

SAVE THE BAY

350 Frank H. Ogawa Plaza Suite 900 Oakland (Lake Merritt/Downtown) 94612
510-452-9261
Mon-Fri 9-5 www.savesfbay.org
Membership organization working exclusively to protect, restore and celebrate
San Francisco Bay. Hands-on wetlands restoration, bay adventures, and
education.

SEQUOIA AUDUBON SOCIETY

P.O. Box 620292 Woodside 94062 650-529-1454
www.sequoia-audubon.org
Volunteer-oriented restoration, preservation, protection and enjoyment of our
native natural resources with emphasis on birds and their habitats. See their
website for classes and activities schedule.

SIERRA CLUB

Loma Prieta Chapter   www.lomaprieta.sierraclub.org
3921 East Bayshore Rd. Suite 204 Palo Alto 94303 650-390-8411
SF Bay Chapter www.sanfranciscobay.sierraclub.org
2530 San Pablo Ave. Suite I Berkeley 94702 510-848-0800
Hours vary by chapter www.sierraclub.org
Sierra Club chapters offer many ways to learn about environmental issues and to get outdoors.

SLOW FOOD SAN FRANCISCO

210 Littlefield Ave. South SF 94080 650-873-6060
www.slowfoodsanfrancisco.com
Promoting ecologically sound food production and consumption to protect the pleasures of the table against modern fast food and life.

SUSTAINABLE SAN MATEO COUNTY

177 Bovet Rd. Suite 600 San Mateo 94402 650-638-2323
Mon-Fri 9-5 www.sustainablesanmateo.org
Educates the community about practical ways to achieve sustainability. Local annual sustainability awards and showcase projects.

SUSTAINABLE WORLD COALITION

79 Sidney Ct. San Rafael 94903 415-785-1888
www.swcoalition.org
Works to educate, inspire, and activate fostering engagement in personal and global sustainability. Produces events and educational materials.

SUSTAINING OURSELVES LOCALLY

1236 23rd Ave. Oakland (Lake Merritt/Downtown) 94606 510-534-9987
Call for work days and times www.oaklandsol.org
Revitalizing the ecology of an urban garbage dump site by planting an organic garden; works with youth by teaching them basic gardening and construction skills, and developing a cottage industry organic nursery.

THOREAU CENTER FOR SUSTAINABILITY

1016 Lincoln Blvd. SF (Presidio/Presidio Heights) 94129 415-561-7823
Mon-Fri 9-5 www.thoreau.org
A community of organizations working for a healthy environment and a just society within the sustainably rehabilitated buildings of Letterman Hospital. A showcase of green re-design and a green building resource web guide.

TRAIL CENTER, THE

3921 East Bayshore Rd. Palo Alto 94303 650-968-7065
Call or send e-mail for office hours, volunteer information, and events
www.trailcenter.org
Volunteer organization to provide and promote non-motorized trails for all people in San Mateo, Santa Clara, and San Francisco counties.

TRANSFAIR USA

1611 Telegraph Ave. Suite 900 Oakland (Lake Merritt/Downtown) 94612
510-663-5260
Mon-Fri 9-5 www.transfairusa.org
Independent, third-party certifier of fair trade products. College credit internships and volunteer programs.

TRANSPORTATION AND LAND USE COALITION

405 14th St. Suite 605 Oakland (Lake Merritt/Downtown) 94612 510-740-3150
Mon-Fri 9-5 www.transcoalition.org
Promotes and expands public participation in transportation and land use decisions.

URBAN CREEKS COUNCIL
1250 Addison St. #107C Berkeley 94702 510-540-6669
www.urbancreeks.org
Watershed protection and restoration in the Bay Area and statewide through affiliate organizations.

URBAN SPROUTS SCHOOL GARDENS
SF 94110 415-648-4596
Hours vary by location   www.urbansprouts.org
Provides school gardens in San Francisco public middle and high schools to help youth learn to grow, harvest, prepare, and eat vegetables from the school garden. Teaches children to eat better and connect with the environment and each other.

EDUCATIONAL ORGANIZATIONS

If you want to study something in the environmental arena in depth, there are a growing number of opportunities for further education. All of the organizations listed below provide ongoing environmental education and many also provide community outreach. Some offer advanced degrees in environmental fields. Others are geared specifically to educate and inspire adults and/or children to become good stewards of the earth. Be sure to check their websites regularly to see when their next class, lecture, or tele-class is being offered.

ARDENWOOD REGIONAL PRESERVE AND HISTORIC FARM
34600 Ardenwood Blvd. Fremont 94555 510-796-0663
Tue-Sun 10-4 www.ebparks.org/parks/arden.htm
Working 19th-century organic farm. Age-specific nature, agriculture, history and cultural programs for children and adults. Seasonal events. Produce stand.

BOTANICAL GARDEN—UNIVERSITY OF CALIFORNIA, BERKELEY
200 Centennial Dr. Berkeley 94720 510-643-2755
Daily 9-5 Free docent-led public tours on Thu, Sat-Sun 1:30
Closed 1st Tue every month   www.botanicalgarden.berkeley.edu
Living laboratory for the conservation and study of native plants. Classes, tours, and plant sales.

CAL STATE UNIVERSITY EAST BAY
220 Robinson Hall CSUEB Hayward 94542 510-885-3193
Mon-Fri 8-5 www.class.csueastbay.edu/geography
Geography and Environmental Studies Program.

CALIFORNIA COLLEGE OF THE ARTS
1111 Eighth St. SF (Potrero Hill) 94107 415-703-9500
Mon-Fri 9-5 www.cca.edu
Classes in sustainable fashion design, environmental impact of building and architecture.

Adding to Your Involvement

CENTER FOR AGROECOLOGY AND SUSTAINABLE FOOD SYSTEMS—UNIVERSITY OF CALIFORNIA, SANTA CRUZ

1156 High St. Santa Cruz 95064 831-459-3240
www.ucsc.edu/ca
A research, education and public service program dedicated to increasing ecological sustainablility and social justice in the food and agricultural system.

CENTER FOR URBAN EDUCATION ABOUT SUSTAINABLE AGRICULTURE

One Ferry Building #50 SF (Embarcadero) 94111 415-291-3276
Mon-Fri 9-4 www.cuesa.org
Educates urban consumers about sustainable agriculture and seasonal eating. Promotes a sustainable food system through its operation of the Ferry Plaza Farmers Market and its educational programs.

COLLEGE OF ENVIRONMENTAL DESIGN, UNIVERSITY OF CALIFORNIA, BERKELEY

202 Wurster Hall Suite 2000 Berkeley 94720 510-642-0324
Mon-Fri 8-5 www.new-laep.ced.berkeley.edu
Undergraduate and graduate degrees in inner-city environmental restoration, community landscape design, regional environmental planning and protection.

COLLEGE OF NATURAL RESOURCES, UNIVERSITY OF CALIFORNIA, BERKELEY

101 Giannini Hall Berkeley 94720 510-642-7171
www.cnr.berkeley.edu
Undergraduate degrees in biology, environmental sciences, forestry, social science, policy, and planning.

COMMON GROUND ORGANIC GARDEN SUPPLY AND EDUCATION CENTER

559 College Ave. Palo Alto 94306 650-493-6072
Tue-Fri 10-5:30 Sat-Sun 10-5 www.commongroundinpaloalto.org
Organic gardening classes and events; library and books for sale; seeds and seedlings; tools and soil conditioners.

COYOTE HILLS REGIONAL PARK

8000 Patterson Ranch Rd. Fremont 94555 510-795-9385
Mon-Sun 8-6 unless otherwise posted Visitor Center: Tue-Sun 9:30-5
www.ebparks.org/parks/coyote.htm
Wildlife refuge, hiking and bike trail; age-specific nature and native culture programs; disabled-accessible.

CROWN MEMORIAL STATE BEACH AND CRAB COVE VISITOR CENTER

1252 McKay Ave. Alameda 94501 510-521-6887
Wed-Sun 10-5 www.ebparks.org
Estuarine marine reserve. 800-gallon aquarium system, interactive stations, nature and culture programs. Wheelchair access to tidepools at low tide. Naturalist-guided programs for school groups and other organized groups.

DOMINICAN UNIVERSITY OF CALIFORNIA, GREEN MBA PROGRAM

50 Acacia Ave. San Rafael 94901 888-323-6763
By appt. www.greenmba.com
A two-year MBA program that promotes financial viability, ecological sustainability, and social justice.

EAST BAY CONSERVATION CORPS

1021 Third St. Oakland (West Oakland) 94607 510-992-7800
Mon-Fri 9-4 www.ebcc-school.org
Educational organization; offers academic and on-the-job training for inner-city youth.

ECOLOGY CENTER
2530 San Pablo Ave. Berkeley 94702 510-548-2220
Tue-Sat 11-6 www.ecologycenter.org
The center promotes environmentally and socially responsible practices
through programs that educate, demonstrate, and provide direct services.

ECOVILLAGE FARM LEARNING CENTER
21 Laurel Lane Richmond 94803 510-223-1693
By appt. www.ecovillagefarm.org
A 5.6 acre organic farm in urban Richmond supports a CSA program, a farmer's
market, and training for youth and young adults in sustainable living skills.

ENVIRONMENTAL EDUCATION DIRECTORY, THE
www.enviroeducation.com
Online database and search engine for worldwide environmental education
accredited degree programs.

ENVIRONMENTAL FORUM OF MARIN
P.O. Box 150459 San Rafael 94915 415-479-7814
www.marinefm.org
Intensive training program and public education services to increase
understanding of ecology, environmental issues, and the planning process.

FOOTHILL COLLEGE ENVIRONMENTAL HORTICULTURE & DESIGN
12345 El Monte Rd. Los Altos Hills 94022 650-949-7402
www.foothill.fhda.edu/bio/programs/hort
Offers A.S. degrees, career certificates or core skills certificate in Environmental
Horticulture and Design. Instructors are green industry professionals in
environmental design, construction, and maintenance practices for urban,
rural, and natural landscapes.

FUTURE LEADERS INSTITUTE, THE
1201 Martin Luther King Jr. Way Suite 104 Oakland (Lake Merritt/Downtown)
94612 510-292-8181
www.thefutureleadersinstitute.org
Offers programs for high school youth to inspire and guide them to transform
their passions into real social and/or environmental solutions for the community.

GAMBLE GARDEN
1431 Waverley St. Palo Alto 94301 650-329-1356
Gardens: Daily dawn to dusk Office/Reference Library: Mon-Fri 9-12
www.gamblegarden.org
Community horticultural organization that tends formal and demonstration
gardens. Intergenerational educational programs.

GOLDEN GATE UNIVERSITY, SCHOOL OF LAW
536 Mission St. SF (Financial District) 94105 800-448-4968
www.ggu.edu
Environmental Law and Justice Clinic. Students directly represent environmental
organizations and community groups in low-income and minority communities
in real-life public health, toxics, and environmental matters.

HIDDEN VILLA
26870 Moody Rd. Los Altos Hills 94022 650-949-8650
Tue-Sun 9 to dusk www.hiddenvilla.org
A 1,600 acre organic farm. Field trips, summer camp, farm tours; wilderness
exploration; gardening and environmental education. Events and facility rental.
Hostel; hiking trails.

MARIN ART AND GARDEN CENTER
30 Sir Francis Drake Blvd. Ross 94957 415-455-5260
Dawn to dusk www.maagc.org
Sustainable gardening, composting classes and workshops.

MERRIT COLLEGE LANDSCAPE HORTICULTURE DEPARTMENT

12500 Campus Dr. Oakland (East Oakland) 94619 510-436-2418
www.merrittlandhort.com
Offers A.S. degrees and certificates in Landscape Design and Construction, Nursery Management, Landscape and Parks Maintenance, Turf and Landscape Management, and Horticultural Therapy.

MILLS COLLEGE ENVIRONMENTAL STUDIES PROGRAM

5000 MacArthur Blvd. Oakland (East Oakland) 94613 510-430-2317
Mon-Fri 9-5 www.mills.edu
Undergraduate degrees in Environmental Sciences and Environmental Studies, focusing on the interaction of humans with the environment. Women's college.

OCCIDENTAL ARTS AND ECOLOGY CENTER

15290 Coleman Valley Rd. Occidental 95465 707-874-1557
By appt. www.oaec.org
Education center, organic farm; developing ecologically, economically, and culturally sustainable communities.

OHLONE COLLEGE

43600 Mission Blvd. P.O. Box 3909 Fremont 94539 510-659-6000
www.ohlone.cc.ca.us/instr/earthscience
Courses and certificate in Environmental Science.

PRESIDIO SCHOOL OF MANAGEMENT

P.O. Box 29502 SF (Presidio/Presidio Heights) 94129 415-561-6590
Mon-Fri 9-5 www.presidiomba.org
Offers an innovative MBA in Sustainable Management, integrating social responsibility and environmental values into all courses.

REGENERATIVE DESIGN INSTITUTE

P.O. Box 923 Bolinas 94924 415-868-9681
www.regenerativedesign.org
A non-profit educational organization providing courses and workshops designed to teach the skills necessary to live a more sustainable life.

SAN FRANCISCO STATE UNIVERSITY ENVIRONMENTAL STUDIES PROGRAM

1600 Holloway Ave. SF (Park Merced) 94132 415-338-1149
Mon-Thu 12-5 http://bss.sfsu.edu/envstudies
Offers B.A. in Environmental Studies: Concentrations in Environmental Sustainability and Social Justice, the Urban Environment, or Humanities and the Environment; B.S. in Environmental Studies: Concentrations in Earth System Science, or Natural Resource Management and Conservation.

SAN JOSE CONSERVATION CORPS & CHARTER SCHOOL

2650 Senter Rd. San Jose 95111 408-283-7171
Mon-Fri 8-4:30 www.sjccccharterschool.org
Provides youth with a high school education and teaches valuable work and life skills in environmental conservation, recycling, and the construction trades.

SAN JOSE STATE UNIVERSITY, ENVIRONMENTAL STUDIES DEPARTMENT

One Washington Square Hall 118 San Jose 95192 408-924-5424
Mon-Thu 9-4 http://sjsu.edu/depts/envstudies
Offers a department dedicated to Environmental Studies.

SANTA CLARA UNIVERSITY

500 El Camino Real Santa Clara 95053 408-551-7086
www.scu.edu/envs
Offers an Environmental Studies program.

SLIDE RANCH
2025 Shoreline Hwy. Muir Beach 94965 415-381-6155
Tue-Sat 9-5 www.slideranch.org
A 134-acre agriculture and environmental education center off Marin's Highway 1.

SOLAR LIVING INSTITUTE
13771 South Hwy. 101 P.O. Box 836 Hopland 95449 707-744-2017
www.solarliving.org
Environmental education organization. Workshops on renewable energy, ecological design, sustainable living, alternative construction techniques.

SONOMA STATE UNIVERSITY
1801 East Cotati Ave. Rohnert Park 94928 707-664-2306
www.sonoma.edu/ensp
Courses in conservation and restoration, energy management and design, environmental education, hazardous material, and water technology.

STANFORD UNIVERSITY—WOODS INSTITUTE FOR THE ENVIRONMENT
Encina Modular C429 Arguello Way Stanford 94305 650-736-8668
Mon-Fri 8-5:30 http://environment.stanford.edu
Interdisciplinary Environmental Research Center. Graduate and undergraduate degrees and programs.

SUNOL REGIONAL WILDERNESS
Southeast end of Geary Rd. Sunol 94586 925-862-2601
Daily 7 to dusk Subject to closure during fire season (June through October)
Regional park. Nature and history programs align with State Content Standards. Hiking, cave exploring. Bird lists at Visitor Center. Parking fee.

THIMMAKKA'S RESOURCES FOR ENVIRONMENTAL EDUCATION
2124 Kitteredge St. PMB 139 Berkeley 94704 510-655-5566
Mon-Fri 9-5 www.thimmakka.org
Seeks to mobilize the urban consumer, particularly the South Asian community, toward environmentalism and social justice.

TILDEN ENVIRONMENTAL EDUCATION CENTER
North End of Central Park Dr. Berkeley 94708 510-525-2233
EEC: Tue-Sun 10-5 The Little Farm: Daily 8:30-4 www.ebparks.org/parks/tilden.htm
Weekday programs by reservation; weekend programs open to all.
Education Center at Tilden Park. Environmental puppet theater. Nature study supplies. Nature craft, garden and farming classes.

UC COOPERATIVE EXTENSION—ALAMEDA COUNTY
1131 Harbor Bay Parkway Suite 131 Alameda 94502 510-639-1371
www.cealameda.ucdavis.edu
Environmental horticulture and master gardener education programs, workshops, and demonstrations.

UC COOPERATIVE EXTENSION—MARIN
1682 Novato Blvd. Suite 150-B Novato 94947 415-499-4204
Mon-Fri 9-4 www.cemarin.ucdavis.edu
Conferences, workshops and demonstrations. Programs in horticulture, master gardening, and organic and sustainable agriculture.

UC COOPERATIVE EXTENSION—SAN MATEO AND SAN FRANCISCO COUNTY
80 Stone Pine Rd. Suite 100 Half Moon Bay 94019 650-726-9059
Mon-Fri 9-5 www.cesanmateo.ucdavis.edu
Richard J. Elkus Ranch, environmental education center. Programs in gardening and master gardening, agriculture, forestry, and marine science.

UC EXTENSION—BERKELEY

1995 University Ave. Berkeley 94720 510-642-4111
Mon-Thu 8-6:30   www.unex.berkeley.edu
Courses and certificate programs for individuals and professionals in
sustainable interior and garden design, ecosystem restoration, and
environmental management. Berkeley, Oakland, San Francisco, and
Redwood City campuses.

UNIVERSITY OF SAN FRANCISCO

2130 Fulton St. SF (Richmond) 94117 415-422-5555
www.usfca.edu
Undergraduate and graduate degrees in Environmental Sciences and
Environmental Studies. Certificate programs in Environmental and Trade law;
Nonprofit Organization Management.

Many great groups are providing a means for activism, learning,
and involvement in environmental issues. What are your
experiences with these groups? Have you checked out any of
the classes and workshops? If so, how would you rate them?
Have you volunteered with any of these organizations? What
was your experience? How effective are their programs? On
www.greenopia.com, you can share your thoughts and also
add your favorite groups to our list.

Eating Out/Eating In

Everyday Greens: Home Cooking from Greens, the Celebrated Vegetarian Restaurant
Annie Somerville
Innovative vegetarian cooking. Title refers to Zen concept of everyday mindfulness. Recipes vary in complexity; all are inspired by readily available fresh and sometimes unusual ingredients.

Full Moon Feast: Food and the Hunger for Connection
Jessica Prentice
Champions locally grown, humanely raised, nutrient-rich foods, and traditional cooking methods. Follows the thirteen lunar cycles of an agrarian year. Includes recipes.

Grub: Ideas for an Urban Organic Kitchen
Anna Lappé and Bryant Terry
Promotes benefits of sustainable eating. Provides how-to's for creating an affordable organic kitchen. Includes dozens of delectable recipes.

The Omnivore's Dilemma: A Natural History of Four Meals
Michael Pollan
Traces two "organic" meals back to their local or corporate sources, then compares these with one from McDonald's and one the author hunts and gathers himself. Illuminates the real sources of our food.

Your Organic Kitchen: The Essential Guide to Selecting and Cooking Organic Foods
Jesse Ziff Cool
Easy-to-prepare, delicious, healthy recipes listed by season. Clear format. Includes main dishes, side dishes, and desserts.

Getting Goods

Stuff: The Secret Lives of Everyday Things (New Report, No. 4)
John C. Ryan and Alan Thein Durning
Documents a day in the life of the average North American consumer and unravels the hidden costs of everything around us. Traces the environmental impact of consumer decisions.

Greening Your Space

Cradle to Cradle: Remaking the Way We Make Things
William McDonough and Michael Braungart
Challenges the belief that human industry must damage the natural world. Guided by the principle that "waste equals food."

Food Not Lawns: How to Turn Your Yard into a Garden and Your Neighborhood into a Community
Heather C. Flores
Practical wisdom on ecological garden design and community-building; a permaculture lifestyle manual.

Green Remodeling: Changing the World One Room at a Time
David R. Johnston and Kim Master
Points out advantages of green remodeling. Discusses simple renovation solutions for homeowners.

Naturally Clean: The Seventh Generation Guide to Safe and Healthy, Non-Toxic Cleaning
Jeffrey Hollender, Geoff Davis, and Meika Hollender
Full of useful information on chemicals and cleaners to avoid. Very good resource section.

The Passive Solar House: The Complete Guide to Heating and Cooling Your Home
James Kachadorian
Proven techniques for building homes that heat and cool themselves using readily available materials and methods.

Seeing the World

Code Green: Experiences of a Lifetime
Kerry Lorimer
Travel publisher Lonely Planet's first ecotourism guide. Offers practical tips for socially and environmentally responsible travelers, including how to immerse oneself in a culture and make a positive economic impact at the same time.

Fragile Earth: Views of a Changing World
Collins UK Staff (ed.)
Stunning photographs of the dramatic changes affecting today's world. Features satellite imaging and outstanding cartography.

Adding to Your Involvement

The Consumer's Guide to Effective Environmental Choices: Practical Advice from the Union of Concerned Scientists
Michael Brower and Warren Leon
A guide to living responsibly. Outlines choices consumers can make to reduce their environmental impact. Includes priority actions in transportation, food, and household operations.

Green Living: The E Magazine Handbook for Living Lightly on the Earth
By the Editors of E/The Environmental Magazine
Practical tips for living a healthier, more eco-friendly life. Smart food choices, natural health care, socially responsible investing, healthy home care. Chapter-by-chapter resource list.

An Inconvenient Truth: The Planetary Emergency of Global Warming and What We Can Do About It
Al Gore
Eloquently outlines the necessity for immediate action to reduce global warming.

Stop Global Warming: The Solution is You! An Activist's Guide
Laurie David
Provides inspiration for global warming activists. Raises public awareness. Invites action. Lots of resource listings.

Worldchanging: A User's Guide for the 21st Century
Alex Steffen (ed.)
A compendium of the latest and most innovative solutions, ideas, and inventions for building a sustainable, livable, prosperous future.

Presidio

WASHINGTON

Seacliff

Presidio Heights

JACK
CL

Laurel
Heights

LAKE

CALIFORNIA

CLEMENT

EUCLID

C

GEARY

ARGUELLO

6th AVE

ANZA

BALBOA

STANYAN

TURK
GOLDEN C

Richmond

CABRILLO

FULTON

FULTO

43rd AVE

38th AVE

36th AVE

32nd AVE

28th AVE

23rd AVE

19th AVE

15th AVE

FUNSTON

LINCOLN

GOLDEN

GATE

PARK

J. F. KENNEDY

Haight-

Cole
Valle

LINCOLN

LINCOLN

4th AVE

PARNASSUS

IRVING

UDAH

43rd AVE

39th AVE

36th AVE

32nd AVE

28th AVE

22nd AVE

19th AVE

15th AVE

FUNSTON

11th AVE

9th AVE

7th AVE

17th AVE

17th AV

KIRKHAM

SUNSET

WARREN

CLARENDON

LAWTON

MORAGA

Twin
Peaks

NORIEGA

ORTEGA

Sunset

OLYMPIA

QUITARA

14th AVE

9th AVE

WOODSIDE

RIVERA

DEWEY

SANTIAGO

Forest
Hill

TARAVAL

ULLOA

West
Portal

TER

ULLOA

VICENTE

WAWONA

SANTA ANA

YERBA BUENA

LANSDALE

Park Merced

SLOAT

SUNSET

OCEAN

Fisherman's Wharf

JEFFERSON
BEACH
BAY
CHESTNUT
LOMBARD

Marina

101

SCOTT
STEINER
FILLMORE
WEBSTER
LAGUNA
GOUGH
VAN NESS

UNION

POWELL
MASON
TAYLOR
JONES
LARKIN

COLUMBUS
GRANT
KEARNY

North Beach

Russian
Hill

Cow Hollow

VALLEJO
BROADWAY

Heights

JACKSON
101 CLAY

Nob Hill

Chinatown

Embarcadero

CALIFORNIA

BUSH

BEALE

80

Western
Addition

Japantown

POST
GEARY
O'FARRELL
ELLIS

Union
Square

Financial
District

2nd ST.
3rd ST.
4th ST.

SCOTT
DIVISADERO
STEINER
FILLMORE
WEBSTER
LAGUNA
GOUGH

Tenderloin

GOLDEN GATE

Hayes
Valley

Civic
Center

MARKET

SOMA

MISSION
HOWARD
6th ST.
9th ST.
FOLSOM
HARRISON

KING

amo Square

VAN NESS

10th ST.
11th ST.

BRYANT
BRANNAN
TOWNSEND
KING
BERRY

BERRY

3rd ST.

WALLER
DUBOCE

101

MARKET

15th ST.
16th ST.
17th ST.
18th ST.
19th ST.

DOLORES
GUERRERO
VALENCIA
MISSION
VAN NESS
FOLSOM
HARRISON
BRYANT
POTRERO
KANSAS
DE HARO

Mission Bay

16th ST.

280

CASTRO
NOE
SANCHEZ

18th ST.

MARIPOSA

eka
lley

19th ST.
20th ST.
21st ST.
22nd ST.
23rd ST.
24th ST.

Mission
District

20th ST.

Potrero
Hill

Dog Patch

WISCONSIN
MISSOURI
PENNSYLVANIA
INDIANA
3rd ST.

Castro

25th ST.

Noe Valley

C. CHAVEZ

C. CHAVEZ

28th ST.

PRECITA

Bernal Heights

NAPOLEON

CARGO

EVANS

30th ST.

CORTLAND

101

TOLAND

JERROLD

280

IOND HTS.

BEACON

Glen Park

CHENERY

ANDOVER
POWHATTAN

BAYSHORE

OAKDALE

INDUSTRIAL

Bayview/Hunter's Pt.

CRESCENT

BOSWORTH

side

280

ALEMANY

SILVER

Visitacion
Valley

NEWHALL
MENDELL
HUDSON
LA SALLE

Excelsior

THORNTON

Emeryville

UNIVERSITY OF CALIFORNIA
AT BERKELEY

ASHBY
BANCROFT
M.L. KING
POWELL
SAN PABLO
STANFORD
SHATTUCK
TELEGRAPH
COLLEGE
CLAREMONT

College Ave

MARITIME
W. GRAND
M.L. KING JR.
TELEGRAPH
BROADWAY
BROADWAY TER.

West Oakland
Temescal
PIEDMONT
OAKLAND
MORAGA

7TH ST.
MARKET
GRAND
GRAND

Montclair
SNAKE

Piedmont

LAKE
MERRIT
14TH ST.
8TH ST.
Downtown
PARK
Oakland
SHEPHERD CYN.

MAIN
WEBSTER
FOOTHILL
PARK
East Oakland
LINCOLN

BUENA VISTA
14TH AV.
23RD AV.
McARTHUR

CENTRAL
SANTA CLARA
ENCINAL
FRUITVALE

SHORE
OTIS
GRAND
35TH AV.
35TH AV.

Alameda
PARK
BROADWAY
HIGH
HIGH
FOOTHILL
CAMPUS

Harbor Bay Isle

INTERNATIONAL
SEMI-NARY

DOOLITTLE
66TH AV.
73RD AV.
McARTHUR
KELLER

82ND AV.
SAN LEANDRO
BANCROFT
SEQUOYAH

OAKLAND
INTERNATIONAL
AIRPORT
98TH AV.

98TH AV.

DOOLITTLE
San
Leandro

DAVIS

WILLIAMS
ESTU-DILLO

MARINA
E. 14TH ST.

MERCED
WASHINGTON

WICKS
San
Lorenzo
HESPERIAN

LEWELLING
GRANT
E. 14TH ST.

ALMITOS
MEEKLAND
Hayward

BUCKMAN

HAYWARD
EXEC.
AIRPORT
W. A ST.
A ST.

HESPERIAN

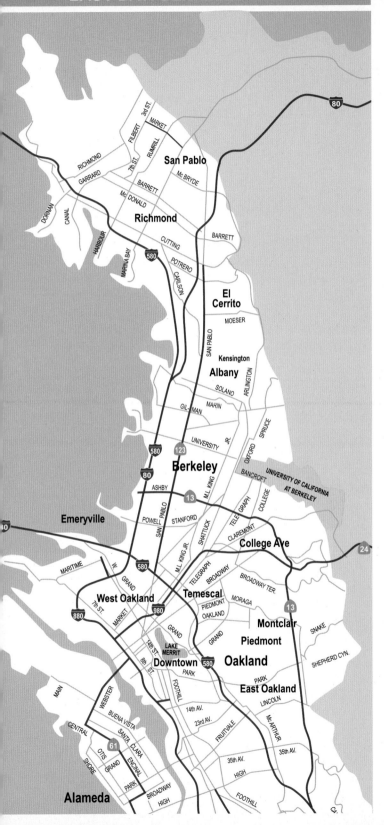

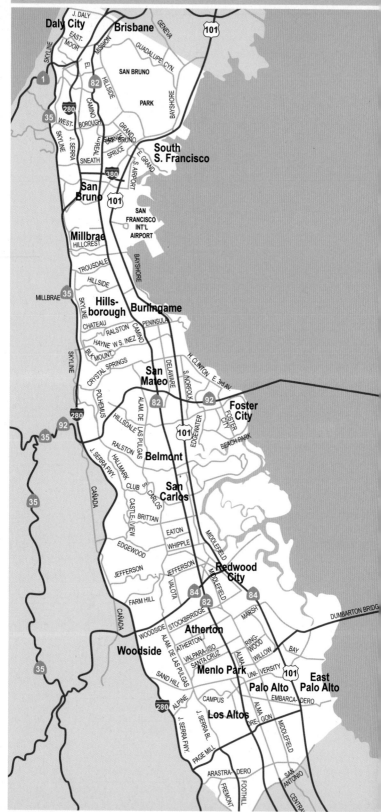

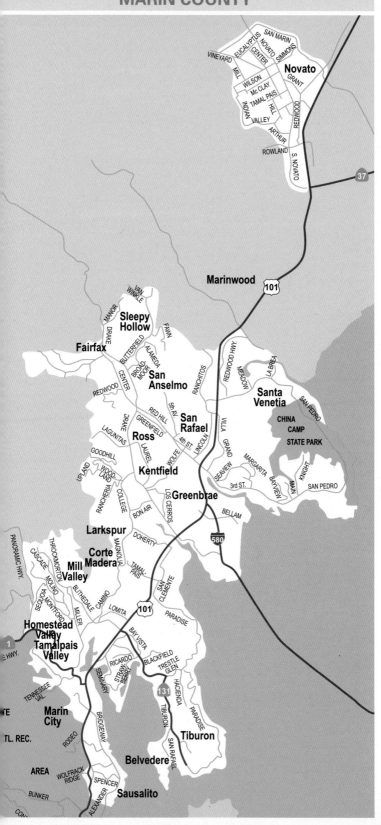

SAN FRANCISCO

Alternative Energy Contractors
Grid Alternatives, 149
Occidental Power, 149
Sunlight Electric, LLC, 150
Sustainable Spaces, 150

Alternative Fuel
(see Fueling Stations)

Alternative Transportation
Bay City Bike Rentals, 168
Bike and Roll, 168
Bike Hut, The, 168
̄ ...y Saddles Bike Rentals, 168
Locksmith Magic/Golden Gate Park
   Skate and Bike, 169
San Francisco Bike Coalition, 169
Scootcar San Francisco, 169
Walk SF, 169
Wheel Fun Rentals, 169

Architects
Full Circle Design Group, 141
Gelfand Partners Architects, 141
Jackson Liles Architecture, 142
Leddy Maytum Stacy Architects, 142
OrganicArchitect, 142
Palter/Donzelli Design, 142
Pfau Architecture, 143
Solutions, 143
Upwall, 143
Urban Structure, 143

Automobiles
(see Eco-Friendly
Vehicle Dealerships)

Baby Products
(see Gifts, Accessories, and
Baby Products)

Bakeries
Boulangerie Bay Bread, 28
Petite Patisserie, 29
Tartine Bakery, 29
Town's End Restaurant and Bakery, 29

Banking and Finance
Calvert Social Investment Foundation, 121
David Dobkin, CFP®, AIF®, 122
Forward Funds / Sierra Club Stock
   Fund, 122
New Resource Bank, 122
Parnassus Investments, 122
RBC Dain Rauscher, SRI Wealth
   Management Group, 123
RSF Social Finance, 123

SKBA Capital Management, 123
Trillium Asset Management, 123
Valencia Green, 123
Vision Capital Investment
   Management, 123
Women's Equity Fund, 123
Your Money & Your Life, 123

Beauty Product Suppliers
Aveda, 66
Bare Necessities, 66
Beauty Company, 67
Body Shop, The, 67
Body Time, 67
Church Street Apothecary, 67
Hydra, 68
Jurlique, 68
L'Occitane en Provence, 68
Lush, 68
Madkat, 68
Nancy Boy, 68
Occasions Boutique, 68
Pharmaca Integrative Pharmacy, 69
Sumbody & Sumtime Spa, 69

Beds, Bedding, and Linens
Down Etc..., 134
Foamorder.com, 135
Happy Planet, A, 134
Ruby Livingdesign, 135
Spring, 135

Bicycles and Bicycling
(see Alternative Transportation)

Biodiesel
(see Fueling Stations)

Building Materials and Supplies
Ceramic Tile & Design, 151
Cliff's Variety, 151
Earthsource Forest Products, 151
Greensage, 151
Spring, 152

Burial Services
Neptune Society of Northern California,
   The, 127

Cafés, Tea Houses, and Juice Bars
Acre Café, 21
Arc Café, 21
Axis Café, 22
Blue Bottle Coffee Co., 22
Boxed Foods Company, 22
Café Benally, 22
Café Crescendo, 22
Café Lo Cubano, 23
Café Gratitude, 22
Café Que Tal, 23

Chat's of San Francisco, 23
Coffee to the People, 23
Crissy Field Center Café, 23
Dish Café, 23
Frog Hollow Farms, 24
Grove, The, 24
Harvest & Rowe, 24
Java Beach, 24
Judahlicious, 24
Juicey Lucy's, 24
Kaila's Corner Cup, 24
Lettus Café Organic, 25
Mission Creek Café, The, 25
Nervous Dog Coffee, 25
New College Café, 25
Organic Coffee Company, 26
Peace Café, 26
People's Café, 26
Philz Coffee, 26
Power Source, 26
Progressive Grounds, 26
Rigolo Café, 26
Ritual Coffee Roasters, 26
Rockin' Java, 26
Samovar Tea Lounge, 27
Sidewalk Juice, 27
Spike's Coffees and Teas, 27
Sundance Coffee, 27
Sunset Café, 27
Warming Hut, The, 27
Zazen Coffee Tea & Organics, 27

Car Rentals
EV Rentals at Fox Rent A Car, 167
Hertz, 167
Specialty Rentals, 167

Car Share Services
City Carshare, 167
Flexcar, 168
Zipcar 168

Carbon Offset Services
Drive Neutral, 171
PG&E ClimateSmart Program, 172
3 Phases, 171

Carpeting
(see Furniture, Flooring, Carpeting,
  and Décor)

Catering Services and Personal Chefs
Cook! SF, 53
Debbie Does Dinner, 54
Earthen Feast, 54
Green Table, The, 54
Healing Hearth, The, 54
Jane Peal Cuisinière, 54
Living Room Events, 54
Marcus Rios Personal Chef & Caterer, 54
Organic Chef Catering, 54
Season: Conscious Catering, 55
Therapeutic Chef, 55
Work of Art Catering, 55

Chocolatiers and Dessert Shops
Bi-Rite Creamery and Bakeshop, 30
Bittersweet, 30
Citizen Cake, 30
Kara's Cupcakes, 30
Maggie Mudd, 31
Miette, 31
Petite Patisserie, 31
San Francisco Chocolate Factory,
  The, 31
Tartine Bakery, 31

Cleaning Services
Greenway Maid, 117
Healthy Choice Carpet Cleaners, 117
SF Earthly Housekeeping, 118
Verde Green Cleaning, 118

Clothing/Shoes
See Jane Run Sports, 83
Giggle, 81
Global Exchange Fair Trade Store, 81
Happy Planet, A, 81
Lululemon, 82
Miranda Caroligne, 82
Mollusk, The, 82
P-Kok, 82
Patagonia, 82
Rabat Shoes, 83
REI, 83
Residents Apparel Gallery, 83
Ruby2, 83

Community-Supported Agriculture
Eating With the Seasons CSA, 48

Compressed Natural Gas
(see Fueling Stations)

Day Spas
Bella Pelle, 73
Belli Capelli, 73
Earth and Sky Oasis, 74
International Orange, 74
Kabuki Springs & Spa, 74
Kamalaspa, 74
Schizandra, 74
Sen Spa, 75
Therapeia, 75

Décor
(see Furniture, Flooring, Carpeting,
and Décor)

Dry Cleaners
(see Wet and Hydrocarbon Cleaners or
Wet and CO_2 Cleaners)

Eco-Friendly Vehicle Dealerships
San Francisco Chrysler Jeep, 163

Educational Organizations

California College of the Arts, 188
Center for Urban Education about
  Sustainable Agriculture, 189
Golden Gate University, School of
  Law, 190
Hidden Villa, 190
Presidio School of Management, 191
San Francisco State University
  Environmental Studies Program, 191
University of San Francisco, 193

Electric Plug-In Stations

(see Fueling Stations)

Electric Vehicles

(see Eco-Friendly Vehicle Dealerships)

Energy

(see Alternative Energy Contractors)

Environmental Consultants

Simon & Associates, Inc., 146

Environmental Organizations

Action for Nature, 178
Amazon Watch, 178
ARC Ecology, 178
As You Sow, 179
Baykeeper/SF Bay Chapter, 179
Bioneers, Youth & Satellite Program, 179
Bluewater Network, 179
Breast Cancer Fund, The, 179
California Academy of Sciences, 179
California Coastal Commission, 180
Californians For Pesticide Reform, 180
City and County of San Francisco Department
  of the Environment Ecocenter, 180
Clean Water Action, 181
Crissy Field Center, 181
Cultural Conservancy, 181
Earth Island Institute, 181
Earth Share of California, 181
Forestethics, 182
Global Exchange, 182
Golden Gate National Parks
  Conservancy, 182
Greenaction for Health and
  Environmental Justice, 183
Greenbelt Alliance, 183
Greenpeace, 183
Literacy For Environmental Justice, 183
Natural Resources Defense Council, 184
Nature in the City, 184
Ocean Conservancy, The, 184
Pesticide Action Network North
  America, 185
Rainforest Action Network, 185
San Francisco Bay Conservation and
  Development Commission, 185
San Francisco Beautiful, 186
San Francisco Bike Coalition, 186
San Francisco Botanical Garden at
  the Strybing Arboretum, 186

San Francisco Neighborhoods Parks
  Council, 186
San Francisco Recreation and Park
Department, Natural Areas & Volunteer
  Programs, 186
San Francisco Tomorrow, 186
Slow Food San Francisco, 187
Thoreau Center For Sustainability, 187
Urban Sprouts School Gardens, 188

Fabric/Yarn Stores

Imagiknit, 84

Farmers' Markets

San Francisco Alemany CFM, 47
San Francisco Crocker Galleria, 47
San Francisco Ferry Plaza Farmers
  Market, 47
San Francisco Fillmore CFM, 47
San Francisco Heart of the City Farmers'
  Markets, 47
San Francisco Kaiser CFM, 47
San Francisco Marina CFM, 47
San Francisco Noe Valley CFM, 47
South San Francisco CFM, 48

Flooring

(see Furniture, Flooring, Carpeting,
  and Décor)

Florists

Church Street Flowers, 88
Ixia, 88
Oak Hill Farm, 88

Fueling Stations, Biodiesel

People's Fuel Cooperative, 165
San Francisco Biofuels Cooperative, 165

Fueling Stations, Compressed
Natural Gas

Clean Energy, 164
PG&E Service Centers, 164

Fueling Stations, Electric Plug-In

Clean Fueling Stations, 164

Furniture, Flooring, Carpeting,
and Décor

Abbey Carpet, 131
Ceramic Tile Design, 131
Earthsource Forest Products, 131
Eco-Terric, 131
Findecor, 132
Greensage, 132
Luxant, 132
Propeller, 133
Ruby Livingdesign, 133
Smith & Hawken, 133
Touch, The, 133

Garden Supplies

(see Nurseries and Garden Supplies)

Gardening and Landscaping

Flora Grubb Gardens, 139
Jennifer Hall, 139
Second Nature Design, 139

General Contractors

Brendan Uniacke Construction, 146
Collier Ostrom, Inc., 146
Jeff King & Company, Inc., 147
Lorax Development, 147

Gifts, Accessories, and Baby Products

Bell and Trunk, 85
Brilliant Earth, 85
Common Scents, 85
Day One - The Center for New and
   Expectant Parents, 86
Earthsong, 86
Giggle, 86
Global Exchange Fair Trade Store, 86
Natural Resources, 87
Planetweavers, 87

Grocery and Produce Delivery

Eating with the Seasons CSA, 49
Organic Express, 50

Grocery Stores

Andronico's Market, 39
Bi-Rite Market, 39
Buffalo Whole Food & Grain
   Company, 39
Church Street Groceteria, 39
Eezy Freezy, 40
Essential Foods, 40
Falletti Foods, 40
Fresh Organics, 40
Fruit Barn, 40
Golden Produce, 40
Good Life Grocery, 40
Haight Fillmore Whole Foods, 40
Harvest Urban Market, 41
Health Haven Produce and Natural
   Food, 41
Mollie Stone's, 41
Nabilas, 41
Nature Stop, 41
Noriega Produce Market, 41
Other Avenues, 42
Rainbow Grocery, 42
Real Food Company, The, 42
Taraval Market, 42
Thom's Natural Foods, 42
Trader Joe's, 43
26th and Guerrero Market, 39
Valencia Whole Foods, 43
Village Market, The, 43
Whole Foods Market, 43

Hair and Nail Salons

Belli Capelli, 71
Chakra Salonspa, 71
Face It Beauty Salon and Spa, 71
Hair Now South Beach, 71
Kamalaspa, 71
Shear Bliss, 72
Treat Aveda Salon, 72
Vierra and Friends, 72

Hazardous Waste

(see Household Hazardous
   Waste Disposal)

Hotels

Argonaut Hotel, 105
Fairmont, San Francisco, The, 106
Harbor Court Hotel, 106
Hilton San Francisco, 106
Hotel Carlton, 106
Hotel Monaco, 106
Hotel Palomar, 106
Hotel Triton, 106
Hyatt at Fisherman's Wharf, 107
Monticello Inn, 107
Orchard Garden Hotel, The, 107
Orchard Hotel, The, 107
Prescott Hotel, 107
Red Victorian Ben & Breakfast and
   Art, 107
Serrano Hotel, 107
Sir Francis Drake Hotel, 107
Tuscan Inn, 108
Villa Hotel Florence, 108

Household Hazardous Waste Disposal

Walgreens, 157

Interior Designers

Caroline Day Design, 145
Eco-Terric, 145
Greensage, 145

Landscaping

(see Gardening and Landscaping)

Linens

(see Beds, Bedding, and Linens)

Nail Salons

(see Hair and Nail Salons)

Nurseries and Garden Supplies

Flora Grubb Gardens, 136
Sloat Garden Center, 137
Smith & Hawken, 137
Urban Farmer Store, The, 137

Office and Paper Products

Cardology, 89
Green Office, The, 89
Kelly Paper, 90
Paper Source, 90
Waldeck's Office Supplies, 90

Paper Products
(see Office and Paper Products)

Personal Services
Big Vision Career and Project
 Consulting, 114
Healing Cuisine, 114
Homegrown Weddings & Events, 114
Sillapere, 114

Pest Control
Hungry Owl Project, 120
Pestec Exterminator Company, 120
San Francisco Department of the
 Environment, 120

**Pet Food, Supplies, Grooming, and
Other Services**
Animal Company, The, 96
Bella and Daisy's Dog Bakery &
 Boutique, 96
Bernal Beast, The, 96
Best in Show, 97
Bowwowmeow, 97
Dog Spa, The, 97
George, 97
Happy Pet, 97
Healthwize for Pets, 97
Jeffrey's Natural Pet Foods, 98
Noe Valley Pet Company, 98
Pawtrero Hill Bathhouse & Feed Co., 98
Pet Camp, 98
Pet Food Express, 98
Puppy Haven, 99
South Paw Bathhouse & Feed Co., 99
Sunset Pet Supply, 99

Pharmacies
Daily Health, 112
Pharmaca Integrative Pharmacy, 113
Scarlet Sage Herb Company, The, 113
Tower of Health, 113
West Portal Nutrition Center, 113

Public Transportation
BART, 170
Blue and Gold Fleet, 170
Caltrain, 170
Eastbay Ferry, 170
Golden Gate Transit, 170
SamTrans, 170
SFMUNI, 170

Recycling Centers/Recycling Services
Ecofinderrr, 153
Green Citizen, 153
South San Francisco Scavenger, 154

Restaurants
Absinthe Brasserie and Bar, 11
Acme Chophouse, 7
Acquerello, 13
Alive!, 20

Ame Restaurant, 6
Americano Restaurant and Bar, 13
Aperto, 13
Aziza, 16
B Restaurant and Bar, 7
Bacar, 8
Bacco Ristorante Italiano, 13
Balboa Cafe, 3
Bar Tartine, 16
Bia's Restaurant and Wine Bar, 16
Blue Plate, The, 4
Boulettes Larder, 4
Boulevard Restaurant, 8
Brickhouse Cafe, 7
Bullshead Restaurant, 3
Burger Joint, 7
Butler and the Chef Bistro, The, 11
Café Colucci, 11
Café de La Paz, 15
Café Gratitude, 20
Campton Place, 16
Cha Cha Cha, 15
Charanga, 15
Chaya Brasserie, 6
Chez Maman, 11
Citizen Cake, 8
Cock-A-Doodle Café, 3
Coco 500, 8
Coi, 8
Côté Sud, 11
Daily Health, 20
De Young Café, 8
Delancey Street Restaurant, 4
Delfina, 14
Delfina Pizzeria, 18
Delica RF-1, 6
Emmy's Spaghetti Shack, 14
Eos Restaurant, 6
Farmer Brown, 3
Faz, 16
Ferry Plaza Seafood, 19
1550 Hyde Café & Wine Bar, 7
Firefly, 4
Fleur De Lys, 11
Fringale, 11
Front Porch, The, 15
Globe, 9
Green Chile Kitchen, 17
Greens Restaurant, 16, 20
Harvest & Rowe, 9
Hog Island Oyster Company, 19
Home, 5
Jack Falstaff Restaurant, 9
Jardinière, 12
Juicey Lucy's, 20
Judahlicious, 20
Kokkari, 16
Legion of Honor café, 9
Let's Be Frank Dogs, 3
Lettus Café Organic, 9
Liberty Café, The, 5
Limon, 15
Masa's Restaurant, 12
Medicine Eatstation, 6
Mijita, 17

206

Millennium, 20
Mistral Rotisserie Provencale, 12
Mixt Greens, 9
Modern Tea, 9
Myth, 10
One Market, 5
Out the Door, 6
Pacific Catch, 19
Paréa Wine Bar and Café, 17
Pauline's Pizza, 18
Peña Pachamama, 15
Pisces California Cuisine, 19
Pizzetta 211, 18
Plumpjack Café, 10
Pomelo, 7
Postrio, 5
Ramblas Tapas Restaurant and Bar, 15
Range, 10
Roosevelt Tamale Parlor, 18
Roti Indian Bistro, 13
Rubicon, 5
Sellers Markets, 10
Slanted Door, The, 6
Slow Club, 5
South Park Café, 12
Subculture Dining, 5
Sutro's, 10
Tablespoon, 5
Town Hall, 4
Town's End Restaurant and Bakery, 5
2223 Restaurant, 4
Universal Café, 5
Velo Rouge, 4
Vignette, 10
Vinorosso, 15
Weird Fish, 19
Yumma's Mediterranean Grill, 17
Zuppa, 15

Salvage Yards

Building Resources, 154
Caldwell Building Wreckers, 154
SCRAP - Scroungers' Center for
   Re-Usable Art Parts, 155

Shoes

(see Clothing/Shoes)

Solar Energy

(see Alternative Energy Contractors)

Spas

(see Day Spas)

Specialty Markets

AK Meats, 51
Cheese Plus, 51
Cowgirl Creamery, 51
Drewes Bros. Meats, 51
Far West Fungi, 51
Golden Gate Meat Company, 51
McEvoy Ranch, 52
Mission Market Fish and Poultry, 52

Prather Ranch Meat Company, 52
San Francisco Fish Company, 52
Tsar Nicoulai Caviar Café, 52
Village Market, The, 52

Taxicabs and Limousines

Yellow Cab Co-Op, 166

Telecommunications

Working Assets, 125

Tradespeople

Earthfirst Electric, 144
Flack + Kurtz, 144
Randy Colosky Design, 144
Woodshanti Cooperative, Inc., 144

Travel Agents

Global Exchange Reality Tours, 104
Green Tortoise Adventure Travel, 104
Himalayan High Treks, 104
Nature Trip, 104
Sierra Club Outings, 104

Wet and Hydrocarbon Cleaners

California Oak Cleaners, 115
Meader's Cleaners, 116
Union French Cleaners, 116

Wine, Beer, and Spirits

Arlequin Wine Merchant, 56
Elixir, 56
Ferry Plaza Wine Merchant, 56
Jug Shop, The, 57
Paréa Wine Bar and Café, 57
Swirl on Castro, 57
Vinorosso, 57
William Cross, 57
Yield Wine Bar, 57

Yarn

(see Fabric/Yarn Stores)

EAST BAY: OAKLAND AREA

Alternative Fuel

(see Fueling Stations)

Alternative Transportation

Alameda Bicycle, 168

Architects

Deboer Architects, 141
GHA/Geoffrey Holton & Associates, 141
Mercedes Corbell Design +
   Architecture, 142
Michelle Kaufmann Designs, 142
Siegel & Strain Architects, 143
Thomas Saxby Architect, 143

Automobiles
(see Eco-Friendly Vehicle Dealerships)

Baby Products
(see Gifts, Accessories, and
Baby Products)

Bakeries
Arizmendi Bakery Cooperative, 28
Feel Good Bakery, 29
Great Harvest Bread, 29
Your Black Muslim Bakery, 29

Banking and Finance
Aegis Capital Management, Inc., 121
Cathedral Financial Group, Inc., 121
Peoples Community Partnership Federal
Credit Union, 122
Progressive Asset Management, 123

Beauty Product Suppliers
Beauty Center, 66
Body Shop, The, 67
Body Time, 67
Sumbody & Sumtime Spa, 69

Beds, Bedding, and Linens
Matsu Bedding, 135
Murasaki, 135

Bicycles and Bicycling
(see Alternative Transportation)

Building Materials and Supplies
Earthsource Forest Products, 151

Cafés, Tea Houses, and Juice Bars
Arizmendi Bakery Cooperative, 21
Bittersweet, 22
Cole Coffee, 23
Hudson Bay Caffe, 24
Julie's Coffee and Tea Garden, 24
L'Amyx Tea Bar, 25
Nomad Café, 25
Spasso Coffeehouse, 27
Zocalo Coffeehouse, 28

Car Rentals
EV Rentals at Fox Rent A Car, 167
Hertz, 167
Specialty Rentals, 167

Car Share Services
Spaceshare, 168

Carpeting
(see Furniture, Flooring, Carpeting,
and Décor)

Catering Services and Personal Chefs
Amiee Alan Custom Catering, 53

Componere Fine Catering, 53
Garden Gourmet, 54
Nourishing the Whole, 54

Chocolatiers and Dessert Shops
Bittersweet, 30

Cleaning Services
Natural Home Cleaning
Professionals, 118
Natural Way, 118
Sunclean Carpet Care, 118

Clothing/Shoes
See Jane Run Sports, 83
August, 81
Twenty Two, 83
Waddle and Swaddle, 83

Compressed Natural Gas
(see Fueling Stations)

Day Spas
Meditrina, 74
Simply Gorgeous, 75

Décor
(see Furniture, Flooring, Carpeting,
and Décor)

Eco-Friendly Vehicle Dealerships
Electric Motorsport, 162
Segway of Oakland, 163

Educational Organizations
Cal State University East Bay, 188
Crown Memorial State Beach and
Crab Cove Visitor Center, 189
East Bay Conservation Corps, 189
Future Leaders Institute, The, 190
Merrit College Landscape Horticulture
Department, 191
Mills College Environmental Studies
Program, 191
UC Cooperative Extension - Alameda
County, 192

Electric Plug-In Stations
(see Fueling Stations)

Electric Vehicles
(see Eco-Friendly Vehicle
Dealerships)

Environmental Organizations
Alameda Creek Alliance, 178
Asian-Pacific Environmental
Network, 179
Bay Localize, 179
California League of Conservation
Voters, 180

Center for Environmental Health, 180
Circle of Life, 180
Coastal Conservancy, 181
Communities for a Better
  Environment, 181
Earthjustice, 181
Ella Baker Center for Human Rights, 182
Environmental Justice Coalition
  for Water, 182
Food First/Institute For Food and
  Development, 182
Hayward Shoreline Interpretive
  Center, 183
International Healthy Cities Foundation,
  The, 183
People's Grocery, 185
Public Health Institute, 185
Regional Asthma Management and
  Prevention, Bay Area Ramp, 185
Save the Bay, 186
Sustaining Ourselves Locally, 187
Trans Fair USA, 187
Transportation and Land Use
  Coalition, 187

Fabric/Yarn Stores
Article Pract, 84

Farmers' Markets
Alameda CFM, 44
East Oakland CFM, 45
East Oakland Senior Center CFM, 45
Hayward CFM, 46
Hayward Kaiser CFM, 46
Mo' Better Food, 46
Oakland Fruitvale CFM, 46
Oakland Grand Lake CFM, 46
Oakland Jack London CFM, 46
Oakland Kaiser CFM, 46
Oakland Montclair Sunday CFM, 46
Oakland Temescal CFM, 46
Old Oakland CFM, 46
San Leandro Bayfair Mall CFM, 47

Flooring
(see Furniture, Flooring, Carpeting,
  and Décor)

**Fueling Stations, Compressed
Natural Gas**
Clean Energy, 164
PG&E Service Centers, 164

Fueling Stations, Electric Plug-In
Clean Fueling Stations, 164

**Furniture, Flooring, Carpeting,
and Décor**
Abbey Carpet, 131
Amber Flooring, 131

Garden Supplies
(see Nurseries and Garden Supplies)

Gardening and Landscaping
Wildheart Gardens, 139

General Contractors
Bashland Builders, 146
Fryer Consulting, 147
Spring Friedlander Remodeling, 147

Grocery and Produce Delivery
Guerrilla Organics, 50
Westside Organics, 50

Grocery Stores
Alameda Natural Grocery, 39
Food Mill, The, 40
Lakeshore Natural Foods, 41
Market Hall Produce, 41
Piedmont Grocery, 42
Savemore Market, 42
Trader Joe's, 43
Village Market, The, 43

Hair and Nail Salons
Piedmont Hairport, 72
17 Jewels, 71

Hazardous Waste
(see Household Hazardous
  Waste Disposal)

Hotels
Courtyard by Marriott, Downtown
  Oakland, 105
Marriott, Oakland City Center, 107

Household Hazardous Waste Disposal
Alameda County Drop-Off, 156
Walgreens, 157

Interior Designers
Beautiful Place, A, 145

Landscaping
(see Gardening and Landscaping)

Linens
(see Beds, Bedding, and Linens)

Nail Salons
(see Hair and Nail Salons)

Nurseries and Garden Supplies
Wildheart Gardens, 137

Office and Paper Products
Kelly Paper, 90
Xpedx Paper and Graphics, 90

Paper Products
(see Office and Paper Products)

Personal Services
Vibrant Events, 115

Pest Control
A-Non-Toxic Live Bee Removal, 119

Pet Food, Supplies, Grooming, and Other Services
Dog Bone Alley, 97
Pet Food Express, 98
Redhound, 99

Public Transportation
AC Transit, 169
BART, 170
Blue And Gold Fleet, 170
Eastbay Ferry, 170

Recycling Centers/Recycling Services
Alameda County Waste Management Authority, 152
Reuse People, The, 155

Restaurants
À Côté, 16
B Restaurant and Bar, 7
Café 817, 13
C'era Una Volta, 13
Di Bartolo, 16
Doña Tomas, 17
Dopo, 14
Garibaldi's, 8
Gregoire Jacquet, 12
Happy Burrito, 17
JoJo, 12
La Estrellita Café, 17
Luka's Taproom & Lounge, 12
Manzanita Restaurant, 20
New World Vegetarian Cuisine, 20
Oliveto's, 14
Pappo, 10
Pizza Pazza, 18
Pizzaiolo, 14
Prism Café, 20
Tamarindo Antojeria Mexicana, 18
Tomatina, 17

Salvage Yards
C & K Salvage, 154
Restore Store, The, 155
Ruiz Antique Lighting, 155

Shoes
(see Clothing/Shoes)

Spas
(see Day Spas)

Specialty Markets
Baron's Meat and Poultry, 51
Hapuku Fish Shop, 51
Numi Organic, 52
Ver Brugge Foods, 52

EAST BAY: BERKELEY AREA

Alternative Energy Contractors
Borrego Solar, 148
Sun Light and Power, 150

Alternative Fuel
(see Fueling Stations)

Alternative Transportation
Solano Avenue Cyclery, 169

Architects
Arkin Tilt Architects, 141
Dan Smith & Associates, 141
Todd Jersey Architecture, 143

Baby Products
(see Gifts, Accessories, and Baby Products)

Bakeries
Acme, 28
Nabolom Bakery, 29
Vital Vittles, 29

Banking and Finance
Cambridge Investment Group, 121
Catherine Woodman, Financial Advisor, 122
David Dobkin, CFP®, AIF®, 122
Effective Assets (Lincoln Payne), 122
North Berkeley Investment Partners, 122
Social Equity Group, The, 123

Beauty Product Suppliers
Aveda, 66
Beauty Center, 66
Body Shop, The, 67
Body Time, 67
Elephant Pharmacy, 67
Hydra, 68
Pharmaca Integrative Pharmacy, 69

Beds, Bedding, and Linens
Earthsake, 134
European Sleepworks, 134

Bicycles and Bicycling
(see Alternative Transportation)

Biodiesel
(see Fueling Stations)

Building Materials and Supplies
Bofings Elmwood Hardware, 150
Ecohome Improvement, 151

Cafés, Tea Houses, and Juice Bars
Bake Shop, The, 22

Café Fanny, 22
Café Gratitude, 22
Far Leaves Tea, 23
Guerilla Café, 24
Juice Bar Collective, 24
Mokka, 25
Pri Pri Café, 26
Raw Energy Organic Juice Café, 26
Tay Tan Café, 27
Village Grounds, 27
Well Grounded Tea & Coffee, 27
Zemocha, 27

Carpeting
(see Furniture, Flooring, Carpeting,
    and Décor)

Catering Services and Personal Chefs
Alive and Radiant Foods, 53
Aubergine Catering, 53
Back to Earth, 53

Chocolatiers and Dessert Shops
Ici, 30
Sketch Ice Cream, 31

Cleaning Services
Eco-Friendly Cleaning, 117
Eco-Safe Cleaning, 117
House Shinning, 118
Natural Care for Carpets, 118

Clothing/Shoes
American Apparel, 81
Bryn Walker, 81
Global Exchange Fair Trade Store, 81
Mephisto, 82
Rabat Shoes, 83
REI, 83

Compressed Natural Gas
(see Fueling Stations)

Day Spas
About Face & Body, 73
Alchemy Skin Spa, 73
Artbeat Salon & Gallery, 73

Décor
(see Furniture, Flooring, Carpeting,
    and Décor)

Dry Cleaners
(see Wet and Hydrocarbon or Wet and
CO_2 Cleaners)

Educational Organizations
Botanical Garden - University of
    California, Berkeley, 188
College of Environmental Design,
    University of California, Berkeley, 189

College of Natural Resources, University
    of California, Berkely, 189
Ecology Center, 190
Ecovillage Farm Learning Center, 190
Thimmakka's Resources For
    Environmental Education, 192
Tilden Environmental Education
    Center, 192
UC Extension - Berkeley, 193

Electric Plug-In Stations
(see Fueling Stations)

Energy
(see Alternative Energy Contractors)

Environmental Consultants
Build It Green, 146
Natural Builders, The, 146

Environmental Organizations
Bay Area Coalition for Headwaters
    Forest, 179
Bay Nature Institute, 179
Chez Panisse Foundation, 180
Ecology Center, 181
Endangered Species Coalition, 182
Ethical Traveler, 182
Golden Gate Audubon Society and
    Nature Store, 182
Health Care Without Harm, 183
Healthy Building Network, 183
Regional Parks Botanic Garden at
    Tilden Park, 185
River of Words, 185
Urban Creeks Council, 188

Fabric/Yarn Stores
Stash Yarn + Inspiration, 84

Farmers' Markets
Bayview/Hunter's Point Farmers'
    Market, 44
Berkeley Saturday CFM, 45
Berkeley Shattuck Organic CFM, 45
Berkeley Tuesday CFM, 45
El Cerrito Plaza Farmers' Market, 45
Farm Fresh Choice, 45
Richmond CFM, 47

Flooring
(see Furniture, Flooring, Carpeting,
    and Décor)

Fueling Stations, Biodiesel
Berkeley Biodiesel Collective, 165
Biofuel Oasis, 165
LC Biofuels, 165

**Fueling Stations, Compressed
Natural Gas**
PG&E Service Centers, 164

Trillium USA, 164

Fueling Stations, Electric Plug-In
Clean Fueling Stations, 164

Furniture, Flooring, Carpeting, and Décor
Abbey Carpet, 131
Ecohome Improvement, 131
Flooring Alternatives, 132
Habitats (formerly Asiantiques), 132
High Cotton Living, 132
Smith & Hawken, 133
Wooden Duck, The, 133

Garden Supplies
(see Nurseries and Garden Supplies)

Gardening and Landscaping
Magic Gardens Landscape
  Nursery, 139

General Contractors
McCutcheon Construction, Inc., 147

Gifts, Accessories, and Baby Products
Earthsake, 86
Global Exchange Fair Trade Store, 86
Juniper Tree Supplies, 87
Soap Sistahs, 87
Twig & Fig, 88

Grocery Stores
Andronico's Market, 39
Berkeley Bowl, 39
Berkeley Natural Grocery, 39
El Cerrito Natural Grocery, 40
Produce Center, The, 47
Trader Joe's, 43
Whole Foods Market, 43
William's Natural Foods, 43

Hair and Nail Salons
Darin David Salon, 71
Elixir, 71
Joi Nail Spa, 71
Nina Homisak Hair Design, 71
Sole Salon & Sanctuary, 72
Thairapeutics, 72

Hazardous Waste
(see Household Hazardous
  Waste Disposal)

Hotels
Doubletree Hotel & EMC Berkeley
  Marina, 106

Household Hazardous Waste Disposal
Walgreens, 157

Interior Designers
Christine Reid, 145

Landscaping
(see Gardening and Landscaping)

Linens
(see Beds, Bedding, and Linens)

Nail Salons
(see Hair and Nail Salons)

Nurseries and Garden Supplies
Berkeley Horticultural Nursery, 136
Friends of the Regional Parks
  Botanic Garden, 136
Garden Shop at UC Berkeley Botanical
  Garden, 136
Magic Gardens Landscape Nursery, 136
Native Here Nursery, 136
Smith & Hawken, 137
Urban Farmer Store, The, 137
Urban Forest Home, 137
Westbrae Nursery, 137
Yabusaki's Dwight Way Nursery, 137

Office and Paper Products
Ecology Center Store, 89
Greener Printer, 89
Inkworks Press, 89
Paper Source, 90

Paper Products
(see Office and Paper Products)

Pest Control
Bio Integral Resource Center, 119
Bzz Bees, 120
Joe's Wildlife Animal Damage
  Control, 120

**Pet Food, Supplies, Grooming, and
Other Services**
Alpha Pet Supply, 96
Holistic Hound, 98
Pet Food Express, 98
Village Dog, The, 99

Pharmacies
Elephant Pharmacy, 112
Pharmaca Integrative Pharmacy, 113
Shen Herbal Pharmacy, 113

Public Transportation
AC Transit, 169
BART, 170

Recycling Centers/Recycling Services
Berkeley Ecology Center Curbside
  Recycling Program, 152
City of El Cerrito Recycling, 153

Community Conservation Centers
- Berkeley Recycling Center, 153

Restaurants
Adagia, 7
Breads of India & Gourmet Curries, 12
Café Gratitude, 20
Café Rouge, 16
Cheeseboard Pizza Collective, The, 18
Chez Panisse, 8
Cugini, 14
Eccolo, 14
Fonda, 15
Gioia, 18
Jerusalem Organic Kitchen &
   Burgers, 18
Jimmy Bean's, 3
Lalime's, 9
Lola's, 3
O'Chame, 7
Razan's Organic Kitchen, 18
Renee's Place, 6
Rivoli, 14
Sea Salt, 19
Sunny Side Café, 3
T-Rex Barbeque, 4
Thai Delight Cuisine, 6
Tacubaya, 18
Venus, 10
Zatar, 17

Salvage Yards
East Bay Depot for Creative Refuse, 154
Gilman Trading Company, Inc., 154
Ohmega Salvage, 155
Omega Too, 155
Sink Factory, The, 155
Urban Ore, 155

Shoes
(see Clothing/Shoes)

Solar Energy
(see Alternative Energy Contractors)

Spas
(see Day Spas)

Specialty Markets
Cheeseboard Collective, The, 51
Stonehouse California Olive Oil
   Company, 52

Tradespeople
Ecocraft, 144
Stonelace Designs, 144

Travel Agents
Seacology, 104
Wilderness Travel, 104

Wet and CO_2 Cleaners
Bob's Cleaners, 115

Wet and Hydrocarbon Cleaners
Norge Cleaners, 116

Wine, Beer, and Spirits
Bison Brewery, 56
Vintage Berkeley, 57

Yarn
(see Fabric/Yarn Stores)

PENINSULA

Alternative Energy Contractors
Green Building Exchange, 149
Owens Electric and Solar, 149
Solar City, 149

Architects
Green Building Exchange, 141
Vox Design Group, 143

Automobiles
(see Eco-Friendly Vehicle Dealerships)

Baby Products
(see Gifts, Accessories, and
   Baby Products)

Banking and Finance
Principled Solutions, 122

Beauty Product Suppliers
Beauty Center, 66
Body Shop, The, 67
Elephant Pharmacy, 67
Fringe Salon, 68
Jouvence Skin Rejuvenation Center, 68
L'Occitane en Provence, 68
Sandra Caron European Spa, 69
Skin and Body Therapy, 69
Skin Envy, 69
Susan's Soap, 69
Willa Home, 69

Building Materials and Supplies
Eco Design Resources, 151
Green Building Exchange, 151

Cafés, Tea Houses, and Juice Bars
Café Capuchino, 22
Café Grillades, 23
Caffé Del Doge, 23

Car Rentals
Specialty Rentals, 167

Car Share Services
Spaceshare, 168

Carbon Offset Services
Terra Pass, 172

Carpeting
(see Furniture, Flooring, Carpeting, and Décor)

Catering Services and Personal Chefs
Cool Eatz Catering, 54

Cleaning Services
Emma's Eco-Clean, 117

Clothing/Shoes
Bare Necessities Clothing and Scents, 81
Footloose Birkenstock Store, 81
Leela, 82
Lululemon, 82
Meyer Bunje, 82
Orapa Gallery of Wearable Arts, 82
Pendleton, 82
Rabat Shoes, 83
REI, 83
World Centric, 83

Community-Supported Agriculture
Hidden Villa CSA, 48

Compressed Natural Gas
(see Fueling Stations)

Day Spas
Sandra Caron European Spa, 74
Skin Envy, 75
Skin Therapy, 75
Spa de Beaute, 75
Star City Salon & Day Spa, 75
Tea Garden Springs, 75
Watercourse Way, 75

Décor
(see Furniture, Flooring, Carpeting, and Décor)

Dry Cleaners
(see Wet and Hydrocarbon or Wet and CO_2 Cleaners)

Eco-Friendly Vehicle Dealerships
Tesla Motors, 163

Educational Organizations
Common Ground Organic Garden Supply and Education Center, 189
Foothill College Environmental Horticulture & Design, 190
Gamble Garden, 190

Stanford University - Woods Institute for the Environment, 192

Energy
(see Alternative Energy Contractors)

Environmental Organizations
Acterra, 178
Palo Alto Green Team Project, 184
Peninsula Open Space Trust, 184
Sequoia Audubon Society, 186
Sierra Club, 187
Sustainable San Mateo County, 187
Trail Center, The, 187

Fabric/Yarn Stores
Knitter's Studio, The, 84
Yarn Paper Scissors, 85

Farmers' Markets
Belmont CFM, 45
Burlingame Fresh Market CFM, 45
Daly City CFM, 45
Larkspur CFM, 46
Menlo Park CFM, 46
Millbrae CFM, 46
Redwood City CFM, 47
Redwood City Kaiser CFM, 47
San Carlos CFM, 47
San Mateo CFM, 47
Sausalito CFM, 48

Flooring
(see Furniture, Flooring, Carpeting, and Décor)

Fueling Stations, Compressed Natural Gas
Trillium USA, 164

Furniture, Flooring, Carpeting, and Décor
Abbey Carpet, 131
Eco Design Resources, 131
Hoot Judkins, 132
Luxant, 132
Smith & Hawken, 133

Garden Supplies
(see Nurseries and Garden Supplies)

Gardening and Landscaping
Yerba Buena California Native Plant Nursery, 139

General Contractors
Drew Maran Construction, Inc., 146
Form + Function Construction, 147
Hammerschmidt Construction, 147
MGS Construction, Inc., 147

Gifts, Accessories, and Baby Products

Artisan Shop, 85
Cheeky Monkey Toys, 85
Learning Express, 87
Letter Perfect, 87
Meyer Bunje, 87
Nature at Play, 87
Play Store, The, 87
Renaissance Spirit, 87
World Centric, 88

Grocery and Produce Delivery

Aha-Yes!, 49

Grocery Stores

Andronico's Market, 39
Country Sun Natural Foods, 39
Draeger's Supermarkets, Inc., 39
Earthbeam Natural Foods, 40
Lunardi's, 41
Mollie Stone's, 41
Piazza's Fine Foods, 42
Trader Joe's, 43
Whole Foods Market, 43
Whole Life Natural Foods, 43

Hair and Nail Salons

Fringe Salon, 71
Incognito, 71
Perfect Ten Nail Salon, The, 72
Star City Salon & Day Spa, 72

Hazardous Waste

(see Household Hazardous
   Waste Disposal)

Hotels

Crowne Plaza Hotel Cabana, 106
Stanford Terrace Inn, 108

Household Hazardous Waste Disposal

San Francisco Recycling and
   Disposal, 157
San Mateo County Household Hazardous
   Waste Program/Recycleworks, 157
Walgreens, 157

Interior Designers

Peché Interiors, 145
Sustainable Home, 145

Landscaping

(see Gardening and Landscaping)

Nail Salons

(see Hair and Nail Salons)

Nurseries and Garden Supplies

Common Ground Organic Garden Supply
   and Education Center, 136
Garden Shed, The, 136
Sloat Garden Center, 137
Smith & Hawken, 137

Office and Paper Products

Kelly Paper, 90
World Centric, 90

Paper Products

(see Office and Paper Products)

Personal Services

Don't Agonize, Organize!, 114
Green Chi, 114

Pest Control

AAA Animal Removal, 119
Donovan's Pest Control, Inc., 120

Pet Food, Supplies, Grooming, and Other Services

Birders' Garden, 97
Bowwowmeow, 97
Dolly's Treasures, 97
Grooming with TLC, 97
Pawsitively Groomed Pet Salon, 98
Pet Food Express, 98
Pet Place, The, 98
Pets Are Us, 98
Plaza De Paws, 99
Scrub a Pup Dog Wash, 99

Pharmacies

Apple Health Foods, 112
Elephant Pharmacy, 112
Health by Heidi, 112

Public Transportation

SamTrans, 170

Recycling Centers/Recycling Services

Allied Waste of San Mateo County
   Curbside Program, 152
Allied Waste Services of Daly City, 152
City of Palo Alto Recycling Program, 153
County of San Mateo Recycleworks, 153

Restaurants

Central Park Bistro, 4
Chez Alexander, 11
Cool Café, 3
Crepes Café, 11
Divino Ristorante Italiano, 14
Don Pico's Original Mexican Bistro, 17
Flea St. Café, 8
John Bentley's Restaurant, 12
JZCool Eatery, 9
Mandaloun, 16
Que Seraw Seraw, 20
Roti Indian Bistro, 13
Sirayvah Organic Thai Cuisine, 6

Trapeze Restaurant, 17
Vino Locale, 10
West Bay Café and Lounge, 11

Salvage Yards
Whole House Building Supply, 155

Shoes
(see Clothing/Shoes)

Solar Energy
(see Alternative Energy Contractors)

Spas
(see Day Spas)

Specialty Markets
Crystal Springs Fish & Poultry, 51
De Martini Orchard, 51
Sigona's Farmers Market, 52

Wet and Hydrocarbon Cleaners
Richard's Dry Cleaners, 116

Wine, Beer, and Spirits
K&L Wine Merchants, 57

Yarn
(see Fabric/Yarn Stores)

MARIN COUNTY

Alternative Energy Contractors
Cooperative Community Energy, 148
Greenlight Solar, 149
Healthy Home Plans, 149
Marin Solar, 149
Renu: Smart Solutions for Healthy
    Homes, 149
Solarcraft, 149
SPG Solar, Inc., 149
Sun First, 150

Architects
Alb Designs, 140
Architecture Studio, 141
Bridget Brewer Associates, 141
Gettman Schow Architecture, 141
Healthy Home Plans, 142
Hubbell Daily Architecture + Design, 142
Inkmoon Architects, 142
Newland + Winnen Design Studio, 142
Sustainable Architecture &
    Consulting, 143
Wagstaff Architects, 144

Baby Products
(see Gifts, Accessories, and
    Baby Products)

Bakeries
Boulangerie Bay Bread, 28
Churro Station, 29
Fat Angel Bakery, 29
Rustic Bakery, 29

Banking and Finance
Estate Conservation Associates, 122
Girton Capital Management, Inc., 122
Mortgagegreen, 122

Beauty Product Suppliers
Aveda, 66
Body Shop, The, 67
Body Time, 67
Cat Murphy's Skin Care Salon, 67
Elephant Pharmacy, 67
Eva Claiborne Skin Institute, 67
Evo Spa, 67
L'Occitane en Provence, 68
Original Swiss Aromatics, 69
Pharmaca Integrative Pharmacy, 69

Beds, Bedding, and Linens
Foam Store of Marin, The, 134
Green Fusion Design Center, 135

Biodiesel
(see Fueling Stations)

Building Materials and Supplies
Black's Farmwood, 150
Fairfax Lumber & Hardware, 151
Green Fusion Design Center, 151
Mill Valley Bamboo Flooring, 151

Cafés, Tea Houses, and Juice Bars
Café Del Soul, 22
Comforts, 23
Marin Coffee Roasters, 25
Muffin Mania, 25
Nelly's Java, 25
Northpoint Coffee Company, 25

Car Rentals
Specialty Rentals, 16

Carpeting
(see Furniture, Flooring, Carpeting,
    and Décor)

Catering Services and Personal Chefs
Are You Being Served, 53

Chocolatiers and Dessert Shops
Fairfax Scoop, 30
Three Twins Ice Cream, 31

Cleaning Services
Oz Cleaning Company, 118

Clothing/Shoes
Dharma Trading Company, 81
Fat Kat Surf Shop, 81
Hip & Zen, 82
Pendleton, 82
REI, 83
Tela D, 83
Yoga of Sausalito, 83
Yoga Studio, 84

Compressed Natural Gas
(see Fueling Stations)

Day Spas
Eva Claiborne Skin Instiute, 74
Evo Spa, 74
Paris Salon and Spa, 74
Rebecca Smith Skin Care, 74
Stellar Spa, 75

Décor
(see Furniture, Flooring, Carpeting,
  and Décor)

Dry Cleaners
(see Wet and Hydrocarbon or Wet and
CO$_2$ Cleaners)

Educational Organizations
Dominican University of California, Green
MBA Program, 189
Environmental Forum of Marin, 190
Marin Art and Garden Center, 190
UC Cooperative Extension - Marin, 192

Electric Plug-In Stations
(see Fueling Stations)

Energy
(see Alternative Energy Contractors)

Environmental Consultants
Energy Management Services, 146

Environmental Organizations
Green Museum, 183
Green Planet Films, 183
Marin Audubon Society, 184
Marin County Open Space District, 184
Marine Mammal Center, The, 184
Richardson Bay Audubon Center
  Sanctuary, 185
San Francisco Bay National Wildlife
Refuge Complex, 186
Sustainable World Coalition, 187

Fabric/Yarn Stores
Amazing Yarns, 84
Ambatalia Fabrics, 84
Atelier Marin, 84

Marin Fiber Arts, 84
Studio Knit, 84

Farmers' Markets
Corte Madera CFM, 45
Fairfax CFM, 45
Novato Downtown CFM, 46
San Rafael Civic Center-Marin CFM, 47
San Rafael Downtown CFM, 47

Flooring
(see Furniture, Flooring, Carpeting,
  and Décor)

Fueling Stations, Biodiesel
Biodiesel
LC Biofuels, 165

**Fueling Stations, Compressed
Natural Gas**
PG&E Service Centers, 164

Fueiling Stations, Electric Plug-In
Clean Fueling Stations, 164

**Furniture, Flooring, Carpeting,
and Décor**
Abbey Carpet, 131
Black's Farmwood, 131
Eco Timber, 131
Grccn Fusion Design Center, 132
Madera, 132
Maison Rêve, 132
Marin Outdoor Living, 132
Mill Valley Bamboo, 133
Skyside Studios, 133
Smith & Hawken, 133

Garden Supplies
(see Nurseries and Garden Supplies)

Gardening and Landscaping
Bridget Brewer Associates, 148
Equinox Landscape Construction
  Corps, 138
Gardener's Guild, 139
Green Fusion Design Center, 139
O'Donnell's Organic Nursery & Habitat
Restoration, 139
Sloat Garden Center, Custom Garden
Design, 139
Suburban Habitat, 139

General Contractors
Ebersole Builders, 147
Equinox Landscape Construction
  Corps, 148
Green Builders of Marin, 147
Renaissance Remodelers, 147

Gifts, Accessories, and Baby Products
Body Wise Massage, 85
Dharma Trading Company, 86
EcoExpress, 86
Fat Kat Surf Shop, 86
Golden Gate School of Feng Shui, 86
Hip & Zen, 87
Yoga of Sausalito, 88

Grocery and Produce Delivery
Gourmet Garden to Go, 50

Grocery Stores
Andronico's Market, 39
Good Earth Natural & Organic Foods, 40
Mollie Stone's, 41
Oasis Natural Foods, 41
Paradise Foods, 42
Trader Joe's, 43
Whole Foods Market, 43
Woodlands Market, 43

Hair and Nail Salons
Paris Salon and Spa, 72
Salon des Artistes, 72
Tizka, 72

Hazardous Waste
(see Household Hazardous
Waste Disposal)

Hotels
Embassy Suites Hotel,
San Rafael/Marin, 106
Hosteling International Marin
Headlands, 106
Inn Marin, 107

Household Hazardous Waste Disposal
Marin County Household Hazardous
Waste Facility, 156
Novato Household Hazardous Waste
Facility, 156
Walgreens, 157

Interior Designers
Atmosphera, 145
Carolyn Robbins Site Design, 145
Green Fusion Design Center, 145

Landscaping
(see Gardening and Landscaping)

Linens
(see Beds, Bedding, and Linens)

Nail Salons
(see Hair and Nail Salons)

Nurseries and Garden Supplies
Green Jeans Garden Supply, 136

O'Donnell's Organic Nursery & Habitat
Restoration, 136
Sloat Garden Center, 137
Smith & Hawken, 137
Suburban Habitat, 137
Urban Farmer Store, The, 137

Office and Paper Products
Marin Ideal Stationers, 90

Paper Products
(see Office and Paper Products)

Personal Services
Green Career Tracks, 114
Green Careers, 114

**Pet Food, Supplies, Grooming, and
Other Services**
For Paws, 97
Pet Club, 98
Top Paws, 99
Who Does Your Dog?, 99
Woodlands Pet Food & Treats, 99

Pharmacies
Elephant Pharmacy, 112
Pharmaca Integrative Pharmacy, 113

Public Transportation
Blue and Gold Fleet, 170

Real Estate
Ecology House, 124
Green Key Real Estate, 124
At Home in Marin, 124
Mortgagegreen, 124
My Marin Homes/Linda Tull, 124

Recycling Centers/Recycling Services
City of Sausalito Recycling - Bay Cities
Refuse, 153
Marin City Community Services
District, 153
Marin Recycling Service, 153
Mill Valley Refuse Service, 154

Restaurants
Angelino Restaurant, 13
Benissimo Ristorante & Bar, 13
Bistro 330, 11
Bubba's Diner, 3
Caprice, The, 4
Comforts, 8
Fork, 8
Frantoio Ristorante & Olive Oil Co., 14
Horizon's, 19
Lark Creek Inn, 5
Marché Aux Fleurs, 12
M&G Burgers, 7
Mountain Home Inn, 9

Ondine, 19
Paradise Bay Restaurant & Bar, 19
Piatti Locali, 14
Sam's Anchor Café, 19
Simmer, 10
Small Shed Flatbreads, 5
Sol Food Puerto Rican Cuisine, 15
Table Café, 13
Three Degrees Restaurant, 3

Salvage Yards
Maison Rêve, 154

Shoes
(see Clothing/Shoes)

Solar Energy
(see Alternative Energy Contractors)

Spas
(see Day Spas)

Specialty Markets
EcoExpress, 51

Tradespeople
Bamboo Cabinets By Altereco, 144
Renu: Smart Solutions For Healthy
   Homes, 144

Wet and Hydrocarbon Cleaning
Alex's Cleaners, 115
Vogue Cleaners, 116

Yarn
(see Fabric/Yarn Stores)

OUT OF REGION

Alternative Energy Contractors
Bay Solar Power Design, 148
Mc Solar Engineering, 149

Architects
Tamley Architectural Design, 143
Van Der Ryn Eco Design
   Collaborative, 143

Auto Clubs
Better World Club, 166

Automobiles
(see Eco-Friendly Vehicle Dealerships)

Bicycles and Bicycling
(see Alternative Transportation)

Burial Services
Colorful Coffins, 126
Eternal Reefs Inc., 126
Family Farewell, A, 126
Fernwood Cemetery, 126
Lifegem, 126
Sea-Urn, 127

Car Rentals
EV Rentals at Fox Rent A Car, 167

Car Share Services
Casual Carpooling, 167
City Carshare, 167
Icarpool, 168
Match & Go, 168
Spaceshare, 168

Carbon Offset Services
Better World Club, 171
Carbon Fund, 171
Climate Trust, The, 171
Cool Driver, 171
My Footprint.org, 172
Native Energy, 172
Renewable Choice Energy, 172
Sky Energy, 172
Solar Electric Light Fund, 172
Stop Global Warming, 172
Sustainable Travel International, 172

Catering Services and Personal Chefs
Rising Sun Catering, 55

Cleaning Services
Elbow-Grease Cleaning, 117
Organic Choice Carpet Cleaning, 118

Community-Supported Agriculture
Full Belly Farm CSA, 48
Riverdog Farm CSA, 48
San Geronimo Valley CSA, 48
Terra Firma Farms CSA, 48
Two Small Farms CSA, 48

Eco-Friendly Vehicle Dealerships
Big Kid Toys, 162
Commuter Cars, 162
Ecomotors, 162
Electric Vehicle Repairs &
   Conversions, 162
Ford Motor Company, 162
General Motors, 162
Honda, 163
Lexus, 163
Mercury, 163
Toyota, 163
Voltage Vehicle, 163
Zap!, 163

Educational Organizations
Ardenwood Regional Preserve and
  Historic Farm, 188
Center for Agroecology and Sustainable
  Food Systems - UC Santa Cruz, 189
Coyote Hills Regional Park, 189
Environmental Education Directory,
  The, 190
Occidental Arts and Ecology Center, 191
Ohlone College, 191
Regenerative Design Institute, 191
San Jose Conservation Corps &
  Charter School, 191
San Jose State University, Environmental
  Studies Department, 191
Santa Clara University, 191
Slide Ranch, 192
Solar Living Institute, 192
Sonoma State University, 192
Sunol Regional Wilderness, 192
UC Cooperative Extension - San Mateo
  and SF County, 192

Electric Plug-In Stations
(see Fueling Stations)

Electric Vehicles
(see Eco-Friendly Vehicle Dealerships)

Energy
(see Alternative Energy Contractors)

Environmental Consultants
Green Living Home, 146

Environmental Organizations
Ardenwood Regional Preserve and
  Historic Farm, 178
California Native Plant Society, 180
California State Parks, 180
Californians For GE-Free Agriculture, 180
Marin Agricultural Land Trust, 184
Natural World Museum, 184
Perry Family Farms at Ardenwood
  Historic Farm, 185

Farmers' Markets
Fremont Centerville CFM, 45
Fremont Irvington CFM, 45
Fremont Kaiser CFM, 45
Fremont Nummi CFM, 46
Santa Clara Kaiser CFM, 48
Union City Kaiser CFM, 48
Union City-Old Alvarado CFM, 48

Fueling Stations, Electric Plug-In
Clean Fueling Stations, 164

**Furniture, Flooring, Carpeting,
and Décor**
Amber Flooring, 131

Earthsource Forest Products, 131

Gardening and Landscaping
Allen Land Design, 138

Gifts, Accessories, and Baby Products
Learning Express, 87

Grocery and Produce Delivery
Farm Fresh to You, 49
Full Belly Farm CSA, 49

Hazardous Waste
(see Household Hazardous
  Waste Disposal)

Hotels
Marriott, Fremont, 107

Household Hazardous Waste Disposal
Alameda County Drop-Off, 156
West Contra Costa Integrated
  Waste Management Authority, 157

Interior Designers
Tranquil Spaces Design Group, 145

Office and Paper Products
Green Earth Office Supply, 89

Paper Products
(see Office and Paper Products)

Personal Services
Big Vision Career and Project
  Consulting, 114
Green Living Home, 114

Pest Control
Ashford Pest Control, 119
Bio-Pest, 119
National Pesticide Telecommunications
  Network, 120

Public Transportation
AC Transit, 169
511.org, 169
Nextbus, 170
VTA, 170

Real Estate
Greener Marin at Keller Williams
  San Francisco, 124

**Recycling Centers/Recycling
Services**
City of Novato Curbside Recycling
  Program, 153

Los Altos Garbage Company Curbside
    Program, 153
Novato Disposal Service, 154
Usedcardboardboxes.com, 154
West Contra Costa Integrated Waste
    Management Authority, 154

Salvage Yards
This & That, 155

Solar Energy
(see Alternative Energy Contractors)

Taxicabs and Limousines
Ecolimo, 166
Planettran, 166

Telecommunications
Better World Telecom, 125
Come From the Heart, 125
Earth Tones, 125
Makana Technologies, 125
Red Jellyfish, 125

Tradespeople
Moondance Painting, 144

Wet and CO_2 Cleaners
Blue Sky Cleaners, 115

À Côté, 16
A-Non-Toxic Live Bee Removal, 119
AAA Animal Removal, 119
Abbey Carpet, 131
About Face & Body, 73
Absinthe Brasserie and Bar, 11
AC Transit, 169
Acme, 28
Acme Chophouse, 7
Acquerello, 13
Acre Café, 21
Acterra, 178
Action for Nature, 178
Adagia, 7
Aegis Capital Management, Inc., 121
Aha-Yes!, 49
AK Meats, 51
Alameda Bicycle, 168
Alameda CFM, 44
Alameda County Drop-Off, 156
Alameda County Waste Management
    Authority, 152
Alameda Creek Alliance, 178
Alameda Natural Grocery, 39
Alb Designs, 140
Alchemy Skin Spa, 73
Alex's Cleaners, 115
Alive!, 20
Alive and Radiant Foods, 53
Allen Land Design, 138
Allied Waste of San Mateo County
    Curbside Program, 152
Allied Waste Services of Daly City, 152
Alpha Pet Supply, 96
Amazing Yarns, 84
Amazon Watch, 178
Ambatalia Fabrics, 84
Amber Flooring, 131
Ame Restaurant, 6
American Apparel, 81
Americano Restaurant and Bar, 13
Amiee Alan Custom Catering, 53
Andronico's Market, 39
Angelino Restaurant, 13
Animal Company, The, 96
Aperto, 13
Apple Health Foods, 112
Arc Café, 21
ARC Ecology, 178
Architecture Studio, 141
Ardenwood Regional Preserve and
    Historic Farm, 178, 188
Are You Being Served, 53
Argonaut Hotel, 105
Arizmendi Bakery Cooperative, 21, 28
Arkin Tilt Architects, 141
Arlequin Wine Merchant, 56
Artbeat Salon & Gallery, 73
Article Pract, 84
Artisan Shop, 85
As You Sow, 179
Ashford Pest Control, 119
Asian-Pacific Environmental Network, 179
At Home in Marin, 124
Atelier Marin, 84
Atmosphera, 145
Aubergine Catering, 53
August, 81
Aveda, 66
Axis Café, 22
Aziza, 16

B Restaurant and Bar, 7
Bacar, 8
Bacco Ristorante Italiano, 13
Back to Earth, 53
Balboa Cafe, 3
Bake Shop, The, 22
Bamboo Cabinets by Altereco, 144
Bar Tartine, 16
Bare Necessities, 66
Bare Necessities Clothing and Scents, 81
Baron's Meat and Poultry, 51
BART, 170
Bashland Builders, 146
Bay Area Coalition for Headwaters
    Forest, 179
Bay City Bike Rentals, 168
Bay Localize, 179
Bay Nature Institute, 179
Bay Solar Power Design, 148
Baykeeper/SF Bay Chapter, 179
Bayview/Hunter's Point Farmers' Market, 44
Beautiful Place, A, 145
Beauty Center, 66
Beauty Company, 67
Bell and Trunk, 85
Bella and Daisy's Dog Bakery & Boutique, 96
Bella Pelle, 73
Belli Capelli, 71, 73
Belmont CFM, 45
Benissimo Ristorante & Bar, 13
Better World Telecom,
Berkeley Biodiesel Collective, 165
Berkeley Bowl, 39
Berkeley Ecology Center Curbside
    Recycling Program, 152
Berkeley Horticultural Nursery, 136
Berkeley Natural Grocery, 39
Berkeley Saturday CFM, 45
Berkeley Shattuck Organic CFM, 45
Berkeley Tuesday CFM, 45
Bernal Beast, The, 96
Best in Show, 97
Better World Club, 166, 171
Better World Telecom, 125
Bi-Rite Creamery and Bakeshop, 30
Bi-Rite Market, 39
Bia's Restaurant and Wine Bar, 16
Big Kid Toys, 162
Big Vision Career and Project Consulting, 114
Bike and Roll, 168
Bike Hut, The, 168
Bio Integral Resource Center, 119
Bio-Pest, 119
Biofuel Oasis, 165
Bioneers, Youth & Satellite Program, 179
Birders' Garden, 97
Bison Brewery, 56
Bistro 330, 11
Bittersweet, 22, 30
Black's Farmwood, 131, 150
Blazing Saddles Bike Rentals, 168
Blue And Gold Fleet, 170
Blue Bottle Coffee Co., 22
Blue Plate, The, 4
Blue Sky Cleaners, 115
Bluewater Network, A Division of Friends
    of the Earth, 179
Bob's Cleaners, 115
Body Shop, The, 67
Body Time, 67
Body Wise Massage, 85
Bofings Elmwood Hardware, 150
Borrego Solar, 148

Botanical Garden - University of California, Berkeley, 188
Boulangerie Bay Bread, 28
Boulettes Larder, 4
Boulevard Restaurant, 8
Bowwowmeow, 97
Boxed Foods Company, 22
Breads of India & Gourmet Curries, 12
Breast Cancer Fund, The, 179
Brendan Uniacke Construction, 146
Brickhouse Cafe, 7
Bridget Brewer Associates, 141, 148
Brilliant Earth, 85
Bryn Walker, 81
Bubba's Diner, 3
Buffalo Whole Food & Grain Company, 39
Build It Green, 146
Building Resources, 154
Bullshead Restaurant, 3
Burger Joint, 7
Burlingame Fresh Market CFM, 45
Butler and the Chef Bistro, The, 11
Bzz Bees, 120

C & K Salvage, 154
Café 817, 13
Café Benally, 22
Café Capuchino, 22
Café Colucci, 11
Café Crescendo, 22
Café Lo Cubano, 23
Café de La Paz, 15
Café Del Soul, 22
Café Fanny, 22
Café Gratitude, 20, 22
Café Grillades, 23
Café Que Tal, 23
Café Rouge, 16
Caffé Del Doge, 23
Cal State University East Bay, 188
Caldwell Building Wreckers, 154
California Academy of Sciences, 179
California Coastal Commission, 180
California College of the Arts, 188
California League of Conservation Voters, 180
California Native Plant Society, 180
California Oak Cleaners, 115
California State Parks, 180
Californians For GE-Free Agriculture, 180
Californians For Pesticide Reform, 180
Caltrain, 170
Calvert Social Investment Foundation, 121
Cambridge Investment Group, 121
Campton Place, 16
Caprice, The, 4
Carbon Fund, 171
Cardology, 89
Caroline Day Design, 145
Carolyn Robbins Site Design, 145
Casual Carpooling, 167
Cat Murphy's Skin Care Salon, 67
Cathedral Financial Group, Inc., 121
Catherine Woodman, Financial Advisor, 122
Center for Agroecology and Sustainable Food Systems - UC Santa Cruz, 189
Center for Environmental Health, 180
Center for Urban Education about Sustainable Agriculture, 189
Central Park Bistro, 4
C'era Una Volta, 13
Ceramic Tile & Design, 151
Ceramic Tile Design, 131
Cha Cha Cha, 15
Chakra Salonspa, 71
Charanga, 15
Chat's of San Francisco, 23
Chaya Brasserie, 6

Cheeky Monkey Toys, 85
Cheese Plus, 51
Cheeseboard Collective, The, 51
Cheeseboard Pizza Collective, The, 18
Chez Alexander, 11
Chez Maman, 11
Chez Panisse, 8
Chez Panisse Foundation, 180
Christine Reid, 145
Church Street Apothecary, 67
Church Street Flowers, 88
Church Street Groceteria, 39
Churro Station, 29
Circle of Life, 180
Citizen Cake, 8, 30
City and County of San Francisco Department of the Environment Ecocenter, 180
City Carshare, 167
City of El Cerrito Recycling, 153
City of Novato Curbside Recycling Program, 153
City of Palo Alto Recycling Program, 153
City of Sausalito Recycling - Bay Cities Refuse, 153
Clean Energy, 164
Clean Fueling Stations, 164
Clean Water Action, 181
Cliff's Variety, 151
Climate Trust, The, 171
Coastal Conservancy, 181
Cock-A-Doodle Café, 3
Coco 500, 8
Coffee to the People, 23
Coi, 8
Cole Coffee, 23
College of Environmental Design, University of California, Berkeley, 189
College of Natural Resources, University of California, Berkeley, 189
Collier Ostrom, Inc., 146
Colorful Coffins, 126
Come From the Heart, 125
Comforts, 8, 23
Common Ground Organic Garden Supply and Education Center, 136, 189
Common Scents, 85
Communities for a Better Environment, 181
Community Conservation Centers - Berkeley Recycling Center, 153
Commuter Cars, 162
Componere Fine Catering, 53
Cook! SF, 53
Cool Eatz Catering, 54
Cool Driver, 171
Cooperative Community Energy, 148
Corte Madera CFM, 45
Côté Sud, 11
Country Sun Natural Foods, 39
County of San Mateo Recycleworks, 153
Courtyard by Marriott, Downtown Oakland, 105
Cowgirl Creamery, 51
Coyote Hills Regional Park, 189
Crepes Café, 11
Crissy Field Center, 181
Crissy Field Center Café, 23
Crown Memorial State Beach and Crab Cove Visitor Center, 189
Crowne Plaza Hotel Cabana, 106
Crystal Springs Fish & Poultry, 51
Cugini, 14
Cultural Conservancy, 181

Daily Health, 20, 112
Daly City CFM, 45
Dan Smith & Associates, 141
Darin David Salon, 71

David Dobkin, CFP®, AIF®, 122
Day One - The Center for New and
   Expectant Parents, 86
De Martini Orchard, 51
De Young Café, 8
Debbie Does Dinner, 54
Deboer Architects, 141
Delancey Street Restaurant, 4
Delfina, 14
Delfina Pizzeria, 18
Delica RF-1, 6
Dharma Trading Company, 81, 86
Di Bartolo, 16
Dish Café, 23
Divino Ristorante Italiano, 14
Dog Bone Alley, 97
Dog Spa, The, 97
Dolly's Treasures, 97
Dominican University of California,
   Green MBA Program, 189
Don Pico's Original Mexican Bistro, 17
Doña Tomas, 17
Donovan's Pest Control, Inc., 120
Don't Agonize, Organize!, 114
Dopo, 14
Doubletree Hotel & EMC Berkeley
   Marina, 106
Down Etc..., 134
Draeger's Supermarkets, Inc., 39
Drew Maran Construction, Inc., 146
Drewes Bros. Meats, 51
Drive Neutral, 171

Earth and Sky Oasis, 74
Earth Island Institute, 181
Earth Share of California, 181
Earth Tones, 125
Earthbeam Natural Foods, 40
Earthen Feast, 54
Earthfirst Electric, 144
Earthjustice, 181
Earthsake, 86, 134
Earthsong, 86
Earthsource Forest Products, 131,151
East Bay Conservation Corps, 189
East Bay Depot for Creative Refuse, 154
East Oakland CFM, 45
East Oakland Senior Center CFM, 45
Eastbay Ferry, 170
Eating With the Seasons CFA, 48, 49
Ebersole Builders, 147
Eccolo, 14
Eco Design Resources, 131, 151
Eco Timber, 131
Eco-Friendly Cleaning, 117
Eco-Safe Cleaning, 117
Eco-Terric, 131, 145
Ecocraft, 144
EcoExpress, 51, 86
Ecofinderrr, 153
Ecohome Improvement, 131, 151
Ecolimo, 166
Ecology Center, 181, 190
Ecology Center Store, 89
Ecology House, 124
Ecomotors, 162
Ecovillage Farm Learning Center, 190
Eezy Freezy, 40
Effective Assets (Lincoln Payne), 122
Elbow-Grease Cleaning, 117
El Cerrito Natural Grocery, 40
El Cerrito Plaza Farmers' Market, 45
Electric Motorsport, 162
Electric Vehicle Repairs & Conversions, 162
Elephant Pharmacy, 67, 112
Elixir, 56, 71
Ella Baker Center for Human Rights, 182

Embassy Suites Hotel, San Rafael/Marin, 106
Emma's Eco-Clean, 117
Emmy's Spaghetti Shack, 14
Endangered Species Coalition, 182
Energy Management Services, 146
Environmental Education Directory, The, 190
Environmental Forum of Marin, 190
Environmental Justice Coalition for
   Water, 182
Eos Restaurant, 6
Equinox Landscape Construction
   Corps, 138, 148
Essential Foods, 40
Estate Conservation Associates, 122
Eternal Reefs Inc., 126
Ethical Traveler, 182
European Sleepworks, 134
EV Rentals at Fox Rent A Car, 167
Eva Claiborne Skin Institute, 67, 74
Evo Spa, 67, 74

Face It Beauty Salon and Spa, 71
Fairfax CFM, 45
Fairfax Lumber & Hardware, 151
Fairfax Scoop, 30
Fairmont, San Francisco, The, 106
Falletti Foods, 40
Family Farewell, A, 126
Far Leaves Tea, 23
Far West Fungi, 51
Farm Fresh Choice, 45
Farm Fresh to You, 49
Farmer Brown, 3
Fat Angel Bakery, 29
Fat Kat Surf Shop, 81, 86
Faz, 16
Feel Good Bakery, 29
Fernwood Cemetery, 126
Ferry Plaza Seafood, 19
Ferry Plaza Wine Merchant, 56
1550 Hyde Café & Wine Bar, 7
Findecor, 132
Firefly, 4
511.org, 169
Flack + Kurtz, 144
Flea St. Café, 8
Fleur De Lys, 11
Flexcar, 168
Flooring Alternatives, 132
Flora Grubb Gardens, 136, 139
Foam Store of Marin, The, 134
Foamorder.com, 135
Fonda, 15
Food First/Institute For Food and
   Development, 182
Food Mill, The, 40
Foothill College Environmental Horticulture
   & Design, 190
Footloose Birkenstock Store, 81
For Paws, 97
Ford Motor Company, 162
Forestethics, 182
Fork, 8
Form + Function Construction, 147
Forward Funds / Sierra Club Stock Fund, 122
Frantoio Ristorante & Olive Oil Co., 14
Fremont Centerville CFM, 45
Fremont Irvington CFM, 45
Fremont Kaiser CFM, 45
Fremont Nummi CFM, 46
Fresh Organics, 40
Friends of the Regional Parks Botanic
   Garden, 136
Fringale, 11
Fringe Salon, 68, 71
Frog Hollow Farms, 24
Front Porch, The, 15

Fruit Barn, 40
Fryer Consulting, 147
Full Belly Farm CSA, 48, 49
Full Circle Design Group, 141
Future Leaders Institute, The, 190

Gamble Garden, 190
Garden Gourmet, 54
Garden Shed, The, 136
Garden Shop at UC Berkeley Botanical
Garden, 136
Gardener's Guild, 139
Garibaldi's, 8
Gelfand Partners Architects, 141
General Motors, 162
George, 97
Gettman Schow Architecture, 141
GHA/Geoffrey Holton & Associates, 141
Giggle, 81, 86
Gilman Trading Company, Inc., 154
Gioia, 18
Girton Capital Management, Inc., 122
Global Exchange, 182
Global Exchange Fair Trade Store, 81, 86
Global Exchange Reality Tours, 104
Globe, 9
Golden Gate Audubon Society and Nature
Store, 86, 182
Golden Gate Meat Company, 51
Golden Gate National Parks Conservancy, 182
Golden Gate School of Feng Shui, 86
Golden Gate Transit, 170
Golden Gate University, School of Law, 190
Golden Produce, 40
Good Earth Natural & Organic Foods, 40
Good Life Grocery, 40
Gourmet Garden to Go, 50
Great Harvest Bread, 29
Green Builders of Marin, 147
Green Building Exchange, 141, 149, 151
Green Career Tracks, 114
Green Careers, 114
Green Chi, 114
Green Chile Kitchen, 17
Green Citizen, 153
Green Earth Office Supply, 89
Green Fusion Design Center, 132, 135, 139,
145, 151
Green Jeans Garden Supply, 136
Green Key Real Estate, 124
Green Living Home, 114, 146
Green Museum, 183
Green Office, The, 89
Green Planet Films, 183
Green Table, The, 54
Green Tortoise Adventure Travel, 104
Greenaction for Health and Environmental
Justice, 183
Greenbelt Alliance, 183
Greener Marin at Keller Williams
San Francisco, 124
Greener Printer, 89
Greenlight Solar, 149
Greenpeace, 183
Greens Restaurant, 16, 20
Greensage, 132, 145, 151
Greenway Maid, 117
Gregoire Jacquet, 12
Grid Alternatives, 149
Grooming with TLC, 97
Grove, The, 24
Guerilla Café, 24
Guerrilla Organics, 50

Habitats (formerly Asiantiques), 132
Haight Fillmore Whole Foods, 40
Hair Now South Beach, 71

Hammerschmidt Construction, 147
Happy Burrito, 17
Happy Pet, 97
Happy Planet, A, 81, 134
Hapuku Fish Shop, 51
Harbor Court Hotel, 106
Harvest & Rowe, 9, 24
Harvest Urban Market, 41
Hayward CFM, 46
Hayward Kaiser CFM, 46
Hayward Shoreline Interpretive Center, 183
Healing Cuisine, 114
Healing Hearth, The, 54
Health by Heidi, 112
Health Care Without Harm, 183
Health Haven Produce and Natural Food, 41
Healthwize for Pets, 97
Healthy Building Network, 183
Healthy Choice Carpet Cleaners, 117
Healthy Home Plans, 142, 149
Hertz, 167
Hidden Villa, 190
Hidden Villa CSA, 48
High Cotton Living, 132
Hilton San Francisco, 106
Himalayan High Treks, 104
Hip & Zen, 82, 87
Hog Island Oyster Company, 19
Holistic Hound, 98
Home, 5
Homegrown Weddings & Events, 114
Honda, 163
Hoot Judkins, 132
Horizon's, 19
Hosteling International Marin Headlands, 106
Hotel Carlton, 106
Hotel Monaco, 106
Hotel Palomar, 106
Hotel Triton, 106
House Shining, 118
Hubbell Daily Architecture + Design, 142
Hudson Bay Caffe, 24
Hungry Owl Project, 120
Hyatt at Fisherman's Wharf, 107
Hydra, 68
Hydrogen Fueling Map, 165

Icarpool, 168
Ici, 30
Imagiknit, 84
Incognito, 71
Inkmoon Architects, 142
Inkworks Press, 89
Inn Marin, 107
International Healthy Cities Foundation,
The, 183
International Orange, 74
Ixia, 88

Jack Falstaff Restaurant, 9
Jackson Liles Architecture, 142
Jane Peal Cuisiniére, 54
Jardiniére, 12
Java Beach, 24
Jeff King & Company, Inc., 147
Jeffrey's Natural Pet Foods, 98
Jennifer Hall, 139
Jerusalem Organic Kitchen & Burgers, 18
Jimmy Bean's, 3
Joe's Wildlife Animal Damage Control, 120
John Bentley's Restaurant, 12
Joi Nail Spa, 71
JoJo, 12
Jouvence Skin Rejuvenation Center, 68
Judahlicious, 20, 24
Jug Shop, The, 57
Juice Bar Collective, 24

Juicey Lucy's, 20, 24
Julie's Coffee and Tea Garden, 24
Juniper Tree Supplies, 87
Jurlique, 68
JZCool Eatery, 9

Kabuki Springs & Spa, 74
Kaila's Corner Cup, 24
Kamalaspa, 71, 74
Kara's Cupcakes, 30
Kelly Paper, 90
K&L Wine Merchants, 57
Knitter's Studio, The, 84
Kokkari, 16

La Estrellita Cafe, 17
Lakeshore Natural Foods, 41
Lalime's, 9
L'Amyx Tea Bar, 25
Lark Creek Inn, 5
Larkspur CFM, 46
LC Biofuels, 165
Learning Express, 87
Leddy Maytum Stacy Architects, 142
Leela, 82
Legion of Honor café, 9
Let's Be Frank Dogs, 3
Letter Perfect, 87
Lettus Café Organic, 9, 25
Lexus, 163
Liberty Café, The, 5
Lifegem, 126
Limon, 15
Literacy For Environmental Justice, 183
Living Room Events, 54
L'Occitane en Provence, 68
Locksmith Magic/Golden Gate Park
    Skate and Bike, 169
Lola's, 3
Lorax Development, 147
Los Altos Garbage Company Curbside
    Program, 153
Luka's Taproom & Lounge, 12
Lululemon, 82
Lunardi's, 41
Lush, 68
Luxant, 132

Madera, 132
Madkat, 68
Maggie Mudd, 31
Magic Gardens Landscape Nursery, 136, 139
Maison Rêve, 132, 154
Makana Technologies, 125
Mandaloun, 16
Manzanita Restaurant, 20
Marché Aux Fleurs, 12
Marcus Rios Personal Chef & Caterer, 54
Marin Agricultural Land Trust, 184
Marin Art and Garden Center, 190
Marin Audubon Society, 184
Marin City Community Services District, 153
Marin Coffee Roasters, 25
Marin County Household Hazardous
    Waste Facility, 156
Marin County Open Space District, 184
Marin Fiber Arts, 84
Marin Ideal Stationers, 90
Marin Outdoor Living, 132
Marin Recycling Service, 153
Marin Solar, 149
Marine Mammal Center, The, 184
Market Hall Produce, 41
Marriott, Fremont, 107
Marriott, Oakland City Center, 107
Masa's Restaurant, 12
Match & Go, 168

Matsu Bedding, 135
Mc Solar Engineering, 149
McCutcheon Construction, Inc., 147
McEvoy Ranch, 52
Meader's Cleaners, 116
Medicine Eatstation, 6
Meditrina, 74
Menlo Park CFM, 46
Mephisto, 82
Mercedes Corbell Design + Architecture, 142
Mercury, 163
Merrit College Landscape Horticulture
    Department, 191
Meyer Bunje, 82, 87
M&G Burgers, 7
MGS Construction, Inc., 147
Michelle Kaufmann Designs, 142
Miette, 31
Mijita, 17
Mill Valley Bamboo, 133
Mill Valley Bamboo Flooring, 151
Mill Valley Refuse Service, 154
Millbrae CFM, 46
Millennium, 20
Mills College Environmental Studies
    Program, 191
Miranda Caroligne, 82
Mission Creek Café, The, 25
Mission Market Fish and Poultry, 52
Mistral Rotisserie Provencale, 12
Mixt Greens, 9
Mo' Better Food, 46
Modern Tea, 9
Mokka, 25
Mollie Stone's, 41
Mollusk, The, 82
Monticello Inn, 107
Moondance Painting, 144
Mortgagegreen, 122, 124
Mountain Home Inn, 9
Muffin Mania, 25
Murasaki, 135
My Footprint.org, 172
My Marin Homes/Linda Tull, 124
Myth, 10

Nabilas, 41
Nabolom Bakery, 29
Nancy Boy, 68
National Pesticide Telecommunications
    Network, 120
Native Energy, 172
Native Here Nursery, 136
Natural Builders, The, 146
Natural Care for Carpets, 118
Natural Home Cleaning Professionals, 118
Natural Resources, 87
Natural Resources Defense Council, 184
Natural Way, 118
Natural World Museum, 184
Nature at Play, 87
Nature in the City, 184
Nature Stop, 41
Nature Trip, 104
Nelly's Java, 25
Neptune Society of Northern California,
    The, 127
Nervous Dog Coffee, 25
New College Café, 25
New Resource Bank, 122
New World Vegetarian Cuisine, 20
Newland + Winnen Design Studio, 142
Nextbus, 170
Nina Homisak Hair Design, 71
Noe Valley Pet Company, 98
Nomad Café, 25
Norge Cleaners, 116

Noriega Produce Market, 41
North Berkeley Investment Partners, 122
Northpoint Coffee Company, 25
Nourishing the Whole, 54
Novato Disposal Service, 154
Novato Downtown CFM, 46
Novato Household Hazardous Waste
  Facility, 156
Numi Organic, 52

Oak Hill Farm, 88
Oakland Fruitvale CFM, 46
Oakland Jack London CFM, 46
Oakland Grand Lake CFM, 46
Oakland Kaiser CFM, 46
Oakland Montclair Sunday CFM, 46
Oakland Temescal CFM, 46
Oasis Natural Foods, 41
Occasions Boutique, 68
Occidental Arts and Ecology Center, 191
Occidental Power, 149
Ocean Conservancy, The, 184
O'Chame, 7
O'Donnell's Organic Nursery &
  Habitat Restoration, 136, 139
Ohlone College, 191
Ohmega Salvage, 155
Old Oakland CFM, 46
Oliveto's, 14
Omega Too, 155
Ondine, 19
One Market, 5
Orapa Gallery of Wearable Arts, 82
Orchard Garden Hotel, The, 107
Orchard Hotel, The, 107
Organic Chef Catering, 54
Organic Choice Carpet Cleaning, 118
Organic Coffee Company, 26
Organic Express, 50
OrganicArchitect, 142
Original Swiss Aromatics, 69
Other Avenues, 42
Out the Door, 6
Owens Electric and Solar, 149
Oz Cleaning Company, 118

P-Kok, 82
Pacific Catch, 19
Palo Alto Green Team Project, 184
Palter/Donzelli Design, 142
Paper Source, 90
Pappo, 10
Paradise Bay Restaurant & Bar, 19
Paradise Foods, 42
Paréa Wine Bar and Café, 17, 57
Paris Salon and Spa, 72, 74
Parnassus Investments, 122
Patagonia, 82
Pauline's Pizza, 18
Pawsitively Groomed Pet Salon, 98
Pawtrero Hill Bathhouse & Feed Co., 98
Peace Café, 26
Peché Interiors, 145
Peña Pachamama, 15
Pendleton, 82
Peninsula Open Space Trust, 184
People's Café, 26
Peoples Community Partnership Federal
  Credit Union, 122
People's Fuel Cooperative, 165
People's Grocery, 185
Perfect Ten Nail Salon, The, 72
Perry Family Farms at Ardenwood
  Historic Farm, 185
Pestec Exterminator Company, 120
Pesticide Action Network North America
  (PANNA), 185

Pet Camp, 98
Pet Club, 98
Pet Food Express, 98
Pet Place, The, 98
Petite Patisserie, 29, 31
Pets Are Us, 98
Pfau Architecture, 143
P&GE ClimateSmart Program, 172
PG&E Service Centers, 164
Pharmaca Integrative Pharmacy, 69, 113
Philz Coffee, 26
Piatti Locali, 14
Piazza's Fine Foods, 42
Piedmont Grocery, 42
Piedmont Hairport, 72
Pisces California Cuisine, 19
Pizza Pazza, 18
Pizzaiolo, 14
Pizzetta 211, 18
Planettran, 166
Planetweavers, 87
Play Store, The, 87
Plaza De Paws, 99
Plumpjack Café, 10
Pomelo, 7
Postrio, 5
Power Source, 26
Prather Ranch Meat Company, 52
Prescott Hotel, 107
Presidio School of Management, 191
Pri Pri Café, 26
Principled Solutions, 122
Prism Café, 20
Produce Center, The, 42
Progressive Asset Management, 123
Progressive Grounds, 26
Propeller, 133
Public Health Institute, 185
Puppy Haven, 99

Que Seraw Seraw, 20

Rabat Shoes, 83
Rainbow Grocery, 42
Rainforest Action Network, 185
Ramblas Tapas Restaurant and Bar, 15
Randy Colosky Design, 144
Range, 11
Raw Energy Organic Juice Café, 26
Razan's Organic Kitchen, 18
RBC Dain Rauscher, SRI Wealth
  Management Group, 123
Real Food Company, The, 42
Rebecca Smith Skin Care, 74
Red Jellyfish, 125
Red Victorian Bed & Breakfast and Art, 107
Redhound, 99
Redwood City CFM, 47
Redwood City Kaiser CFM, 47
Regenerative Design Institute, 191
Regional Asthma Management and
  Prevention, Bay Area Ramp, 185
Regional Parks Botanic Garden at
  Tilden Park, 185
REI, 83
Renaissance Remodelers, 147
Renaissance Spirit, 87
Renee's Place, 6
Renewable Choice Energy, 172
Renu: Smart Solutions for Healthy
  Homes, 144, 149
Residents Apparel Gallery, 83
Restore Store, The, 155
Reuse People, The, 155
Richard's Dry Cleaners, 116
Richardson Bay Audubon Center
  Sanctuary, 185

Richmond CFM, 47
Rigolo Café, 26
Rising Sun Catering, 55
Ritual Coffee Roasters, 26
River of Words, 185
Riverdog Farm CSA, 48
Rivoli, 14
Rockin' Java, 26
Roosevelt Tamale Parlor, 18
Roti Indian Bistro, 13
RSF Social Finance, 123
Rubicon, 10
Ruby2, 83
Ruby Livingdesign, 133, 135
Ruiz Antique Lighting, 155
Rustic Bakery, 29

Salon des Artistes, 72
Samovar Tea Lounge, 27
Sam's Anchor Café, 19
SamTrans, 170
San Carlos CFM, 47
San Francisco Alemany CFM, 47
San Francisco Bay Conservation and
    Development Commission, 185
San Francisco Bay National Wildlife
    Refuge Complex, 186
San Francisco Beautiful, 186
San Francisco Bike Coalition, 169, 186
San Francisco Biofuels Cooperative, 165
San Francisco Botanical Garden at the
    Strybing Arboretum, 186
San Francisco Chocolate Factory, The, 31
San Francisco Chrysler Jeep, 163
San Francisco Crocker Galleria, 47
San Francisco Department of the
    Environment, 120
San Francisco Ferry Plaza Farmers
    Market, 47
San Francisco Fillmore CFM, 47
San Francisco Fish Company, 52
San Francisco Heart of the City Farmers'
    Markets, 47
San Francisco Kaiser CFM, 47
San Francisco Marina CFM, 47
San Francisco Neighborhoods Parks
    Council, 186
San Francisco Noe Valley CFM, 47
San Francisco Recreation and Park Department,
    Natural Areas & Volunteer Programs, 186
San Francisco Recycling and Disposal, 157
San Francisco State University Environmental
    Studies Program, 191
San Francisco Tomorrow, 186
San Geronimo Valley CSA, 48
San Jose Conservation Corps &
    Charter School, 191
San Jose State University, Environmental
    Studies Department, 191
San Leandro Bayfair Mall CFM, 47
San Mateo CFM, 47
San Mateo County Household Hazardous
    Waste Program/Recycleworks, 157
San Rafael Civic Center-Marin County
    CFM, 47
San Rafael Downtown CFM, 47
Sandra Caron European Spa, 69, 74
Santa Clara Kaiser CFM, 48
Santa Clara University, 191
Sausalito CFM, 48
Save the Bay, 186
Savemore Market, 42
Scarlet Sage Herb Company, The, 113
Schizandra, 74
Scootcar San Francisco, 169
SCRAP - Scroungers' Center for Re-Usable
    Art Parts, 155

Scrub a Pup Dog Wash, 99
Sea Salt, 19
Sea-Urn, 127
Seacology, 104
Season: Conscious Catering, 55
Second Nature Design, 139
See Jane Run Sports, 83
Segway of Oakland, 163
Sellers Markets, 10
Sen Spa, 75
Sequoia Audubon Society, 186
Serrano Hotel, 107
17 Jewels, 71
SF Earthly Housekeeping, 118
SFMUNI, 170
Shear Bliss, 72
Shen Herbal Pharmacy, 113
Sidewalk Juice, 27
Siegel & Strain Architects, 143
Sierra Club, 187
Sierra Club Outings, 104
Sigona's Farmers Market, 52
Sillapere, 114
Simmer, 10
Simon & Associates, Inc., 146
Simply Gorgeous, 75
Sink Factory, The, 155
Sir Francis Drake Hotel, 107
Sirayvah Organic Thai Cuisine, 6
SKBA Capital Management, 123
Sketch Ice Cream, 31
Skin and Body Therapy, 69, 75
Skin Envy, 69, 75
Skin Therapy, 75
Sky Energy, 172
Skyside Studios, 133
Slanted Door, The, 6
Slide Ranch, 192
Sloat Garden Center, 137, 139
Slow Club, 5
Slow Food San Francisco, 187
Small Shed Flatbreads, 5
Smith & Hawken, 133, 137
Soap Sistahs, 87
Social Equity Group, The, 123
Sol Food Puerto Rican Cuisine, 15
Solano Avenue Cyclery, 169
Solar City, 149
Solar Electric Light Fund, 172
Solar Living Institute, 192
Solarcraft, 149
Sole Salon & Sanctuary, 72
Solutions, 143
Sonoma State University, 192
South Park Café, 12
South Paw Bathhouse & Feed Co., 99
South San Francisco CFM, 48
South San Francisco Scavenger, 154
Spa de Beaute, 75
Spaceshare, 168
Specialty Rentals, 167
Spike's Coffees and Teas, 27
Spring, 135, 152
Spring Friedlander Remodeling, 147
Stanford Terrace Inn, 108
Stanford University - Woods Institute for
    the Environment, 192
Star City Salon & Day Spa, 72, 75
Stash Yarn + Inspiration, 84
Stellar Spa, 75
Stonehouse California Olive Oil Company, 52
Stonelace Designs, 144
Stop Global Warming, 172
Studio Knit, 84
Subculture Dining, 5

Suburban Habitat, 137, 139
Sumbody & Sumtime Spa, 69
Sun First, 150
Sun Light and Power, 150
Sunclean Carpet Care, 118
Sundance Coffee, 27
Sunlight Electric, LLC, 150
Sunny Side Café, 3
Sunol Regional Wilderness, 192
Sunset Café, 27
Sunset Pet Supply, 99
Susan's Soap, 69
Sustainable Architecture & Consulting, 143
Sustainable Home, 145
Sustainable San Mateo County, 187
Sustainable Spaces, 150
Sustainable Travel International, 172
Sustainable World Coalition, 187
Sustaining Ourselves Locally, 187
Sutro's, 10
Swirl on Castro, 57

T-Rex Barbeque, 4
Table Café, 13
Tablespoon, 5
Tacubaya, 18
Tamarindo Antojeria Mexicana, 18
Tamley Architectural Design, 143
Taraval Market, 42
Tartine Bakery, 29, 31
Tay Tah Café, 27
Tea Garden Springs, 75
Tela D, 83
Terra Firma Farms CSA, 48
Terra Pass, 172
Tesla Motors, 163
Thai Delight Cuisine, 6
Thairapeutics, 72
Therapeia, 75
Therapeutic Chef, 55
Thimmakka's Resources For Environmental
   Education, 192
This & That, 155
Thom's Natural Foods, 42
Thomas Saxby Architect, 143
Thoreau Center For Sustainability, 187
Three Degrees Restaurant, 3
3 Phases, 171
Three Twins Ice Cream, 31
Tilden Environmental Education Center, 192
Tizka, 72
Todd Jersey Architecture, 143
Tomatina, 17
Top Paws, 99
Touch, The, 133
Tower of Health, 113
Town Hall, 4
Town's End Restaurant and Bakery, 5, 29
Toyota, 163
Trader Joe's, 43
Trail Center, The, 187
Tranquil Spaces Design Group, 145
TransFair USA, 187
Transportation and Land Use Coalition, 187
Trapeze Restaurant, 17
Treat Aveda Salon, 72
Trillium Asset Management, 123
Trillium USA, 164
Tsar Nicoulai Caviar Café, 52
Tuscan Inn, 108
Twenty Two, 83
2223 Restaurant, 4
26th and Guerrero Market, 39
Twig & Fig, 88
Two Small Farms CSA, 48

UC Cooperative Extension - Alameda
   County, 192
UC Cooperative Extension - Marin, 192
UC Cooperative Extension - San Mateo
   and San Francisco County, 192
UC Extension - Berkeley, 193
Union City Kaiser CFM, 48
Union City-Old Alvarado CFM, 48
Union French Cleaners, 116
Universal Café, 5
University of San Francisco, 193
Upwall, 143
Urban Creeks Council, 188
Urban Farmer Store, The, 137
Urban Forest Home, 137
Urban Ore, 155
Urban Sprouts School Gardens, 188
Urban Structure, 143
Usedcardboardboxes.com, 154

Valencia Green, 123
Valencia Whole Foods, 43
Van Der Ryn Eco Design Collaborative, 143
Velo Rouge, 4
Venus, 10
Ver Brugge Foods, 52
Verde Green Cleaning, 118
Vibrant Events, 115
Vierra and Friends, 72
Vignette, 10
Villa Hotel Florence, 108
Village Dog, The, 99
Village Grounds, 27
Village Market, The, 43, 52
Vino Locale, 10
Vinorosso, 15, 57
Vintage Berkeley, 57
Vision Capital Investment Management, 123
Vital Vittles, 29
Vogue Cleaners, 116
Voltage Vehicle, 163
Vox Design Group, 143
VTA, 170

Waddle and Swaddle, 83
Wagstaff Architects, 144
Waldeck's Office Supplies, 90
Walgreens, 157
Walk SF, 169
Warming Hut, The, 27
Watercourse Way, 75
Weird Fish, 19
Well Grounded Tea & Coffee, 27
West Bay Café and Lounge, 11
West Contra Costa Integrated Waste
   Management Authority, 154, 157
West Portal Nutrition Center, 113
Westbrae Nursery, 137
Westside Organics, 50
Wheel Fun Rentals, 169
Who Does Your Dog?, 99
Whole Foods Market, 43
Whole House Building Supply, 155
Whole Life Natural Foods, 43
Wilderness Travel, 104
Wildheart Gardens, 137, 139
Willa Home, 69
William Cross, 57
William's Natural Foods, 43
Women's Equity Fund, 123
Wooden Duck, The, 133
Woodlands Market, 43
Woodlands Pet Food & Treats, 99
Woodshanti Cooperative, Inc., 144
Work of Art Catering, 55
Working Assets, 125
World Centric, 83, 88, 90

Xpedx Paper and Graphics, 90

Yabusaki's Dwight Way Nursery, 137
Yarn Paper Scissors, 85
Yellow Cab Co-Op, 166
Yerba Buena California Native Plant
  Nursery, 138, 139
Yield Wine Bar, 57
Yoga of Sausalito, 83, 88
Yoga Studio, 84
Your Black Muslim Bakery, 29
Your Money & Your Life (James Frazin), 123
Yumma's Mediterranean Grill, 17

Zap!, 163
Zatar, 17
Zazen Coffee Tea & Organics, 27
Zemocha, 27
Zipcar, 168
Zocalo Coffeehouse, 28
Zuppa, 15